学堂在线"高级综合英语写作"慕课的数字版教材

高级综合英语写作教程

慕课版

Advanced Comprehensive English Writing

樊玲 常波 / 主 编
戴云 盛海燕 曹晓蕾 张淑芳 / 副主编
杨洪 刘璇 陈星 何华 李鹏雁 唱宇 / 参 编

机械工业出版社
CHINA MACHINE PRESS

《高级综合英语写作教程（慕课版）》是一本集实用性和操作性于一体的数字版英语写作教程，主体部分为学堂在线"高级综合英语写作"课程的讲稿，此外，也包含针对课程中各项写作技能的精准操练以及写作能力拓展内容。本书中的英语写作技能训练适用于非英语专业本科到硕士研究生和博士研究生阶段的学生，也适用于对英语写作感兴趣的学习者。

    本书内容包括选词造句、段落写作技巧、应用文写作、四种文体的写作、学术论文写作以及国际会议报告撰写与宣读。本书为立体数字化教材，利于翻转课堂教学（既可以作为慕课教材，也可以独立使用）；内容突出写作难点，语言纯正；讲解结构清晰，形式多样；阶梯式的分模块内容设计，包含15周的学习内容，由易到难，学习者可以灵活选用；讲练结合，精讲精练，每周学习内容均包含写作练习（附参考答案）。

图书在版编目（CIP）数据

高级综合英语写作教程：慕课版 / 樊玲，常波主编. —北京：机械工业出版社，2022.9

ISBN 978-7-111-71609-9

Ⅰ. ①高⋯　Ⅱ. ①樊⋯ ②常⋯　Ⅲ. ①英语–写作–教材　Ⅳ. ①H319.36

中国版本图书馆 CIP 数据核字（2022）第 171861 号

机械工业出版社（北京市百万庄大街22号　邮政编码100037）
策划编辑：尹小云　　　　　责任编辑：尹小云
责任校对：张若男　　　　　责任印制：任维东
北京富博印刷有限公司印刷
2023年1月第1版第1次印刷
184mm×260mm・20.5印张・453千字
标准书号：ISBN 978-7-111-71609-9
定价：68.00元

电话服务　　　　　　　　　网络服务
客服电话：010-88361066　　机　工　官　网：www.cmpbook.com
　　　　　010-88379833　　机　工　官　博：weibo.com/cmp1952
　　　　　010-68326294　　金　书　网：www.golden-book.com
封底无防伪标均为盗版　　　机工教育服务网：www.cmpedu.com

前 言
PREFACE

自 2019 年 12 月上线以来，由北京化工大学教学团队主讲的学堂在线课程——高级综合英语写作在线学习人数已超出 8000 人。为了让学习者便捷、高效地掌握该慕课的学习内容，主讲教师团队经过一年多的编写和修订，完成了此教材书稿。

本书中的英语写作技能训练适用于非英语专业本科到硕士研究生和博士研究生阶段的学生，也适用于对英语写作感兴趣的学习者。

本书是配有学堂在线视频课程的立体化数字教材，包含 15 周的阶梯式分模块内容设计，学习者可以针对不同的学习目标自行选取。内容包括基础阶段的选词造句、段落写作技巧；提升阶段的应用文写作、四种文体的写作、学术论文写作以及国际会议报告撰写与宣读。本书中系统的技巧讲解能够为学习者顺利完成论文发表并参加国际会议奠定基础。每周的讲座包括三个部分：（一）概述；（二）慕课讲稿，这部分是本书的核心内容，通常含 Lead-in，Objectives，Tasks，Key Points，Language Focus，Summary 等板块。为了便于读者理解和自学，编者为此部分的重点和难点内容增加了中文注释；（三）写作练习。

本书主要特色：

1. **可读性强**。本书编写者都是具有多年写作教学经验的一线教师，教材的重点和难点突出，所有文字稿均根据美国 Jean Alvares 教授的建议进行了反复修改，语言地道，符合书面语特点。

2. **可操作性强**。本书讲座内容采用"任务型"教学模式，有针对性地破解学习者常见的写作问题和难题，问题导入、问题解答和知识点输入的策略都是根据具体任务精心设计的，学习者通过完成任务可以掌握写作的基本技能。每周讲座后的写作练习可用于巩固所学知识。学习者学完每周的讲座内容（可观看在线视频课程）后，可以通过写作练习来检验学习成果，从而取得事半功倍的效果。本书中的练习题多为主观题，是对慕课测试（客观题）的进一步补充，完成后可以自行核对参考答案。

3. **针对性强**。本书中阶梯式的分模块内容是针对不同目标学习主体而设计的，学习者可以根据自身的需求来选取学习内容。例如，应用文写作适合专业学位硕士学习，不同文体写作适合学术学位硕士学习，学术论文写作和国际会议报告撰写与宣读更适合有需求的博士生。

本书既可以结合学堂在线的视频课程学习，也可以作为独立的教材来学习。本书附赠针对每周讲座内容的写作知识拓展（中文）部分，可以帮助英语基础较弱的学习者，使其进一步加深对各讲座（英文）中知识点的理解。此外，本书还附赠慕课课程的 14 套单元测试题，供学习者检测其学习效果。

　　教师可以利用本书采用线上和线下相结合的教学模式，线上学生自学学堂在线的慕课课程，线下利用此教材进行课堂教学。

　　本书在编写和出版过程中获得了北京化工大学研究生院的大力支持，而机械工业出版社编辑为本书的结构体例、内容设计和出版做了大量工作并给出了宝贵建议，在此我们一并表示深深的谢意。由于时间仓促，编者水平有限，敬请同仁和读者批评指正。

编　者

2022 年 10 月

目 录
CONTENTS

前言

第1周 词义的选择（Word Choice） ... 001

Ⅰ. 概述 ... 001

Ⅱ. 慕课讲稿 ... 001

　讲座1　如何准确用词：理解词义——词的内涵与外延（How to Choose Words Accurately：Understand Word Meaning—Denotation and Connotation） ... 001

　讲座2　如何恰当选词——正式与非正式词（How to Use Words Appropriately—Formal and Informal） ... 006

　讲座3　如何选择有说服力的词：特指词和泛指词（How to Use Words Compellingly—Specific and General） ... 011

　讲座4　需要避免使用的词（Some Don'ts in Word Choice） ... 015

Ⅲ. 写作练习 ... 020

第2周 语句的变化及常见句子错误（Sentence Variety and Common Sentence Errors） ... 022

Ⅰ. 概述 ... 022

Ⅱ. 慕课讲稿 ... 023

　讲座1　语句的变化（Sentence Variety） ... 023

　讲座2　常见句子错误Ⅰ（Common Sentence Errors Ⅰ） ... 028

　讲座3　常见句子错误Ⅱ（Common Sentence Errors Ⅱ） ... 033

Ⅲ. 写作练习 ... 037

第3周 段落结构及段落的统一性和连贯性（The Structure of a Paragraph; the Unity and Coherence of a Paragraph） 040

  Ⅰ．概述 040
  Ⅱ．慕课讲稿 040
    讲座1　段落结构（The Structure of a Paragraph） 040
    讲座2　段落的统一性和连贯性（The Unity and Coherence of a Paragraph）
    045
  Ⅲ．写作练习 050

第4周 段落展开方法——过程分析法和分类法（Developing a Paragraph by Process Analysis and Classification） 052

  Ⅰ．概述1 052
  Ⅱ．慕课讲稿1 052
    讲座1　过程分析法（Process Analysis） 052
  Ⅲ．写作练习1 056
  Ⅳ．概述2 057
  Ⅴ．慕课讲稿2 057
    讲座2　分类法（Classification） 057
  Ⅵ．写作练习2 062

第5周 应用文写作Ⅰ（Practical Writing Ⅰ） 063

  Ⅰ．概述 063
  Ⅱ．慕课讲稿 063
    讲座1　概要（Summary） 063
    讲座2　求职信（Job Application Letters） 068
    讲座3　简历（Résumé） 073
    讲座4　商务电子邮件（Business Emails） 079
    讲座5　备忘录（Memo） 082
  Ⅲ．写作练习 088

第6周 应用文写作 II (Practical Writing II) ... 091

- I. 概述 ... 091
- II. 慕课讲稿 ... 091
  - 讲座1 图表写作的类型（Essays Based upon Graphs）... 091
  - 讲座2 线图写作：趋势（Line Graph：Trends）... 097
  - 讲座3 饼图：百分比（Pie Chart：Percentage）... 101
  - 讲座4 柱状图：对比（Bar Chart：Contrast）... 105
- III. 写作练习 ... 110

第7周 篇章写作 I (Essay Writing I) ... 113

- I. 概述 ... 113
- II. 慕课讲稿 ... 113
  - 讲座1 判断好文章的标准（Features of Good Effective Essays）... 113
  - 讲座2 开头和结尾的写法（Effective Introduction and Conclusion）... 118
- III. 写作练习 ... 124

第8周 篇章写作 II (Essay Writing II) ... 128

- I. 概述 ... 128
- II. 慕课讲稿 ... 128
  - 讲座1 记叙文（Narrative Essays）... 128
  - 讲座2 描写文（Descriptive Essays）... 132
- III. 写作练习 ... 136

第9周 因果作文 (Cause and Effect Essays) ... 140

- I. 概述 ... 140
- II. 慕课讲稿 ... 140

讲座 1　什么是因果（What Causes and Effects Are） ……………… 140
讲座 2　如何撰写因果作文（How to Write Cause and Effect Essays） … 144
讲座 3　范文分析（Sample Essays） ……………………………… 148
讲座 4　常用表达（Useful Expressions） ………………………… 152
Ⅲ．写作练习 …………………………………………………………… 157

第 10 周　对照与对比作文（Comparison and Contrast Essays） …………… 160

Ⅰ．概述 ………………………………………………………………… 160
Ⅱ．慕课讲稿 …………………………………………………………… 160
讲座 1　理解对照与对比（Understanding Comparison and Contrast） …… 160
讲座 2　如何撰写比较类作文（How to Write Comparison and Contrast Essays） …………………………………………………… 164
讲座 3　如何避免"无意义主旨句"（How to Avoid So-what Thesis Statements） ……………………………………………… 170
讲座 4　常用表达（Useful Expressions） ………………………… 174
Ⅲ．写作练习 …………………………………………………………… 179

第 11 周　定义型作文（Writing a Definition Essay） ……………………… 183

Ⅰ．概述 ………………………………………………………………… 183
Ⅱ．慕课讲稿 …………………………………………………………… 184
讲座 1　什么是定义（What a Definition Is） …………………… 184
讲座 2　如何下定义（How to Make a Definition） ……………… 187
讲座 3　如何撰写定义型作文Ⅰ（Writing a Definition Essay Ⅰ） ……… 192
讲座 4　如何撰写定义型作文Ⅱ（Writing a Definition Essay Ⅱ） ……… 196
Ⅲ．写作练习 …………………………………………………………… 201

第 12 周　议论文写作（Writing an Argumentative Essay） ………………… 203

Ⅰ．概述 ………………………………………………………………… 203

Ⅱ. 慕课讲稿 204
　　讲座1　什么是论证（What Argumentation Is） 204
　　讲座2　论证方法（Methods to Present Argumentation） 208
　　讲座3　议论文写作的准备阶段（Pre-writing an Argumentative Essay） 213
　　讲座4　议论文写作（Writing an Argumentative Essay） 217
Ⅲ. 写作练习 222

第13周　学术论文写作Ⅰ（Academic Writing Ⅰ） 224

Ⅰ. 概述 224
Ⅱ. 慕课讲稿 224
　　讲座1　学术论文写作介绍（Overview of Academic Writing） 224
　　讲座2　如何拟论文题目和主旨陈述（How to Prepare the Title and Thesis Statement） 230
　　讲座3　如何写文献综述（How to Present a Literature Review） 234
　　讲座4　如何写开题报告（How to Make a Thesis Proposal） 241
　　讲座5　如何写引言（How to Write the Introduction） 247
Ⅲ. 写作练习 252

第14周　学术论文写作Ⅱ（Academic Writing Ⅱ） 255

Ⅰ. 概述 255
Ⅱ. 慕课讲稿 255
　　讲座1　如何描述材料和方法（How to Describe the Materials and Methods Used in Research） 255
　　讲座2　如何汇报与讨论结果（How to Report and Discuss the Results of Research） 262
　　讲座3　如何写结论（How to Write the Conclusion） 268
　　讲座4　如何写摘要（How to Write the Abstract） 272
　　讲座5　如何引用文献（How to Cite the References） 278
Ⅲ. 写作练习 287

第15周　国际会议（International Conferences） ... 290

Ⅰ. 概述 ... 290

Ⅱ. 慕课讲稿 ... 290

　　讲座 1　课程和授课教师简介（Introduction to Course and Instructor's Name） ... 290

　　讲座 2　开始准备：投怎样的会议论文，投向何处？征文通知（Getting Started: What Paper Should You Send and Where? The Call for Papers） ... 293

　　讲座 3　撰写会议论文摘要（Writing the Abstract） ... 297

　　讲座 4　精心准备学术会议演讲（Crafting the Oral Presentation） ... 301

　　讲座 5　参加学术会议、宣读会议论文和接受提问（Tips on Attending a Conference, Presenting the Conference Paper, and Taking Questions） ... 305

Ⅲ. 写作练习 ... 308

写作练习参考答案 ... 310

第1周
词义的选择(Word Choice)

>> I. 概述

本周课程将探讨写作中如何选词和有效用词,主要从正反两个方面探讨措辞时词义的选择和注意避免使用某些类别的词汇。主要内容包括:如何正确选词、如何准确用词、如何精彩用词以及如何避免不恰当用词。

首先,什么是有效用词及其标准?我们所说的使用高级词汇是指在写作中使用了一定范围的高级词汇,这包括能够使用有效词汇、固定表达和习语,会使用正确的词形(word form)和符合语域(register)要求的用词。选择正确的词包括要了解词义的两个方面,即内涵和外延。区分这两个概念有助于学习者在同义词之间做出正确的选择,同时也有助于学习者洞悉英汉两种语言在词义色彩方面的差异。选词正确是最基本的要求,还需要选择恰当的词,分清什么是正式与非正式用词;最后还要学会使用能够给读者留下深刻印象的词汇,其中包括要区分泛指词和具体词。

其次,在选词上要学会尽量避免赘述、陈词滥调和卖弄辞藻,这样会使语言的使用更加地道、更加符合目标语的规范。

>> II. 慕课讲稿

讲座1 如何准确用词:理解词义——词的内涵与外延(How to Choose Words Accurately: Understand Word Meaning—Denotation and Connotation)

知识概要 本讲座首先对本周的学习内容做了简要的概括,之后回答了什么是正确选词的标准以及如何选择正确的词。主要内容有:1. 明白什么是措辞;2. 了解什么是词的内涵和外延,这有助于学习者准确用词;3. 需要注意因文化差异而导致的词的外延的差异。

关 键 词　diction（措辞）；denotation（内涵）；connotation（外延）；synonym（同义词）

Lead-in

Welcome to our Advanced Comprehensive English Writing Course—Basic writing: word meaning and effective word choice.

What are the criteria for effective word choice or the good use of vocabulary?

What we mean by excellence in respect to your use of vocabulary in your writing is that your choice of vocabulary should show a sophisticated range, effective word or idiom choice and usage, a mastery of word forms, and the use of appropriate register(tone) of words.

In Lectures 1-4: I will teach you some do's and don'ts regarding word choice. First, we learn some do's. **Lecture 1: How to use words accurately: about denotation and connotation**; **Lecture 2: How to use words effectively: formal and informal words**; **Lecture 3: How to use words compellingly: general and specific words.**

We also learn some don'ts in Lecture 4. They are: wordiness, cliché and pretentious words.

Objectives

- Understand the definition of word choice.
- Know about the two levels of meaning found in the denotations and connotations of words, which can help us make accurate word choice.
- Be cautious about the different connotations due to cultural differences.

Tasks

Read the following paragraph and answer the questions.

The Life of German Tycoons: The Reticent Rich

If they think their ranking on the list of rich individuals is too low (e.g. the *Forbes* 500), American tycoons fume. German ones kick up a fuss when their ranking looks suspiciously high, explains Heinz Dürr. When a magazine called him a billionaire a few years ago, Mr Dürr rang the editor to remonstrate. The reporters had double-counted his ownership of Homag, a maker of wood-processing machines that Dürr, his family's mechanical-engineering firm, bought in 2014. Plutocrats have reached the top of politics in America and Italy, while in Asian the super-

译文：如果美国**大亨们**认为自己在富豪榜上的排名太低（例如《福布斯》500强），他们就会大发雷霆。亨氏·杜尔解释说，当德国**富豪们**的排名看起来很可疑地靠前时，他们会骚动不安。几年前，当一家杂志称杜尔先生为**亿万富翁**时，他打电话给编辑提出抗议，说记者对他的Homag所有权进行了重复统计，Homag是一家木材加工机械制造商，也是2014年杜尔收购的一家家族机械工程公司。在美国和意大利，**富豪们**已经登上了政坛的顶峰，而在亚洲，

rich often display their wealth in ostentatious style. German's magnates love to shun the limelight.

超级富豪们往往以炫耀的方式展示他们的财富。德国的巨头们喜欢避开聚光灯。

Question 1

What are the images that come to your mind? Do the above five synonyms of "the rich" convey the author's same emotional preference?

You might say they have similar literal meanings, but the author adds a different flavor by using each word. Now let's look at the slightly different meanings.

Tycoon refers to a person who is successful in business and so has become rich and powerful. It is neutral and often disapproving. **Billionaire:** it is neutral. **Plutocrat** is a person who is powerful because of their wealth. It is neutral or negative. **The super rich** is neutral or negative. **Magnate** is someone who has earned a lot of money from a particular business or industry. It is neutral or positive. Of course, we can use other terms to refer to the rich people with positive or neutral meaning. For example, **the affluent**, **the better off**. So now you have different images of the rich.

✎ "the rich(富人)" 的同义词

中性词和贬义词	中性词	中性词和褒义词	褒义词
tycoon 大亨，指一个人在生意上成功，有钱又有权	billionaire 亿万富翁	magnate 巨头；大亨；富豪。指因某种特殊生意和工业而挣了很多钱的人	the affluent, the better off 富人；富裕阶层
plutocrat 有钱有势的人；财阀。指因有钱而变得有势的人			

Question 2

Why does the author use five synonyms instead of one term "the rich"?

Synonyms are words that have a similar or same meaning. Using synonyms can help move the reader easily from one thought to the next. Now you have a vivid picture about different kinds of rich people and the author's attitude toward wealth. Likewise, as you work on your academic essays, you need to create sentences that express clear and precise ideas, while at the same time not sounding dull. The author creates a varied picture to make the article more interesting and increase variety by avoiding needless repetition.

✎ 范文段落中使用 "the rich" 的 5 个同义词来分别表达作者对不同国家富豪的不同情感色彩，从而为我们生动形象地描绘出了不同面孔的富豪。使用同义词不仅可以为文章增色、避免枯燥乏味，还可以让文章的表达千变万化、生动有趣，避免不必要的重复。

Key Points

So what is Word Choice?

Word choice is the skillful use of language to create meaning. Word choice is also known as "**Diction**". It refers to a writer's selection of words determined by a number of factors like: **1. the significance of your idea; 2. specificity; 3. tone; 4. audience.**

> 词义的选择（word choice）是为了产生意义而有技巧地使用语言，也称为措辞（diction），由以下几个因素决定：1. 观点的意义；2. 具体性；3. 语气；4. 读者。

To achieve an excellent score in your use of vocabulary, the first step is to choose the accurate word every time.

Accuracy refers to "how well the target language is produced in relation to the rule system of the target language" (Skehen 1996).

> 准确性指"在目标语的规则系统中，目标语的产出质量高"（Skehen 1996）。

Semantically there are two kinds of word meaning: **Denotation**（内涵）and **Connotation**（外延）. **Denotation** is the dictionary meaning of a word—it's literal meaning. Some technological words and terminology only have denotative meaning, e.g. ESL, sodium（钠）, cartography（制图学）. **Connotation** refers to the meaning a word has in conversational and informal usage. Connotative meanings are the associations or emotional overtones that words have acquired.

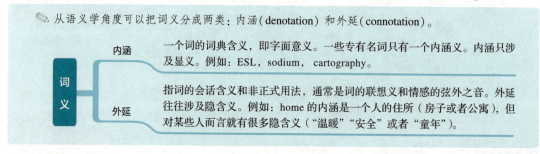

It tends to be concerned with implicit meaning. Wierzbicka (1986) shows that while *only*, *merely*, and *just* all denote "It is more than X" in the frame.

> I am going to buy that pen, if it is **only/merely/just** 10 cents.

Their connotations for English speakers are different. *Only* is more neutral, whereas *merely* is deprecating and *just* in mildly positive. *Just for fun* could be used as an advertising slogan, but *merely for fun* won't sell anything well. The various feelings, images and memories that surround a word make up its connotations. Connotations can be negative, neutral and positive.

> **only/merely/just** *adv.* 词义辨析
> 本义都是"It is more than X（只有，仅仅是）"，但对于以英语为母语的人士，它们的外延却不尽相同。

only	中性词。强调数量少或只是整体中的一小部分。例如：There are **only** two cars on the island. 这个岛上仅有两辆汽车。
merely	偏向贬义的词。用于强调数量之小。例如：The brain accounts for **merely** three percent of body weight. 大脑仅占体重的3%。
just	偏向褒义的词。在非正式文体中，just 可作"非常，简直，太"解，起强调作用（加强语气）。例如：I **just** love this book. 我太喜欢这本书了。**just** for fun"只是为了好玩；就是闹着玩的"。

Good writers are sensitive to both the denotations and the connotations of words.

For example, many words in English have synonyms, or words with very similar denotations, but with different connotations. For example, we might say, "There was a *crowd* at the lecture," but not "There was a *mob* at the lecture."

Quiz: In the left column the words are positive/neutral and could you give the negative words in the right column?

Positive/Neutral	Negative
scrupulous: praise somebody for being careful	meticulous: describe somebody being somewhat fussy
public servant	bureaucrat
financier	speculator
investigator	spy

Here are **two tips** on making an accurate word choice. When we use connotative word meanings we should pay more attention to:

1. Understand that we cannot expect a word or concept in one language to have an equivalent in another. For an example, there is no English word that conveys the full range of meanings that the Chinese term **"face"** possesses. Even concrete concepts, such as *mouse* have culture-specific associations, determined by speakers' interests and attitudes as much as by any denotations. For another example, *pine tree*（松）, *bamboo*（竹）, and *plum blossom*（梅）, *orchid*（兰）, *chrysanthemum*（菊）are simply common plants to English speakers but are embodiments of uprightness, perseverance, endurance, and loftiness in Chinese under the pens of many Chinese poets and artists since ancient times.

2. Be cautious about words with a positive meaning on surface but which imply the author's satiric or unfriendly tone. Read the following paragraph from *New York Time*.

China's Film Industry Finally Joins the Space Race
By Steven Lee Myers

The openings also come as China reached a milestone in space: the landing of a probe on the far side of the moon in January. Although decades behind Russia and the United States, China has now put astronauts in orbit and has *grandiose* plans to join—or even lead—a new age of space exploration.

> ✎ Pay attention to the word "*grandiose*". On the surface, it conveys a positive attitude toward China's achievement made in space exploration, but it implies the author's satiric and skeptical tone. We prefer the word "*ambitious*" here.

The connotations of a particular word choice can greatly impact the meaning of what you write. Obviously, the examples above are only the tip of the iceberg in regard to possible word choice. One strategy is to use a thesaurus (同义词词典) to check for synonyms. There are many of these online. You type in a word, and the thesaurus gives synonyms. For example, if I type in *smart*, I get many synonyms. Now have a look.

> agile, astute, bold, brainy, bright, brilliant, canny, crafty, good, nimble, quick, resourceful, sharp, shrewd, slick, wise, acute, adept, alert, brisk, genius, keen, knowing, pointed, ready, skull, whiz, apt, clever, effective, eggheaded, fresh, impertinent, ingenious, long-haired, nervy, on the ball, pert, quick-witted, sassy

> ✎ Instead of "*smart*", we use "*talented*" "*ingenious*" "*resourceful*" "*shrewd*" in formal writing. Pay more attention to the connotations of each word.

Today, we have learned how to choose words accurately by understanding their denotative and connotative meanings. Always be aware of words' connotative meanings and whether you are promoting positive or negative attitudes toward your subject. When it's time to write and revise, you make more word choices. Ask yourself: "Is this really what I mean?" "Does this sound right?"

讲座2 如何恰当选词——正式与非正式词
(How to Use Words Appropriately—Formal and Informal)

知识概要 本讲座强调恰当选词的重要性以及如何选择恰当的词。首先，要学会区分词的正式程度。根据语体风格，常用词可分为三类：正式的、半正式或通用的和非正式的；其次，要学会使用最常用的正式词。正式的学术文章要使用正式用词，体现客观性。注意：1. 选择第三人称代词；2. 用正式词汇而不用俚语；3. 如果要在单个的词和同义词组之间做出选择，尽量选用单个的词。

关 键 词 正式程度(formality)；行话(jargon)；口语的(colloquial)

Lead-in

British writer Jonathan Swift said, "Proper words in proper places make the true definition of a style." Diction is appropriate when it suits the intended occasion. Choosing words that are appropriate in your writing can convince your readers that your work is serious and important.

Objectives

- Learn what are formal, popular and informal words.
- Be able to choose formal/popular words for essay writing.
- Be able to present the most frequently used formal words.

Tasks

Look at the following paragraph and answer the questions.

English Language Learning Styles

1) We all know that students have their own individual styles of learning. Learning styles are a hot topic for analysis nowadays. 2) One expert says that there are six different general learning styles. 3) Do you know what they are called? They are dependent, independent, collaborative, competitive, participant, and avoidant. However, regarding English specifically, 4) another expert says there are only four different styles: the concrete, the analytical, the communicative and the authority-oriented. In the following paragraphs, 5) I'll tell 6) you more about this classification and explain some of the pros and cons of each one.

Question: Is this paragraph writing formal, semi-formal or informal?

Answer: This is an informal writing. If you intend to write in a formal way, you should not use first and second personal pronouns such as 1), 3), 5) and 6), nor use informal vocabulary, and acknowledge sources with accurate references, like 2) and 4). Do not ask questions in essays unless they are rhetorical questions, like 3), and do not use contractions, like 5).

> 如果给这个段落的写作打分的话，由于典型的问题是用词不规范(虽然内容较完整，使用了衔接词，符合段落写作要求)，一般给出的分数为6分(满分10分)。这也是写作成绩中等偏下的同学无法提高成绩的主要原因。这个段落的主要问题：1. 使用了第一人称和第二人称；2. 使用了口语词汇；3. 没有明确指出文献的来源；4. 使用了问句。正常情况下，除了修辞问句，不要使用问句；5. 使用了缩写词。

Key Points

What are the levels of formality?

Formality means the state of being formal. The level | 正式程度就是正式的状态。正

of formality of a piece of writing is determined by the purpose, the audience and the type of writing. There are three levels of formality in English: formal, semi-formal/popular and informal.

式程度是由写作目的、读者和写作类型决定的。英语正式程度分为三个层次：正式、半正式/通用和非正式。

【Formal】 We have talked about informal level of diction. Now let's come to the formal level of diction which is serious and dignified, such as textbooks, official reports, academic articles, essays, business letters, contracts, official speeches. Formal diction is often written in the third person, tends to include long sentences and multisyllabic words, and contains no slang or contractions. It has a slow, rhythmic flow and an authoritative, distant, and impersonal tone.

✎ 采用正式文体的通常是教材、政府工作报告、学术文章、论文、商务信函、合同、官方演讲等。除了使用第三人称，往往还会使用长难句、多音节词，表达舒缓、权威、疏远和非主观的语气。

Formal diction is also used in scholarly publications, in operation manuals, and in most academic fields. Notice in the following excerpt from a chemistry textbook that the language is concise, exact, and marked by specialized terms, called jargon(行话), used within the particular field of study. The examples of jargon are in italics(斜体).

✎ 下表段落中正式的或学术性的词汇很多，使用的语言简洁、准确，最为显著的是特殊术语，也叫行话。这些术语是非常正式的用语。

> A *catalyst* is classified as homogeneous if it is present in the same phase as that of the *reactants*. For *reactants* that are gases, a *homogeneous catalyst* is also a gas.

【Semi-formal/popular】 Formal writing and informal writing are the extremes. Most writing falls between these two extremes and is a blend of formal and informal elements that best fit the context, such as day-to-day interaction with colleagues and teachers, popular magazines/books, newspapers, interviews, when talking with someone in authority or who you respect. It sounds more conversational and personal than formal diction. Contractions may be used, and sentences tend to be shorter and less varied than in formal diction. The first person(*I, me, mine, we*) or second person(*you, your*) may be used.

Example

In the summer of 1987, I graduated from a public high school in Austin, Texas, and headed northeast to attend Yale. I then spent nearly 15 years studying at various universities—the London School of Economics, the University of Oxford, Harvard, and finally Yale Law School—picking up a string of degrees along the way. Today, I teach at Yale Law, where my students unnervingly(令人不安地) resemble my younger self: They are, overwhelmingly, products of professional parents and high-class universities. I pass on to them the advantages that my own teachers bestowed on me. They, and I, owe our prosperity and our caste(社会等级) to meritocracy(英才教育).

Though the author used five first person pronouns, his language is basically formal, being neither too serious nor too casual. In this excerpt, the writer conveys a light, conversational tone. There are also many action verbs(实义动词), few abstract words and more concrete words.

Since we have learned the three levels of formality, we now can consider which types of formality we should use in our essay writing and academic writing. IELTS[①] uses a semi-formal/popular or formal style. The IELTS website (www.ielts.org) says academic essays may use "a neutral or slightly formal style of writing". However, the more formal the vocabulary and the more complex the grammar, the higher writing scores your essay will receive. In the case of vocabulary, for instance, the scoring scheme gives higher scores when "less common" or "uncommon lexical items(words or phrases)" are used—which is what formal vocabulary is.

【Informal】If the situation is informal, for example, the writing may be colloquial; that is, the words may be chosen to suggest the language of everyday speech and conversation. It is friendly and casual. E.g. a friendly email. Contractions(*wasn't*, *I'll*), slang expressions(*cops*, *chill out*, *What's up?*), sentence fragments, and first-person and second-person pronouns are all common in informal diction. This level of diction should not be used in essays and academic writing, except when it is part of a quotation or a block of dialogue. Look at the style in the previous task: The language is casual; the sentences are shorter; the tone is familiar and friendly.

Here are some guidelines for understanding what vocabulary to employ for academic papers and essays.

Language Focus

1. **Choose formal/popular vocabulary:** Anglo-Saxon words are less formal than those of Latin/French origin. Native English words can be used both in oral and written English, while Latin and French derived-words are multi-syllabic, and frequently used in your thesis or dissertation writing. Here are the examples.

---

① IELTS：雅思考试，全称为"国际英语测试系统(International English Language Testing System)"。

高级综合英语写作教程（慕课版）

Anglo-Saxon	French	Latin
fire	flame	conflagration
goodness	virtue	probity
fast	firm	secure
fear	terror	trepidation
tiredness	weariness	lassitude
rise	mount	ascend
work	endeavor	toil
holy	sacred	consecrated

Now let's look at the following words. On the right of each pair are the formal words which can be used in the formal writing.

deep—profound	room—accommodation	tooth—dental
body—physique	begin—commence	end—terminate
leave—depart	quit—resign	help—aid
buy—purchase	have—possess	use—utilize
wet—humid	inner—interior	lonely—solitary
deadly—mortal	find out—discover	cut down—reduce
blow up—explode	look into—investigate	on time—punctual

2. **Phrasal verbs & single-word equivalents:** single-word equivalents in the brackets are the formal words which can be used in the formal writing.

ask for (request)	go down with (contract)	set up (establish)
deal with (handle)	find out (discover)	take in (deceive)
look at (examine)	devise (come up)	check up (investigate)

She **caught on** (understood) very quickly.
She **made up for** (compensated) it with an early night.
He **went down** (contracted) with a fever.
The cost of living **went up** (increased/rose).

However, don't think that a few phrasal verbs in your essay writing will make it too informal. In fact, there are many situations—even in quite formal texts—when a phrasal verb is the most natural-sounding way of expressing an idea.

Summary

To summarize, formality and impersonality prevail in a formal research paper.

1. Use the third person (*he*, *she*, *it*) rather than the first person (*I*, *we*), unless you are expressing a personal opinion.
2. Use standard vocabulary, not slang or a regional or an ethnic dialect.
3. Use a more formal one-word verb if it sounds more appropriate than its phrasal verb equivalent.
4. Informal writing tends to be characterized by slang, contractions, references to the reader, and concrete nouns.

Formal writing places a high value on **objectivity** and **accuracy**. Be sure to choose the proper words for your academic writing; consider using more words of French or Latin origin, or the precise terminology employed for the topic under consideration.

讲座3 如何选择有说服力的词：特指词和泛指词(How to Use Words Compellingly—Specific and General)

知识概要　首先，要学会区分抽象词和具体词、泛指词和特指词。其次，在写作中要学会交替使用泛指词和特指词。

关 键 词　抽象词(abstract word)；具体词(concrete word)；
泛指词(general word)；特指词(specific word)

Lead-in

Now we are going to explore **how to use words compellingly**. When you write, have you ever asked yourself the question "Am I trying too hard to impress my readers?" How will you impress your readers? William Blake in his poem *The Auguries*(预兆) *of Innocence* wrote, "To see the world in a grain of sand, and a heaven in a wild flower(一粒沙看世界，一朵花看天堂)." This English poet, rather like the Chinese Zen poets, informs us we can know something, even something about the world and the heaven, by studying what is in front of our noses. *The world* and *the heaven* are general nouns. *A grain of sand* and *a wild flower* are specific words. *Flower* can become a general noun, and, to be more specific, we can say *geranium*(天竺葵) or *rose*. They are specific nouns. Learning how to use general and specific words can make our writing more vivid and interesting, or at least less confusing.

Objectives

- Be able to distinguish abstract and concrete words, general and specific words.
- Be able to use the general words or specific words alternatively.

Tasks

Revise the first draft.

First draft: Let's begin our new life. To **cherish** every day.

Revised version: So let's **hop into** our new life with a new perspective! To *live* every fleeting minute *to the fullest*, to **savor** every bite of a juicy apple, and to **digest** every word in a poem.

* In the revised version the author uses a lot of concrete verbs: *hop into*, *live to the fullest*, *savor*, *digest* rather than the general word *cherish*. These are the types of details that writers should strive to show. The revised one is more interesting, because it includes more concrete, specific details.

Now it is your turn. In the following sentence pair, notice how the underlined words in the first sentence provide little information, whereas those in the revised sentences provide interesting details.

First draft: On Black Friday people **rushed to** the counters.

Revised version: On Black Friday people **elbowed** and **shoved** their way to the counters.

* In the second draft we use strong verbs to spice up our writing.

In order to write compellingly, we should use more specific and concrete words instead of general and abstract words in most cases. Now let's distinguish concrete words and abstract words: *Concrete* comes originally from the Latin *concresco*, (*cresco*: to grow; *con*: together), usually referring to a physical process (like "concrete hardening"). Often concrete terms are words or details that appeal to one or more of the five senses, or words identifying persons and things that can be perceived by the senses or understood by the mind—seen, heard, tasted, felt, smelled, remembered, e. g. table, boy, rose, chair, book, teacher, honking, *Hamlet* or *the Boxer Rebellion*.

写作要有说服力，在大多数情况下，我们应该使用更具体的词，而不是笼统、抽象的词。具体词源于拉丁语 concresco, cresco（to grow）con（together），通常指的是一个物理过程（如混凝土硬化）。具体词通常指的是涉及五个感官中的一个或多个感官的词或细节，或者指能够被感官感知或被头脑理解的词。例如：seen, heard, tasted, felt, smelled, remembered; table, boy, rose, chair, book, teacher, honking; *Hamlet*, *the Boxer Rebellion*.

Here are different types of Concrete Noun:

- **common nouns** (e. g., man, dog)
- **proper nouns** (e. g., Simon, Bonzo)
- **countable nouns** (e. g., bear, country)
- **uncountable nouns** (e. g., music, tennis)
- **collective nouns** (e. g., choir, group)

Key Points

Abstract: *abstract* comes from the Latin word *abtraho*, *traho* means to *draw off*, *ab* means *from*. It often means to strip away material details to leave only the bare essence of the item under consideration. They tend to be words that do not refer to material objects or suggest a direct engagement with any of the five senses. *Courage*, *truth*, *justice*, *honor* and *education* are a few abstract terms.

✎ *abstract* 一词源于拉丁词 *abtraho*，其中 *traho* 的意思是"抽出（draw off）"，*ab* 的意思是"来自（from）"，指剥去事物的细节，只考虑留下该事物本质的东西。这种词不是指物体以及与五种感官联系的直接关系。例如：courage, truth, justice, honor, education。区分一个词是具体名词还是抽象名词要取决于语境，甚至是"可感知的"这个词的定义。

Be aware that classifying a noun as concrete or abstract may depend on context or even the classifier's definition of perceivable.

Some nouns will be abstract in one meaning but concrete in another. For example:

◇ You may be able to fool the voters but not *the atmosphere*. （American environmental scientist Donella Meadows）
（When *atmosphere* refers to the envelope of gases surrounding the Earth, it's concrete.）

◇ Moscow had an intense *atmosphere* of darkness and secrecy. （American author Alan Furst）
（When *atmosphere* refers to the pervading mood of a place, it's abstract.）

General: The most general terms refer to classes or groups. These terms are very broad. For example, flower and dog are general terms.

Specific: The most specific terms stand for definite, precise things. Specific words convey much more information than general words. Most words are neither wholly general nor specific. They exist between the two extremes. A useful exercise in learning to be specific is to see the words we use for people, places, things and ideas as being positioned somewhere on a "**ladder of abstraction**".

✎ 泛指词（general words）和特指词（specific words）是相对的、非绝对的概念。相比较而言，有些词比另外一些词的含义更广泛、更具体。

The following examples show how you might move from general to specific word choice:

Very General	==	Less General	==	More Specific	==	Quite Specific
college student		freshman		boy in math class		Bill Jones
organism		plant		flower		Irises（鸢尾花）

Words that are concrete rather than abstract are more powerful in certain types of writing, specifically in academic works and works of nonfiction. However, abstract words can be powerful tools when creating poetry, fiction, or persuasive rhetoric. They are often used in philosophical and other academic writing. Abstract terms are useful, for we must often write about ideas and concepts, and we need terms that represent those concepts. Abstract terms are useful and even necessary when we want to name ideas (as we do in thesis statements and some paragraph topic sentences), but they're not likely to make points clear or interesting without specific details which clarify them.

在某些类型的写作中，在具体专业的学术著作和非小说类作品中，使用具体词会更有说服力。在诗歌创作、小说或劝说性修辞中，抽象词可以成为强有力的工具。抽象词也经常用于哲学和其他学术写作中。当我们必须表达观点和概念并给这些观点命名时，需要给出能够表述这些概念的术语。这时需要使用抽象术语，比如我们所写的文章主旨句和一些段落主题句。但是，如果没有具体的细节，抽象术语不可能使我们的观点更加清晰或者更加有趣。

Language Focus

✓ Choose specific verbs

In reporting what you have gathered from reading, you will need to use a variety of verbs that suit your purpose. Rather than using the words *say*, *show* or *report* all the time, you may use more specific verbs in academic writing as illustrated below:

In the article, *Euthanasia*, the author **outlines** the origins of the practice in the Nazi regime. Many medical studies have **demonstrated** a clear correlation between smoking and the incidence of lung cancer…The researcher **maintains** that nanoparticles are likely to remain lodged…The paper **concludes** that university education must remain accessible to all who qualify and that none should be denied the opportunity…Available literature **seems to support the view** that one acquires a second language…The report **notes that** there are inconsistencies in the way the economic data have been presented…

Other useful words for reporting what you have gathered in your secondary research are *assert*, *claim*, *argue*, *infer*, *reason*, *postulate* and *illustrate*.

Avoid using unsophisticated adjectives such as *good*, *bad*, *bit*, *little*.

选择具体的词：在一个段落中，不要总是使用 say, show or report, 还可以使用动词 outline, demonstrate, maintain, conclude, seem 和 note 等。此外，类似的用于表达所收集的二手研究的词还有 assert, claim, argue, infer, reason, postulate, illustrate 等。避免使用 good, bad, bit, little 这样的小词。

Summary

Abstract and general words enable us to express ideas. Specific and concrete words enable us to define entities. Both types of words are indispensable, and an accomplished writer can use the two kinds of diction alternatively.

✎ 尽管泛指词和具体词在写作中都应该使用，但是要更多更好地使用具体词，因为具体词的使用会使文章更准确、清晰、生动和鲜活，也更细致、更精彩，表达力更强，能给人留下深刻的印象。

讲座 4　需要避免使用的词（Some Don'ts in Word Choice）

知识概要　本讲座介绍如何避免选词上的三种常见错误类型：赘述、套话和卖弄辞藻；此外也包含避免赘述的四个规则。

关 键 词　赘述（wordiness），套话（cliché），卖弄辞藻（pretentious words）

Lead-in

So far we have learned some do's in word choice to make your diction accurate, appropriate and compelling. Failure to decide precisely what you want to say, or failure to determine how you want to say it, results in sentences that convey blurred, weak thoughts. Here are some typical don'ts in word choice based on common mistakes: **wordiness**, **cliché** and **pretentious words**.

Objectives

- Learn what are the three types of common mistakes in word choice.
- Be able to find four rules for avoiding wordiness.
- Be able to identify the three types of common mistakes.

Tasks

Do you think the following words in bold characters are necessary words?

1. To accelerate **the pace of** economic reform...（to accelerate ＝ increase the pace of）
2. Living standards **for the people**...（The notion of living standards applies only to people.）
3. We should adopt **a series of** measures to ensure that...（Here the plural form of "measures" covers the sense of "series".）
4. In my opinion, **I think** ...
5. What's more, **besides** ...
6. Account for the reason **why**...

✎ 以上例子都是大家在写作中经常出现的赘述问题，主要原因是受到了中式英语的影响。

高级综合英语写作教程（慕课版）

Key Points

So we need to cut out all the words in bold characters. "Vigorous writing is concise. A sentence should contain no unnecessary words, a paragraph no unnecessary sentences, for the same reason that a drawing should have no unnecessary lines and a machine no unnecessary parts." Conciseness is also a mark of good academic writing. To write an effective essay, you should learn to write precisely and concisely, using only as many words as are necessary to convey what you want to say. Do not add words just to lengthen your essay or create fancy expressions. It is far more important to get your message across effectively. To weed out redundancy, ask yourself whether what you have written is essential to the meaning you intend to communicate.

> "雄浑的文字是简洁的。一个句子不应该包含不必要的词语，一个段落不应该包含不必要的句子，出于同样的原因，一幅画不应该有不必要的线条，一台机器不应该有不必要的零件。"简洁是学术写作的标志，不要为了文章的长度或者标新立异的表达增加一些不必要的词。为了避免冗余的词汇，一定要问问自己你所写下的内容是否是你想要表达的。

1 **Redundancy** is commonly seen in the use of *more* or *most* as in the following two examples:

Example 1 There is a *more* preferable method to do this.

（If you prefer something, you like it more than something else; therefore, *more* is redundant.）

Example 2 This is the *most* unique case we have yet seen.

（In the second case, *unique* means one of its kind, with no equal, so strictly speaking, you cannot have varying degrees of uniqueness. So delete *more* or *most*.）

Based on Joan Pinkham's book *The Translator's Guide to Chinglish*, here are four main types of superfluous（多余的）words: Words are superfluous when they can be replaced with fewer words that mean the same thing.

> *more* 和 *most* 是比较容易产生赘述的两个副词，因此要留意哪些词不能加这两个副词来修饰。例如，preferable（例1）和 unique（例2），perfect 和 unique 本身就是表达绝对含义的词。有冗余的词就说明同样的意思本来可以用较少的词来替代。

（1）Omit superfluous unnecessary phrases

Sometimes you can use a simpler word for these phrases, so use the words on the right instead of the words on the left:

- in order to→to
- in the event that→if
- subsequent to→after
- prior to→before
- despite the fact that→although
- because of the fact that→because, since
- in light of→because, since
- owing to the fact that→because, since

◇ came to the realization→realized	◇ due to the fact that→because
◇ is of the opinion→thinks	◇ in all cases→always
◇ regardless of the fact that→although	◇ at that point in time→then

(2) Omit *the* + general noun + *of*

There is one type of noun that deserves special mention, because it is the commonest type of unnecessary word in Chinglish. This is the general noun that serves only to introduce a specific noun (or gerund) to follow: "a serious mistake in **the work of planning**." In such constructions, the first noun announces the category of the second; in this case, it tells readers that "planning" falls into the category of "work". That is something they already know. Accordingly, the first noun should be deleted, to produce "a serious mistake in planning". Now it's your turn. Consider "promoting **the cause of** peaceful reunification". We should remove "the cause of".

✎ 省略"**the** + 泛指名词(**general noun**) + **of**"是中式英语中常见的名词赘述情况。例如短语"a serious mistake **in the work of planning**"中的"**in the work of planning**"这个结构,前面的泛指名词用于介绍后面的具体名词(或者动名词)。第一个名词表明第二个名词的类别。"planning"属于"work"的一个类别,是我们已知的信息,所以需要去掉"work of"。与此类似,"promoting **the cause of** peaceful reunification"需要把"the cause of"去掉。

(3) Unnecessary verb + noun

Most unnecessary verbs in Chinglish occur in phrases. Usually, they are combined with nouns(plus the inevitable articles and prepositions that nouns bring with them).

Example: We must **make an improvement** in our work.

Here the verb(make) is a weak, colorless, all-purpose word having no very specific meaning, while the real action is expressed in the noun(improvement). Since the verb contributes nothing to the sense, remove it! So we say "We must **improve** our work".

✎ 省略"不必要的动词 + 名词":在例句中,动词"make"是无色彩的、万能的、没有特定含义的弱动词,而真正的动作是由名词"improvement"表达的。可以将improvement改为相应的动词,即"We must **improve** our work"。

Now it is your turn: **Can you simplify the following wordy phrases?**

◇ to make an investigation of →to investigate	◇ to make a careful study of →to study carefully

高级综合英语写作教程（慕课版）

◇ to make an analysis→to analyze
◇ to make an application→to apply
◇ to make a determination→to determine
◇ to make a distribution→to distribute
◇ to have a dislike for→to dislike
◇ to have respect for→to respect
◇ to give guidance to→to guide
◇ to carry out the struggle against
　→to struggle against

We can remove the weak verb, and use the verb form of the noun.

(4) Unnecessary verb + unnecessary noun + third word

Example: our *efforts* to *reach* the *goal* of *modernization*

There are three nouns: *efforts*, *goal* and *modernization*. The third word is usually a noun (or gerund). Since this new noun is in fact performing the function of a verb, it should be given the form of a verb. So we need to say "our efforts to **modernize**".

Sometimes the problem isn't choosing exactly the right word to express an idea—it's being "wordy", or using words that your readers may regard as "extra" or superfluous.

Keep an eye out for wordy constructions and see if you can replace them with more concise words or phrases.

省略"不必要动词＋不必要名词＋第三个词"：例句中有三个名词"efforts""goal"和"modernization"。第三个词通常是名词或者动名词。因为第三个词是在执行前面动词的动作，应该使用动词形式，所以要变成"our efforts to modernize"。

以上例子不是说这样使用就是错误的，而是说这样的措辞会让读者认为你使用了多余的词，是赘述，因此，一定要留意你使用的短语结构，看看是否可以用更为简洁的词和短语来替代。

 Clichés（套话）

Can you summarize the common features of the following phrases?

every coin has two sides; with the development of; it dawned on me; sigh of relief; last but not least; work like a dog; all work and no play; it goes without saying; saw the light; easier said than done; on top of the world; time and time again

Yes, they are **clichés**.

A cliché is an expression that has been worn out through constant use, overused word phrases and statements such as, "Don't judge a book by its cover." In everyday speech, we might use clichés, but academic writing requires more thoughtful ideas and originality. This also means that you

套话（Clichés）就是过度、高频使用的短语和陈述，例如"Don't judge a book by its cover.（不要以貌取人。）"日常交流可以使用套话，但是学术写作要求有思想且为原

should avoid using clichés because they do not show original thought and lack specific meaning. It is a better strategy to think of more original and specific ways of stating your idea.

创。良好的写作策略是避免使用套话。

❸ Pretentious Words（卖弄辞藻）

Can you make some unnatural-sounding sentences into natural-sounding ones?

（1）We relished the delicious repast.

（We can say "We enjoyed the delicious meal."）

（2）The officer apprehended the intoxicated operator of the vehicle.

（It should be "The officer arrested the drunken driver."）

We can see that the same thoughts can be expressed more clearly and effectively by using plain, natural language.

✎ 卖弄辞藻（pretentious words）：相对于小词（small words），很多人喜欢用大词，也就是通过卖弄辞藻来展示自己丰富的词汇量和高超的用词技巧。下面的两个例子中完全不必卖弄辞藻来生硬地表达一个简单的陈述。

（1）We relished the delicious repast.

口语中可以用"We enjoyed the delicious meal."来替换上面的句子。

relish：If you relish the idea, thought, or prospect of something, you are looking forward to it very much.

Jacqueline is not relishing the prospect of another spell in prison.

杰奎琳可不想再蹲一阵子监狱。

repast：（old-fashioned or formal）餐；饭菜，相当于 a meal。这是个不常用、过于正式的词。

（2）The officer apprehended the intoxicated operator of the vehicle.

（It should be "The officer arrested the drunken driver."）

We can see that the same thoughts can be expressed more clearly and effectively by using plain, natural language.

apprehend vt. 逮捕；拘押 If the police apprehend someone, they catch them and arrest them.

Police have not apprehended her killer. 警察还未抓获谋杀她的凶手。

这个动词过于正式。

Summary

Some people feel that they can improve their writing by using fancy, elevated words rather than simple, natural words. They use artificial, stilted language that more often obscures their meaning than communicates it clearly. One of the biggest mistakes students made in academic writing is trying too hard to sound "academic". Be sure to avoid writing stiff, overly formal sentences; using big words just for the sake of it, and therefore expressing ide-

✎ 语言使用是否地道也是考查写作能力的主要方面。遣词造句地道，不是指文章通篇都用难词、偏词和长句，而是要变化着使用一些英美人常用的语句，用原汁原味的英文把自己的想法表达清楚。避免生搬硬套过时和过于正式的字眼，不要为了用大词而用大词。

as indirectly.

Remember to check that you use formal vocabulary and that you write concisely—without redundancy and precisely—with words that accurately convey your intended meaning. In addition, you may encounter other examples of uncertainty or confusion regarding word choice. The best guide would be a good dictionary, one that gives you examples of word usage. You can also refer to online corpus resources such as the British National Corpus to check how words are used in published works. If help is not available, it is safer to choose to be simple and clear rather than risk confusing your readers.

We have learned what some don'ts are in your word choice. Now best wishes to get ready for your writing journey.

Ⅲ. 写作练习

1. Choose the correct word in each sentence. Use A to stand for the first word, and B to stand for the second word.

1) His conclusions were **quiet/quite** interesting, but controversial.
2) Millions of people are attempting to **lose/loose** weight.
3) Doctors have great **stature/status** in most countries.
4) Professor Li received their **compliments/complements** politely.
5) The ancient symbol depicted a snake eating **it's/its** tail.
6) Both social and **economical/economic** criteria need to be examined.
7) The tourists went to **claim/exclaim** their luggage at the station.
8) The first prize was **rewarded/awarded** to the youngest competitor.
9) They have the **sole/single** right to sell these products.
10) Sunspots have been known to **affect/effect** radio communication.

2. The following pairs of words are close in meaning but one word in each case is pejorative(贬义的). Pick up the one.

1) terrorist/freedom-fighter   2) slim/skinny   3) fluent/wordy
4) mean/thrifty   5) cunning/shrewd   6) generous/extravagant

3. Select the better alternative (more formal) in each case.

1) The survey **proved/yielded** a surprising amount of information on student politics.
2) This question **arose/manifested** when older students were examined.
3) Both writers attempt to **demonstrate/imply** that older employees are more reliable.
4) Darwin **held/indicated** very strong views on this issue.
5) It must be **proved/emphasized** that these results are only provisional.

6) One of the chimpanzees **supplemented/exhibited** signs of nervousness.

7) Freud was **concerned/identified** primarily with middle class patients.

8) The study was **generated/carried out** to explore the issue of religious tolerance.

4. Certain words are italicized in the following sentences. In the space provided on the left, identify the words as slang (S), a cliché (C), or pretentious words (PW). Then replace the words with more effective diction.

_____ 1) Losing weight *is easier said than done* for someone who loves sweets.

_____ 2) After dinner, we washed the *culinary utensils* and wrapped the *excess* food.

_____ 3) After we set up camp, we watched a beautiful sunset, and then *hit the sack*.

_____ 4) Michelle spent the summer *watching the tube and catching rays*.

_____ 5) The stew I made contained *everything but the kitchen sink*.

_____ 6) My parents never *laid guilt trips on me* when I was a *kid*.

_____ 7) Most colleges *commence* on September 1.

_____ 8) Since I decided to study harder, math no longer seems *clear as mud*.

5. Try to revise the following sentences with better word choice.

1) This signing of the document is ineligible.

2) I received third place in the contest.

3) She understands deeply that I would do everything for her.

4) We can keep in contact by means of WeChat.

5) As the price for an apartment in Beijing is very expensive this year, I cannot afford it.

6) The government has made good progress in solving environmental problems.

7) Our university provides convenience for study.

8) I support him in my mind.

9) He is a person of much ambition and full of great expectation of future.

10) Self-conception is the basis of one's attitude towards success and failure.

第2周
语句的变化及常见句子错误
(Sentence Variety and Common Sentence Errors)

❯❯ I. 概述

本周我们将首先学习如何在写作中使用多样的语句。使用不同类型和不同长度的语句，则文章可读性强，反之，则呆板和单调。具体而言，我们将学习长短句交替使用；变换句子开头；使用倒装句；使用平行结构这四种技巧。

短句通常为简单句，用词较少，短句的优点在于表达简洁、易读并且清楚有力。长句修饰成分多，可以准确地表达复杂的思想。长句包括并列句、复合句和并列复合句。可以使用并列连词或从属连词把短句连接起来，也可以使用分词短语或不定式短语将短句合并成一个长句，其中分词短语或不定式短语将充当状语成分。

如果一篇文章从头到尾都以主语开头必然枯燥乏味，读来无趣。因此，我们要尝试以副词、分词短语、不定式短语、从句等作为句子的开头，灵活多样的句子结构会使文章生动活泼，给文章添彩。

本周第二项重点内容是常见的句子错误，概括起来大致有以下五种：破句、串句、修饰语错置、垂悬修饰语和错误的平行结构。

破句是缺少主语或谓语而无法表达完整意思的错句。串句是错误地将两个独立的分句串在一起。串句有两种形式：一种是用逗号隔开的，也叫"逗号误接句（comma splices）"；另一种不使用任何标点符号，叫作"熔合句（fused sentences）"。修饰语错置是修饰语与被修饰语摆放的位置不恰当。修饰语可以是单词、词组、从句，也可以是句子，为避免修饰语错置，修饰语和被修饰的对象要尽量靠近。垂悬修饰语是修饰语在逻辑上与它所修饰的词语分离，或找不到逻辑上被修饰的对象，因而看起来好像与句子的其他部分无关。平行结构可以是单词、词组、从句，也可以是句子。并列成分需要用相同的语法结构表达出来。

Ⅱ. 慕课讲稿

讲座 1　语句的变化（Sentence Variety）

知识概要　在写作中使用多样的语句会使文章节奏富于变化，可读性强，否则，则单调乏味。本讲座主要涉及**增强句子多样性的三个技巧——长句和短句、复合句和简单句应当交替使用；句子的开头可以使用副词、分词短语、不定式短语等，而不是始终用句子的主语充当开头；在多数为正常顺序的语句中穿插使用倒装句和恰当地使用并列平行结构**。

关 键 词　语句的变化(sentence variety)；句子长度(sentence length)；
　　　　　　句子开头(sentence beginning)；倒装句(inverted sentence)；
　　　　　　平行结构(parallel structure)

Lead-in

In this lecture we'll focus on **how to add sentence variety to your writing**. Using sentences of different types and lengths makes your writing more engaging. If too many of your sentences are short, simple sentences, your writing may sound monotonous. Compare the given two paragraphs. Which one is better written?

Paragraph 1　Being a veterinarian is hard work. Sometimes the veterinarian has to handle heavy animals. Some dogs can weigh more than 100 pounds. Rural veterinarians must care for large animals on-site. That means they must travel from farm to farm. Of course, there are also late-night emergencies. Still, there are many rewards. Veterinarians know the joy of helping animals. They have the satisfaction of relieving their pain.

Paragraph 2　Being a veterinarian is hard work. A veterinarian must be able to handle heavy animals, including dogs that can weigh more than 100 pounds. In addition, rural veterinarians must care for large animals on-site, which means they must travel from farm to farm. Of course, there are also late-night emergencies to deal with. Still, there are many rewards, especially knowing the joy and satisfaction of helping animals and relieving their pain.

> In Paragraph 1, all of the sentences have the same basic length. Using short simple sentences often produces writing that does not flow well. Paragraph 2 is an improvement because now the sentences vary in type and length. How does the writer do that? He/She combines shorter sentences with phrases and conjunctions.

Objectives

In this lecture we'll learn four techniques to add sentence variety.

- Vary sentence lengths.
- Vary sentence beginnings.
- Use inverted sentences.
- Use parallel structures.

Key Points

✓ Vary sentence lengths

Ideas from shorter sentences can be combined into one sentence using an infinitive phrase(不定式短语)or a participial phrase(分词短语).

> Short sentences:
> 1. Annetta searched the Internet. She needed information about the Serengeti Plain.
> 2. I would really like to go to Africa. That's my dream vacation.
>
> Combined sentences:
> 1. Annetta searched the Internet to find information about the Serengeti Plain.
> 2. To go to Africa is my dream vacation.

Example 1 Why did Annetta search the Internet? "To find information about the Serengeti Plain." We could use this infinitive phrase as an adverbial of purpose(目的状语).

Example 2 An infinitive phrase can also serve as the subject of a sentence, so we could use "to go to Africa" to replace "that".

> Short sentences:
> 1. Kyle walked barefoot in the garden. He stepped on a hornets' nest.
> 2. Shannon covered her ears. She was annoyed by the sound of the air hammer.
>
> Combined sentences:
> 1. Kyle, walking barefoot in the garden, stepped on a hornets' nest.
> 2. Annoyed by the sound of the air hammer, Shannon covered her ears.

Example 1 we learned that while Kyle was walking barefoot he stepped on a hornets' nest. So we could use a present participial phrase to combine these two short sentences.

Example 2 Why did Shannon cover her ears? Because she was annoyed by the sound of the air hammer. Thus a past participial phrase is needed to combine these two short sentences.

✓ Vary sentence lengths

Ideas from shorter sentences can be combined into a compound sentence, using coordinating conjunctions(并列连词) like *and*, *but*, *yet*, *or*, *so*, etc.

> **Short sentences:**
> These deformities(畸形) have been difficult to accept. They have provided me with a unique life and greatly influenced the development of my character.
> **Combined sentences:**
> These deformities have been difficult to accept, but they have provided me with a unique life and greatly influenced the development of my character.

We could easily see the contrast between these two sentences. Thus "but" or "yet" is needed to connect these two sentences.

✓ Vary sentence lengths

Ideas from shorter sentences can be combined into a complex sentence(主从复合句). The two clauses can be connected with a subordinating conjunction(从属连词) or a relative pronoun/adverb(关系代词/副词).

> **Short sentences:**
> Mt. Mckinley rises 20,320 feet above sea level. It is the highest peak in the United States.
> **Combined sentences:**
> Mt. Mckinley, which rises 20,320 feet above sea level, is the highest peak in the United States.

Now read through the two short sentences. We could change the first sentence into a dependent clause(从句) and use the second sentence as an independent clause(主句) and thus combine these two sentences into a complex sentence.

✓ Vary sentence beginnings

> **Begin with a subject:**
> Chaya spilled some of the chemicals used in the safety drill.
> The other students followed safety procedures.
> **Begin with a modifying word or phrase:**
> Quickly, they pulled on safety gloves and switched on the ventilation hoods.
> Standing quietly at the door, the teacher made notes on a clipboard.
> As the seconds ticked by, the class worked to clean up the chemicals.
> Because they had gone through the practice many times, the students knew exactly what to do.

In paragraphs and essays, varied sentence beginnings can make your writing more interesting. In addition to beginning with a subject, you can begin with a modifying word or phrase. To be more specific, you can try beginning with **an adverb**, **a participial phrase**, **a preposition phrase** or **a dependent clause**. These different beginnings will add variety to your sentences.

✔ **Use inverted sentences**

> Normal: Traffic is lighter in a gated community.
> Inverted: In a gated community, there is less traffic.
> Normal: A nervous Ray Brown stood on the free throw line with two seconds left.
> Inverted: On the free throw line, with two seconds left, stood Ray Brown.

Another way to add variety to your sentences is to include inverted sentences in your writing. This type of sentences delays the main information until the end, giving it added emphasis.

In the first pair of examples, the second sentence ends with the subject to give added emphasis to the main point: less traffic. In the second pair of examples, the second sentence gives emphasis to the subject: Ray Brown.

✔ **Use parallel construction**

Using parallel construction gives your writing rhythm. You could try repeating similar grammatical elements (words or phrases). Please note this: all repeated words and phrases should have the same structure, otherwise they are not parallel.

Sentence elements	Examples	Technique used
Words (All the words in a series should be the same parts of speech.)	**Not parallel:** Opera can amuse, sadden, or make you think.	
	Parallel: Opera can amuse, sadden, or inspire.	All the words in the series are verbs.
	Parallel: Opera can be amusing, depressing, or inspiring.	All the words in the series are adjectives.
Phrases (All the phrases in a series should be the same type.)	**Not parallel:** The audience members reacted to the show by jumping to their feet, cheering for an encore, and with calls of "Bravo".	
	Parallel: The audience members reacted to the show by jumping to their feet, cheering for an encore, and calling "Bravo".	All the phrases are participial phrases.
	Parallel: The audience began to cheer, to jump to their feet, and to call "Bravo".	All the phrases are infinitive phrases.

In **Example** 1, three verbs are used. "Amuse" and "sadden", the first two verbs, have no objects(宾语)while the third one "make" has one. Thus the sentence is not parallel. We could correct the sentence by using three verbs, none of which has objects. We could also try using three adjectives. In **Example** 2, "jumping to their feet" "cheering for an encore" and "with calls of Bravo" are not parallel either. The third phrase should be changed to "calling 'Bravo'".

Samples

Read through the following sample and find out what techniques the writer has used to add sentence variety.

1) When I was 13 years old[start with a dependent clause], my family—my grandparents, my little sister, and I—moved to the United States from Mexico. 2) I still remember worrying about leaving my lifelong friends behind and having to make new ones in a completely foreign land[parallel structure]. 3) My grandparents had made this decision to move and there was no changing their minds[compound sentence]. 4) "We are moving to make a better life for you and your sister, and you will thank us one day[compound sentence]," they explained. 5) I did not believe them[vary sentence length]. 6) All I could think was that my grandparents, whom I loved and trusted, were doing something that would be the end of happiness as I knew it[complex sentence]. 7) I was sure that I would never forgive them[complex sentence]. 8) In my teen years[start with a preposition phrase], I lacked perspective, above all, the perspective that comes from looking beyond yourself.

Sentence 1 begins with a dependent clause. In Sentence 2, parallel structure is used. Sentences 3 & 4 are compound sentences. Sentence 5 is a short sentence. Sentences 6 & 7 are both complex sentences. The last sentence begins with a preposition phrase and is a complex sentence.

Summary

We've learned about four techniques to add sentence variety. In addition to combining short sentences and creating compound as well as complex sentences, you could try using different beginnings, inverted sentences and parallel construction.

✎ 本讲要点思维导图如下：

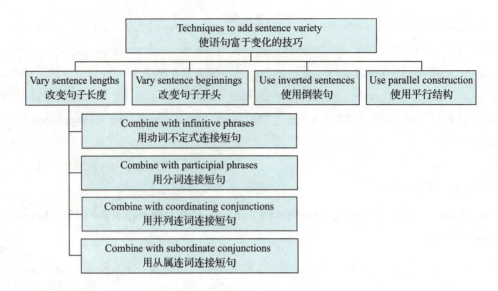

讲座 2 常见句子错误 I（Common Sentence Errors I）

知识概要 本讲座主要涉及两种常见的句子错误，包括**破句**和**串句**。**破句**是缺少主语或谓语而无法表达完整意思的错句。**串句**是错误地将两个独立的分句串在一起。串句有两种形式：一种用逗号隔开，也叫"逗号误接句（comma splices）"；另一种不使用任何标点符号，叫作"熔合句（fused sentences）"。

关 键 词 常见句子错误（common sentence errors）；破句（sentence fragments）；
串句（run-ons）；逗号误接句（comma splices）；熔合句（fused sentences）

Lead-in

In this lecture, we'll focus on **common sentence errors**.

Have you ever written sentences like the given examples? Could you identify the errors?

1. The desire of all mankind to live in peace and freedom, for example.
2. The best movie that I saw last year.
3. Although people want to believe that all men are created equal.
4. Getting married is easy, staying married is a different matter.
5. An encyclopedia is a valuable source of information, it contains summaries of every area of knowledge.
6. San Francisco is a very cosmopolitan city there are people from many cultures and ethnic groups living there.
7. Hang-gliding is a dangerous sport you can easily break your leg.

No. 1-3, obviously, are sentence fragments.

No. 4-7 are run-on sentences; that is, two sentences are run together without adequate punctuation(标点符号) or a conjunction(连词).

Objectives

The most common sentence errors are **fragments**, **run-ons**, **misplaced and dangling modifiers**, and unparalleled structure. Today we'll focus on **fragments** and **run-ons**.

Key Points

✔ Watching for sentence fragments

A sentence fragment lacks a subject, a verb, or some other essential part. Because of the missing part, the thought is incomplete.

> **Examples:**
> 1. Sleep is important for good health. Makes the brain ready for the next day.
> 2. I never get enough sleep. I tired all the time.

We need to make sure that a sentence has a subject and a verb. In the first example, a subject is missing, so we should add "it". In the second example, a verb is missing. It should be "I am tired..."

> **Examples:**
> 1. I'm going to the gym. When I finish this homework.
> 2. Niko is tired. Because he got only four hours of sleep last night.

We also need to make sure that a sentence with a subordinating conjunction has two clauses. "When I finish this homework" is a dependent clause and cannot stand alone. So we need to connect it to the independent clause. Similarly, the last example should be changed to "Niko is tired because he got only four hours of sleep last night."

✎ 破句可能缺少的成分如下：

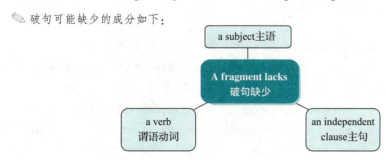

Tasks

Underline the fragments in the following paragraph. Rewrite the paragraph, making the fragments into complete sentences. Add a subject or a verb or connect the fragment to a related sentence in the paragraph.

Hundreds of people have reported seeing a large animal in Loch Ness. <u>A lake in northern Scotland</u>. <u>The Loch Ness monster, nicknamed "Nessie"</u>. Observers say the creature has a long, slender neck. <u>Like a dinosaur</u>. It also has one or two humps and flippers. Scientific expeditions have used sonar to explore the lake. <u>Have detected large moving objects</u>. <u>Not sure whether the objects are one large creature or a school of fish</u>. Underwater photographs have been taken, although many experts question their validity. <u>Despite the doubts about Nessie's very existence</u>. Tourists still flock to Loch Ness in the hopes of catching a glimpse.

Now check your answers. Did you underline all the sentence fragments in the paragraph? Here's the rewritten paragraph.

Hundreds of people have reported seeing a large animal in Loch Ness, <u>a lake in northern Scotland</u>. <u>The Loch Ness monster is nicknamed "Nessie"</u>. Observers say the creature has a long, slender neck—<u>like a dinosaur</u>. It also has one or two humps and flippers. Scientific expeditions have used sonar to explore the lake <u>and have detected large moving objects</u>. <u>The scientists are not sure whether the objects are one large creature or a school of fish</u>. Underwater photographs have been taken, although many experts question their validity. <u>Despite the doubts about Nessie's very existence</u>, tourists still flock to Loch Ness in the hopes of catching a glimpse.

Key Points

✔ Checking for run-ons

A **run-on** is two (or more) sentences joined without adequate punctuation or a conjunction. There are two types of run-ons. **Read through the given examples and find out the differences between the two types of run-ons.**

> **Type A**
> - My grades are very good this semester my social life rates only a C.
> - Our father was a mad man in his youth he would do anything on a dare.
>
> **Type B**
> - My grades are very good this semester, my social life rates only a C.
> - Our father was a mad man in his youth, he would do anything on a dare.

Some sentences are run together with no signs to mark the break between them. Such run-ons are known as fused sentences: They are fused, or joined together, as if they were only one thought. The sentences in Type A are fused sentences.

The other type of run-ons is known as comma splices. A comma splice results when two independent clauses are connected or "spliced" with only a comma. However, a comma alone is not enough to connect two complete thoughts. Some connection stronger than a comma alone is needed. The sentences in Type B are comma splices.

Let's take a look at more examples of fused sentences and comma splices.

> **Fused sentences**
>
> **Run-on**: A creative mind-set and bipolar disorder share certain characteristics such as independence and nonconformity both lead to thinking "outside the box".
>
> **Correct**: A creative mind-set and bipolar disorder share certain characteristics such as independence and nonconformity. **Both** lead to thinking "outside the box".
>
> **Correct**: A creative mind-set and bipolar disorder share certain characteristics such as independence and nonconformity, **and** both lead to thinking "outside the box".

In this example, two complete thoughts are run together with no punctuation or a conjunction. We could use a period(句号) and a capital letter to correct it. We could also use a comma and a coordinating conjunction to correct it.

> **Fused sentences**
>
> **Comma splice**: Countless writers and artists since Aristotle's time have believed that creativity and madness are linked, experts today say that it isn't quite the case.
>
> **Correct**: Countless writers and artists since Aristotle's time have believed that creativity and madness are linked, **but** experts today say that it isn't quite the case. (A coordinating conjunction has been added.)
>
> **Correct**: Countless writers and artists since Aristotle's time have believed that creativity and madness are linked; experts today say that it isn't quite the case. (A semicolon replaces the comma.)

In this example, two complete thoughts are connected with only a comma. We could use a comma and a coordinating conjunction to correct it. Also we could use a semicolon instead of a comma.

How to correct a run-on?

There are four common methods of correcting a run-on. We've mentioned three of them so far.

1. Use a period and a capital letter to break the two complete thoughts into separate sentences.
2. Use a comma plus a coordinating conjunction (*and*, *but*, *for*, *or*, *nor*, *so*, *yet*) to connect the two complete thoughts.
3. Use a semicolon to connect the two complete thoughts. A semicolon is made up of a period above a comma and is sometimes called a strong comma. The semicolon signals more of a pause than a comma alone but not quite the full pause of a period.
4. Use subordinating conjunctions. For instance, the two previously given run-ons could be changed to:

   - Although my grades are very good this semester, my social life rates only a C.
   - Our father was a mad man in his youth because he would do anything on a dare.

如何修改串句？

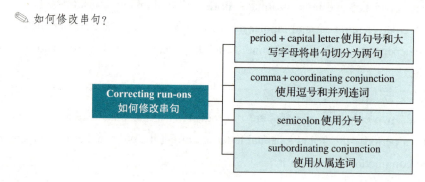

Tasks

Rewrite the following sentences.

Incorrect:

1. The commuters had been bottlenecked on the freeway for two hours, some of the commuters had a crazed look in their eyes, the others were napping.
2. I thought the test would never end I had a classic case of finger cramps. In addition, I had severe brain-drain complications only a long nap would restore me.

Correct:

1. The commuters had been bottlenecked on the freeway for two hours; some of the commuters had a crazed look in their eyes; the others were napping. (We could use semicolons to separate these three sentences.)
2. I thought the test would never end. (This is a complete thought, so we should put a period here.) I had a classic case of finger cramps. (Period.) In addition, (comma) I had severe brain-drain complications, and (comma, *and*) only a long nap would restore me.

Summary

We've learned that a sentence fragment might lack a subject, a verb or a dependent clause.

There are four methods to correct two types of run-ons. Remember that both punctuation and conjunctions matter.

讲座3 常见句子错误 II (Common Sentence Errors II)

知识概要 本讲座主要涉及修饰语错置、悬垂修饰语和错误的平行结构三种常见的句子错误。**修饰语错置**是修饰语与被修饰语摆放的位置不恰当。修饰语可以是单词、词组、从句，也可以是句子。为了避免修饰语错置，修饰语和被修饰的对象要尽量靠近。**垂悬修饰语**是修饰语在逻辑上与它所修饰的词语分离，或者找不到逻辑上被修饰的对象，因而看起来好像与句子的其他部分无关。**平行结构**可以是单词、词组、从句，也可以是句子。平行结构中的并列成分需用同等的语法结构表达出来。

关键词 常见句子错误(common sentence errors)；修饰语错置(misplaced modifiers)；悬垂修饰语(dangling modifiers)；平行结构(parallel structures)

Lead-in

In this lecture we'll focus on **common sentence errors**.
Underline the modifiers in the following sentences.

1. The magazine on the cafeteria table was picked up by someone walking by.
2. Fred realized the gallon of milk he got at the convenience store was sour.
3. He uses a lotion prescribed by his doctor to prevent itching.
4. The students listened as Mr. Smith, in obvious frustration, repeated the homework assignment for the third time.
5. Yolanda looked on the Internet for an attorney to represent her.
6. A diesel engine cannot be repaired without special tools.

A modifier is usually placed next to what it modifies. **No. 1** Where is the magazine? "On the cafeteria table." "On the cafeteria table" modifies "the magazine". Who picked it up? "Someone walking by." "Walking by" modifies "someone". **No. 2** Where did the gallon of milk come from? "He got at the convenience store." **No. 3** What lotion did he use? "Prescribed by his doctor." Similarly, these underlined phrases are all modifiers in **No. 4-6**.

What literary devices are used?

"It was the best of times, it was the worst of times, it was the age of wisdom, it was the age of foolishness, it was the epoch of belief, it was the epoch of incredulity, it was the season of Light, it was the season of Darkness, it was the spring of hope, it was the winter of despair."

—*A Tale of Two Cities* (By Charles Dickens)

In the beginning of *A Tale of Two Cities* by Charles Dickens, we see the repetition of "It was" many times. With such repetitions, the readers are prompted to focus on the traits of the "age" they will read about in the succeeding passages. The repeating of similar words, phrases, or clauses is called **parallelism**.

"I have a dream that one day this nation will rise up and live out the true meaning of its creed: 'We hold these truths to be self-evident; that all men are created equal.'"

"I have a dream that my four little children will one day live in a nation where they will not be judged by the color of their skin but by the content of their character."

"I have a dream today."

—*I Have a Dream*(By Martin Luther King Jr.)

In this speech, Martin Luther King, Jr. repeats the phrase "I have a dream" several times. It is also the title of the speech. This is a good example of parallelism.

"My fellow citizens: I stand here today humbled by the task before us, grateful for the trust you have bestowed, mindful of the sacrifices borne by our ancestors."

—*Presidential Inauguration Speech*(By Barack Obama)

In this speech, U.S. President Barack Obama also uses structural parallelism, giving his speech beauty and unity.

Objectives

The most common errors with sentences are fragments, run-ons, misplaced and dangling modifiers, and unparalleled structure. Last time we focused on fragments and run-ons. Today we'll focus on misplaced and dangling modifiers and unparalleled structure.

Key Points

✓ Misplaced modifiers

Misplaced modifiers are awkwardly placed words that do not describe the words the writer intended them to describe. Misplaced modifiers often obscure the meaning of a sentence. To avoid this, place words as close as possible to what they describe.

Example 1

◇ Tony bought an old car from a crooked dealer with a faulty transmission.

✎ "with a faulty transmission" describes the old car instead of the dealer, so we should put it next to the old car.

Correct: Tony bought an old car with a faulty transmission from a crooked dealer.

Example 2

◇ I nearly earned two hundred dollars last week.

✎ Does it mean you just missed earning two hundred dollars, but in fact earned nothing? The writer probably means he/she earned a little less than two hundred dollars. So we should put "nearly" next to "two hundred dollars".

Correct: I earned nearly two hundred dollars last week.

Example 3

◇ Bill yelled at the howling dog in his underwear.

✎ In this example, it seems like the dog wore underwear. It cannot be right. The words describing Bill should be placed next to Bill.

Correct: Bill, in his underwear, yelled at the howling dog.

✔ Dangling modifiers

A modifier that opens a sentence must be followed immediately by the word it is meant to describe. Otherwise, the modifier is said to be dangling and appears to modify the wrong word.

Example 1

Incorrect: While smoking a pipe, my dog sat with me by the crackling fire.

✎ Who was smoking a pipe? It can't be my dog, right? I was smoking.

Correct: While smoking a pipe, I sat with my dog by the crackling fire.

Example 2

Incorrect: Having unexpectedly turned red, I had to brake suddenly for the stoplight.

✎ Who or what turned red? Is it I that turned red? No, it should be the stoplight that turned red.

Correct: I had to brake suddenly for the stoplight, which had unexpectedly turned red.

✔ How to correct dangling modifiers?

How do we correct dangling modifiers? The key is to decide on the subject of the modifier. Then use one of the following methods: Place the subject within the opening modifier; place the subject right after the opening modifier.

Example 1

Incorrect: Swimming at the lake, a rock cut Sue's foot.

✎ Who was swimming at the lake? The subject is Sue. We could place the subject within the modifier.

Correct: When Sue was swimming at the lake, a rock cut her foot.

✎ We could also place the subject right after the modifier.

Correct: Swimming at the lake, Sue cut her foot on a rock.

Example 2

Incorrect: Getting out of bed, the tile floor was so cold that Yoko shivered all over.

✎ Who got out of bed? The answer is not the tile floor but Yoko.

Correct: When Yoko got out of bed, the tile floor was so cold that she shivered all over.

Correct: Getting out of bed, Yoko found the tile floor so cold that she shivered all over.

Example 3

Incorrect: To join the team, a C average or better is necessary.
✏️ Who is to join the team? The answer is not C average but you.

Correct: For you to join the team, a C average or better is necessary.

Correct: To join the team, you must have a C average or better.

✔ Parallel structures

You need parallel structures when your sentence has two or more items in a list. **All items in the list should use the same part of speech.**

Examples

◇ A good nanny must have patience, creativity, and the ability to multitask. (nouns)
◇ Money is important because it provides us with basic needs, allows us to support our family, and makes it possible to help others in society. (verb phrases)

When you use parallel structures, **do not mix the parts of speech in a list.**

Example 1

◇ A nanny cooks dinner, feeds the baby, is a helper with homework, and plays games.
✏️ The underlined phrase, "is a helper with homework", doesn't match the other phrases. Let's change it to "helps with homework".

Example 2

◇ Happiness comes from achievement and being creative.
✏️ "Being creative" is a gerund. To match "achievement", we should change the gerund to "creativity".

Example 3

◇ My work environment is enjoyable, fun, and has friendly co-workers.
✏️ Obviously, the last item should be changed to "friendly".

You should also make **each item in a list the same or similar in length.**

Example 1

◇ In his free time, Jeremy enjoys dinner with friends at his own home because he is a fabulous cook and hikes in the mountains.
✏️ The first item has a rather long adverbial phrase, which should be deleted.

Example 2

◇ Alison's new job pays well, offers educational opportunities at the company or at a local college, and allows for fun.
✏️ Similarly, the underlined part should be deleted.

Example 3

◇ The world is very different from 100 years ago because of advances in technology, education, and better healthcare.
✏️ "Better" should be left out to maintain the parallel structure.

Samples

Please underline all parallel structures in the following paragraph.

Chapin Howard, her father, operated the town's tannery, a business that turned raw animal skins into leather for <u>sturdy shoes and stout harnesses</u>. An <u>ambitious, public-spirited, likable</u> man, Chapin later <u>owned a hotel, served three terms in the state legislature, helped organize and finance a Baptist seminary in Townshend, and made a fortune with his son Aurelius buying and selling land in territorial Michigan</u>. By the time Clarina Howard was grown, her father was one of the wealthiest men in town, but because he was <u>generous, tactful, and unassuming</u>, Mr. Howard was respected by <u>rich and poor</u> alike.

Summary

As to modifiers, we should remember to put them next to the modified noun/noun phrase. Also, a modifier can't do without its subject. Otherwise, a dangling modifier will result.

Items in a parallel structure should be the same part of speech and a similar length. Parallel structures give rhythm and balance, emphasis and effect, as well as unity and organization to writing. Professional writers use this kind of repetition to give their passages impact. Public speakers use it to give their messages rhythm and emphasis. There's a good chance your writing will improve if you use repetition of similar words, phrase, and clauses. So give it a try!

Ⅲ. 写作练习

1. Read the information. Complete the sentences using parallel structures. You may have to add some words of your own.

1) Sonia Sotomayor is the first Supreme Court Justice of Hispanic heritage.
   She is also one of the youngest Supreme Court justices.
   Sonia Sotomayor is not only the first Supreme Court Justice of Hispanic heritage, but she is also _____.

2) Sotomayor graduated from Princeton University. She also received a degree from Yale Law School. She served as editor of the *Yale Law Journal*.
   Sotomayor graduated from Princeton University, received a degree from Yale Law School, and _____.

3) When Sotomayor first started college, she thought that she did not have the skills to be a good student. She also felt that she did not have enough knowledge to succeed. In addition, she suffered from a lack of confidence.
   When Sotomayor first started college, she thought that she did not have enough _____, _____, or _____ to succeed academically.

4) Sotomayor's biography, *My Beloved World*, does not discuss her political views. It also does not include her judicial philosophy.

Sotomayor's biography does not discuss her political views or _____.

5) Sotomayor visits Puerto Rico frequently because she has family there. She also has many fans there. In addition, she also visits Puerto Rico because she is often invited to speak.

Sotomayor visits Puerto Rico frequently because she has family there, she _____, and she _____.

2. Each word group in the student paragraph following is numbered. In the space provided, write C if a word group is a complete sentence; write F if it is a fragment. You will find seven fragments in the paragraph.

A Disastrous First Date

1) My first date with Donna was a disaster. 2) I decided to take her to a small Italian restaurant. 3) That my friends told me had reasonable prices. 4) I looked over the menu and realized I could not pronounce the names of the dishes. 5) Such as "veal piccata" and "fettucini alfredo". 6) Then I noticed a burning smell. 7) The candle on the table was starting to blacken. 8) And scorch the back of my menu. 9) Trying to be casual, I quickly poured half my glass of water onto the menu. 10) When the waiter returned to our table. 11) He asked me if I wanted to order some wine. 12) I ordered a bottle of Blue Nun. 13) The only wine that I had heard of and could pronounce. 14) The waiter brought the wine, poured a small amount into my glass, and waited. 15) I said, "You don't have to stand there. We can pour the wine ourselves." 16) After the waiter put down the wine bottle and left. 17) Donna told me I was supposed to taste the wine. 18) Feeling like a complete fool. 19) I managed to get through the dinner. 20) However, for weeks afterward, I felt like jumping out of a tenth-story window.

1) _____   11) _____
2) _____   12) _____
3) _____   13) _____
4) _____   14) _____
5) _____   15) _____
6) _____   16) _____
7) _____   17) _____
8) _____   18) _____
9) _____   19) _____
10) _____   20) _____

3. Revise the underlined unparalleled part of each sentence so that it matches the other item or items in the sentence.

1) As the elderly woman climbed the long staircase, she breathed hard and <u>was grabbing</u> the railing tightly.

2) Making a big dinner is a lot more fun than <u>to clean up</u> after it.

3) Many people want a career that pays wages, provides a complete benefit package, and <u>offering</u> opportunities for promotion.

4) Many of today's action movies have attractive actors, fantastic special effects, and <u>dialogue that is ridiculous</u>.

5) The neighborhood group asked the town council to repair the potholes(坑洼) and <u>that a traffic signal be installed</u>.

6) Pesky mosquitoes, <u>humidity that is high</u>, and sweltering heat make summer unpleasant in Louisiana.

7) Penicillin, the first wonder drug, has many uses: to treat syphilis, to fight bacterial infections, and even <u>curing</u> eye and ear infections.

8) The state of Georgia offers a varied landscape with the Blue Ridge Mountains in the north and the Okefenokee Swamp <u>is found in the south</u>.

9) The old historic house had a broken garage door, <u>shutters that were peeling</u>, and a crumbling chimney.

10) The professor warned his students that he would give surprise tests, <u>the assignment of term papers</u>, and allow no makeup exams.

第3周
段落结构及段落的统一性和连贯性
(The Structure of a Paragraph; the Unity and Coherence of a Paragraph)

Ⅰ. 概述

本周我们开始学习段落写作。一般来讲，段落由三个部分构成，即**主题句、支持句和结尾句**。每一段落通常包含一个中心思想，表达这一中心思想的句子就是主题句。支持句围绕段落主题展开，以具体的原因、例子、数字、事实等支撑段落主题。结尾句重申主题，呼应段落的开头。

统一性是一个好的段落应具有的一个重要特点。一个段落中写出的所有句子都必须为此段的中心思想服务，要牢记此段的主题，任何与主题无关的内容均应予以删除，以确保段落的统一性。同时还要注意人称代词和动词时态的一致。

统一性要求一段话只能贯穿一个主题，所有的句子都必须为主题服务，而连贯性要求句子之间转承自然，能够体现句子与句子之间的逻辑关系，从而使整个段落结构浑然一体。要做到这一点，可采用以下三种方法：使用过渡性的单词或短语；使用人称代词，避免随意更换代词；指代前文出现过的人、物或观点时可使用指示代词、定冠词等。过渡性的单词和短语能起到连接句子与意义的作用，为读者指明前进的方向，但也并不是说每句话之间都要有过渡性的单词或短语，过多使用过渡词，会显得机械呆板、毫无生趣。写作中要避免随意更换代词这一经常出现的错误，例如，当叙述任何人都会遇到的事情时，有的习作中出现了第一人称 us，第二人称 you 以及第三人称 a person 等。这样会使读者感到困惑，也会使段落缺乏连贯性。另外，前文出现过的名词再次出现时可使用指示代词、定冠词等来体现段落的连贯性。

Ⅱ. 慕课讲稿

讲座1 段落结构（The Structure of a Paragraph）

知识概要　一个段落通常由三个部分构成，即**主题句、支持句和结尾句**。每一段落通常包含一个中心思想，表达这一中心思想的句子就是主题句。支持句围绕段落主题展开，以具体的原因、例子、数字、事实等支撑段落主题。结尾句重申主题，呼应段落的开头。有时，段落中还有过渡句，在思想和内容上起承上启下的作用。

关 键 词 段落结构(the structure of a paragraph)；过渡句(transitional sentences)

Lead-in

In this lecture we'll focus on the **structure of a paragraph**.

In the following groups of statements, one statement is the general point and the other statements provide specific support for the point. **Identify each point with a P and each statement of support with an S**.

_____ The library subscribes to more than five hundred magazines and newspapers.

_____ Students have online access to thirty-five academic databases to which the college subscribes.

_____ Several expert librarians are always present to help students locate resources.

_____ Our college library has excellent resources.

_____ The library's DVD collection has recently been expanded.

✎ Which statement is the general point? "Our college library has excellent resources." Then it will be demonstrated through 4 aspects: subscription of magazines and newspapers; on-line academic databases; librarians' help and DVD collection.

_____ Because sending emails is so simple, family and friends may use email messages to stay in close touch.

_____ When people are upset, they may send off an angry email before they consider the consequences.

_____ The jokes, petitions, and other emails that friends so easily forward can become a real nuisance.

_____ The ease of using emails can be both a blessing and a curse.

✎ Which statement is the general point? "The ease of using emails can be both a blessing and a curse." The other statements show the advantages and disadvantages of using emails.

Objectives

- Understand the basic structure of a paragraph.
- Understand the function of transitional sentence.

WEEK 3

Tasks

✓ Which paragraph is more effective?

Your first step in writing is to decide what point you want to make and to write that point in a single sentence. As a guide to yourself and to the reader, put that point in the first sentence of your paragraph. Everything else in the paragraph should then develop and support in specific ways the single point given in the first sentence.

You may pause here, so that you will have enough time to read through the following two paragraphs and find out **which one is more effective**.

Paragraph A

Changes in the Family

Changes in our society in recent years have weakened family life. First of all, today's mothers spend much less time with their children. A generation or two ago, most households got by on Dad's paycheck and Mom stayed home. Now many mothers work, and their children attend an after-school program, stay with a neighbor, or go home to an empty house. Another change is that families no longer eat together. In the past, Mom would be home to fix a full dinner—salad, pot roast, potatoes, and vegetables, with homemade cake or pie to top it off. Dinner today is more likely to be takeout food or frozen dinners eaten at home, or fast food eaten out, with different members of the family eating at different times. Finally, television has taken the place of family conversation and togetherness. Back when there were traditional meals, family members would have a chance to eat together, talk with each other, and share events of the day in a leisurely manner. But now families are more likely to be looking at the TV set than talking to one another. Most homes even have several TV sets, which people watch in separate rooms. Clearly, modern life is a challenge to family life.

Paragraph B

Family togetherness is very important. However, today's mothers spend much less time at home than their mothers did, for several reasons. Most fathers are also home much less than they used to be. In previous times, families had to work together running a farm. Now children are left at other places or are home alone much of the time. Some families do find ways to spend more time together despite the demands of work. Another problem is that with parents gone so much of the day, nobody is at home to prepare wholesome meals for the family to eat together. The meals Grandma used to make would include pot roast and fried chicken, mashed potatoes, salad, vegetables, and delicious homemade desserts. Today's takeout foods and frozen meals can provide good nutrition. Some menu choices offer nothing but high-fat and high-sodium choices. People can supplement prepared foods by eating sufficient vegetables and fruit. Finally, television is also a big obstacle to togetherness. It sometimes seems that people are constantly watching TV and never talking to each other. Even when parents have friends over, it is often to watch something on TV. TV must be used wisely to achieve family togetherness.

Paragraph A starts with a point—that changes in our society in recent years have weakened family life—and then supports that idea with examples about mothers' working, families' eating habits, and television.

Paragraph B, on the other hand, does not make and support a single point. At first we think the point of the paragraph may be that "family togetherness is very important". But there is no supporting evidence showing how important family togetherness is or why it is important. Instead, the line of thought in Paragraph B swerves about like a car without a steering wheel. In the second sentence, we read that "today's mothers spend much less time at home than their mothers did, for several reasons". Now we think for a moment that this may be the main point and that the author will list and explain some of those reasons. But the author does not. The author seems to be writing about people spending less time together because of work, but he also mentions "some families do find ways to spend more time together despite the demands of work", which itself could be the point of a paragraph. When writing about fewer wholesome meals at home, the author mentions "takeout foods and frozen meals can provide good nutrition" and "people can supplement prepared foods by eating sufficient vegetables and fruit", both of which are off the point. The paragraph ends with yet another idea that doesn't support any previous point and that itself could be the point of a paragraph: "TV must be used wisely to achieve family togetherness."

Overall, instead of one point, the author makes several points and shows inadequate support for any of his points. The result for the reader is confusion.

Key Points

✓ Basic paragraph structure

Make a point; Support the point with specific evidence; Restate the point

We've learned the first essential step in writing effectively is to start with a clearly stated point. The second step is to support that point with specific evidence. Consider the point in the sample that you just read: Changes in our society in recent years have weakened family life.

The supporting evidence is needed so that we see and understand for ourselves that the writer's point is sound. The author of *Changes in the Family* has supplied specific supporting examples of how changes in our society have weakened family life.

The point that opens a paragraph is a general statement. The evidence that supports a point

is made up of specific examples, like what we read in *Changes in the Family*, reasons and facts, etc. The evidence support and explain a writer's point.

Samples

A paragraph usually ends with a restatement of the point made at the beginning. Writers do not include new ideas in the concluding sentence. No matter what your purpose for writing—to inform, persuade, or entertain—or what form your writing takes—story, explanation, or personal narrative—try to include a strong ending sentence. It should retell the topic sentence in a new way.

Read this sample. The ending sentence retells the topic sentence in a new way.

<u>Gold, a precious metal, is prized for two important characteristics</u>. First of all, gold has a lustrous beauty that is resistant to corrosion. Therefore, it is suitable for jewelry, coins, and ornamental purposes. Gold never needs to be polished and will remain beautiful forever.

For example, a Macedonian coin remains as untarnished today as the day it was minted twenty-three centuries ago. Another important characteristic of gold is its usefulness to industry and science. For many years, it has been used in hundreds of industrial applications. The most recent use of gold is in astronauts' suits. Astronauts wear gold-plated heat shields for protection outside the spaceship. <u>In conclusion, gold is treasured not only for its beauty, but also for its utility.</u>

Let's read one more sample. The concluding sentence gives readers a warning as to the use of synonyms in addition to the retelling of the topic sentence.

Synonyms

1) <u>Synonyms, words that have the same meaning, do not always have the same emotional meaning.</u> 2) For example, the words "stingy" and "frugal" both mean "careful with money". 3) However, to call a person stingy is an insult, while the word "frugal" has a much more positive connotation. 4) Similarly, a person wants to be slender but not skinny and aggressive but not pushy. 5) <u>Therefore, you should be careful in choosing words because many so-called synonyms are not really synonymous at all.</u>

Summary

We've learned that a paragraph usually begins with a general point, or topic sentence, followed by specific evidence and ends with a restatement of the point. This point is commonly called the main idea. All of the sentences are connected to the main idea. A good paragraph has three parts: a topic sentence; supporting sentences; a concluding sentence.

An easy way to picture the structure of a paragraph is to think of a hamburger. A hamburger has two slices of bread(the topic and concluding sentences). The main part of the sandwich is the filling(the supporting sentences).

✔ **Transitional sentences**

Black African Nations

1) During the decade of the 1960s, most of the European colonies of Sub-Saharan Africa achieved independence. 2) In the west, Nigeria(1960), Sierra Leone(1961), and Gambia (1965)—all former British colonies-joined the family of free and independent nations. 3) In the east, Tanzania(1961), Uganda(1962), Kenya(1963), and Zambia(1964) also became sovereign states free of British rule. 4) As the African empire of Great Britain was being dismantled, France, the other major European colonizer, withdrew from vast areas south of the Sahara. 5) Thirteen former French colonies gained national status in the single year 1960: Mauritania, Senegal, Mall, Ivory Coast, Upper Vilta, Togo, Dahomey, Niger, Chad, Central African Republic, Cameroon, Gabon, and Congo. 6) Although a few European colonialists still occupy African territory, the 1960s witnessed the birth of more than twenty free black nations.

In addition to the three essential elements, a topic sentence, supporting sentences, and a concluding sentence, a paragraph sometimes has transitional sentences to shift smoothly in ideas. Sentence 4) serves as a transition.

讲座2 段落的统一性和连贯性(The Unity and Coherence of a Paragraph)

知识概要 一个段落中的所有句子都必须围绕本段的中心思想,以确保段落的统一性,同时还要注意人称代词和动词时态上的一致。**连贯性要求句子之间转承自然,能够体现句子与句子之间的逻辑关系,从而使整个段落结构浑然一体**。要做到这一点,可采用以下三种方法:使用过渡性的单词或短语;使用人称代词,避免随意更换代词;指代前文出现过的人、物或观点时可使用指示代词、定冠词等。

关 键 词 段落的统一性(the unity of a paragraph);
段落的连贯性(the coherence of a paragraph)

Lead-in

In this lecture we'll learn **techniques to promote paragraph unity and coherence**.

Before you begin to write, you should prepare a scratch outline, which can be the single most helpful technique for writing a good paragraph. In a scratch outline, you think carefully about the point you are making, the supporting items for that point, and the order in which you will arrange those items. The scratch outline is a plan or blueprint to help you achieve a unified, supported, and well-organized paragraph.

In each of the following outlines, cross out the items that do not support the opening point.

1. The twentieth century achieved much toward the control of infectious diseases.

    A. Penicillin and other antibacterial medicines were discovered.

    B. Sanitary sewer systems were built in many cities.

    C. School lunch programs offered low-cost meals to students.

    D. Many communities developed water purification systems.

    E. More was learned about psychological diseases.

     CE

    Statement C is about school lunch programs. Statement E is about advances in the research of psychological diseases. Neither of them is related to the point that the 20th century achieved much toward the control of infectious diseases.

2. There are several ways to get better mileage in your car.

    A. Check air pressure in tires regularly.

    B. Drive at no more than fifty-five miles per hour.

    C. Orange and yellow cars are the most visible.

    D. Avoid jackrabbit starts(快速启动) at stop signs and traffic lights.

    E. Always have duplicate ignition and trunk keys.

     CE

    The color of a car and having a spare key are irrelevant to the point.

Objectives

- Understand the unity of a paragraph and how to achieve it.
- Understand the coherence of a paragraph and how to achieve it.
- Understand the consistency of a paragraph and how to achieve it.

Tasks

All of the sentences in a paragraph need to be about the main idea in the topic sentence. This is called paragraph unity. These supporting sentences work together to describe, clarify, and explain that main idea. If supporting sentences do not directly relate to the main idea, it confuses the reader.

Read through the following paragraph and find out which sentence doesn't relate to the

main idea.

A Dean's List

A dean's list consists of students in higher education who get excellent grades during a semester in college or university. It is similar to an honor roll, but an honor roll is generally only used in high schools. To be on the dean's list, students usually need a G.P.A. of 3.5 or above. This means their grade point average for all classes must be above 3.5. <u>I think this is unfair and students who get 3.0 and above should be included.</u> The G.P.A. is based on the A-F grading scale. For example, on this scale an A is 4, a B is 3, a C is 2, a D is 1, and an F is 0. It is an honor to be on the dean's list, and many students work hard to achieve this each semester.

In this example paragraph, the opinion about the unfairness of the grading system is out of place in the middle of the explanation.

Read through another paragraph and find out which sentence is off the point.

Homework

Homework is work that a teacher gives students to do at home. Homework can be an important part of a student's education. Besides learning from doing the homework, students also learn other important skills, such as responsibility and time management. It is very common for teachers to give homework in elementary, middle, and high school. <u>Some teachers say they don't like to correct homework.</u> In universities, homework becomes less common. The teacher may still assign work to do at home, but it's usually an "assignment", not homework. A teacher in a university is also less likely to check to see if a student has completed the work at home. It is the students' responsibility to make sure they have completed any work that is assigned by a teacher.

The underlined sentence is irrelevant to the main idea that students gain a lot from doing homework. Thus it should be deleted.

Key Points

How to gain "Unity"?

<u>Unity</u> means a paragraph discusses only one main idea from beginning to end. Every supporting sentence must directly explain or prove the main idea.

✔ Coherence

Coherence in writing means that the sentences and paragraphs flow well, and that ideas are connected clearly in a way that is easy for the reader to follow. Here are some of the techniques writers use to create coherence.

No. 1 is to use transition words and phrases.

To add information, use *also*, *in addition*, *moreover*, *furthermore*, etc.

To shift focus to a new idea, use *with respect to*, *with regard to*, *regarding*, etc.

To show the order of a process, use *first*, *next*, *followed by*, *finally*, etc.

To summarize or conclude, use *in conclusion*, *in summary*, *in sum*, etc.

Tasks

Let's read through the following paragraph and see how we can improve its coherence and make it easier for readers to follow.

Another difference among the world's seas and oceans is that the salinity varies in different climate zones. <u>For example</u>, the Baltic Sea in Northern Europe is only one-fourth as saline as the Red Sea in the Middle East. There are <u>two</u> reasons for this. <u>First of all</u>, in warm climates, water evaporates rapidly. <u>Therefore</u>, the concentration of salt is greater. <u>Second</u>, the surrounding land is dry and, <u>consequently</u>, does not contribute much fresh water to dilute the salty sea water. In cold climate zones, <u>on the other hand</u>, water evaporates slowly. <u>Furthermore</u>, the runoff created by melting snow adds a considerable amount of fresh water to dilute the saline sea water.

This is an example showing salinity varies in different places. So we should add "for example" here. How many reasons are mentioned? Two, right? First or first of all. With water evaporating rapidly, the concentration of salt is greater. Did you see the cause-effect relationship here? So we'll need "**therefore**" here. Second, "the surrounding land is dry and", again we'll need a connector here to show the cause-effect relationship. Then the writer shifts from the warm climate zones to the cold climate zones, so we need "on the other hand". To add another reason why seas and oceans in cold climate zones are less saline, we need "**furthermore, moreover, additionally**," etc.

Key Points

✓ **Coherence**

Writers also create coherence with demonstratives, pronouns, and the use of articles.

1. Use **demonstratives this/that/these/those + noun** to refer to specific ideas from previous sentences.

2. Use **demonstratives with certain nouns** to label a previous idea. These nouns include argument, belief, effect, experience, fact, opinion, process, setting, situation, study, etc.

3. Use **pronouns** to refer to specific nouns in previous sentences.
4. Use **indefinite articles(a/an)** the first time something is mentioned, and **the definite article(the)** after that.

✓ Consistency with Verbs

We need to **be consistent with verb tenses**. Do not shift verb tenses unnecessarily. If you begin writing a paper in the present tense, don't shift suddenly to the past. If you begin in the past, don't shift without reason to the present. Notice the inconsistent verb tenses in the following example.

Incorrect: The shoplifter <u>walked</u> quickly toward the front of the store. When a clerk <u>shouts</u> at him, he started to run. (Past tense should be consistently used in this example.)

Correct: The shoplifter <u>walked</u> quickly toward the front of the store. When a clerk <u>shouted</u> at him, he started to run.

✓ Consistency with Pronouns

We also need to **be consistent with pronouns**. Pronouns should not shift point of view unnecessarily. When writing a paper, you should be consistent in your use of first-, second-, or third-person pronouns.

Any person, place or thing, as well as any indefinite pronoun like *one*, *anyone*, *someone*, and so on is a third-person word.

> ◇ <u>I</u> enjoy movies like *The Return of the Vampire* that frighten <u>me</u>.
> ◇ As soon as <u>a tourist</u> enters Arlington National cemetery, where many of America's military heroes are buried, <u>he or she</u> begins to realize how costly the price of liberty is.

Summary

Uni- is a Latin prefix meaning "one". When we talk about paragraph unity, we mean that one paragraph focuses on only one idea, i.e., the main idea of the paragraph. If we start to discuss a new idea, we should start a new paragraph. To achieve paragraph unity, all sentences should be related to and supportive of the single main idea.

Co- is a Latin prefix that means "together" or "with". The verb "cohere" means "hold together". Coherence in writing means that each sentence in a paragraph naturally leads to the next sentence. A traveler will easily get lost without signposts giving directions. Similarly, a paragraph without coherence will confuse readers. Use transitions and other techniques to achieve coherence.

They are like signposts telling readers "this way" "over here" and "follow me".

In writing, we should be consistent with verb tenses and pronouns. Don't shift them unless when it's necessary.

III. 写作练习

1. Read the following paragraphs and point out their three major structural parts.

Cooking Methods and Some English Colloquialisms

1) Basic methods of preparing food show great similarity throughout the world. 2) For example, almost all cultures have devised some means of baking, that is cooking bread or other food in an oven. 3) Boiling, or cooking food in water or some other liquid, is another universal practice. 4) A related process, stewing, means to boil slowly or gently a mixture usually of meat, vegetables, and water. 5) Still another cooking process, roasting, means to cook meat in its own juice over an open fire or in an oven.

6) While the terms to describe the various cooking have a literal meaning in formal English, in informal English they are sometimes used to describe human behavior in a colorful or humorous way. 7) "Half-baked", for instance, may refer to a foolish idea or a stupid person. 8) "Boiling" or "boiling mad" means very angry. 9) "In a stew" means to be worried or to be in a difficult situation, and "to stew in one's own juice" means to suffer, especially from one's own actions. 10) "To roast a person" means to criticize or ridicule him without mercy. 11) In other cases, a person, through his excessive relish of life, might "get pickled" and "end up in a jam". 12) This brief list demonstrates the use of cooking terms as colloquial expressions to picture human conduct more vividly.

Paragraph 1:
Topic Sentence _____
Supporting Sentences _____
Paragraph 2:
Topic Sentence _____
Supporting Sentences _____
Concluding Sentence _____

2. Identify the sentence that does not fit logically into the paragraph.

1) Mount Lassen, 10,453 feet high, is one of the most active volcanoes in the United States. 2) It had strong eruptions in 1914-1917 and minor activity as late as 1921. 3) Gold was first discovered in California in 1849. 4) Nature has softened down most of the rough spots on Mount Lassen's slopes, softening them with vegetation. 5) But it is still a place of jagged cliffs,

bubbling mud pots, fuming vents, boiling lakes, and weird lava formations. 6) Although volcano activity in Hawaii has been more spectacular recently, California's Mount Lassen might erupt at any time.

3. Correct the inconsistent pronouns in the following sentences. You may have to change the form of the verb as well.

1) If a student organizes time carefully, you can accomplish a great deal of work.
2) Although I know you should watch your cholesterol intake, I can never resist an ear of corn dripping with melted butter.
3) I read over my notes before class because one can never tell when there will be a quiz.
4) Our time was limited, so we decided not to go to the Gettysburg National Military Park because you would need to spend an entire day for a worthwhile visit.
5) Good conversationalists have the ability to make the person they were talking to feel as if they are the only other person in the room.

第4周
段落展开方法——过程分析法和分类法
（Developing a Paragraph by Process Analysis and Classification）

▶▶ Ⅰ．概述 1

　　段落展开的方法多种多样，本周重点之一是讲解"过程分析法"。内容包括："过程分析法"简介、过程分析写作方法的应用场景和写作特点。

　　首先，什么是"过程"？过程是事情进行或事物发展所经过的程序。学习目标：1）能复述"过程分析法"的特点；2）熟练掌握"过程分析法"，能够运用该方法进行写作。

　　其次，过程分析写作方法的应用场景。我们在解释事情进行的经过或者事物发展的历程时必须运用过程分析写作方法。试举以下几例：实验报告中对实验过程的描述；学校迎新日，高年级学生向低年级学生介绍注册流程；水处理工程师解释城市饮用水的消毒过程等等。以上场景中，我们都在提供实用的信息，所以在过程分析中最重要的是信息要精准、清晰，易于理解。

　　通过范文分析，我们可以总结过程分析写作方法的特点：1）包含清晰明了的主题句；2）按照时间顺序展开；3）预判可能出现的问题，提供规避或解决方案。当运用过程分析法时，需要注意以下三点：1）听众/观众需要什么信息？2）听众/观众期待的细致程度？3）需要特别留意或者重点解释的部分。

▶▶ Ⅱ．慕课讲稿 1

讲座 1　过程分析法（Process Analysis）

　　知识概要　过程分析法是说明文和描写文的常见写作方法。过程分析的要点是清晰、有序，所以过程分析法一般遵循时间顺序。

　　关　键　词　过程（process）；过程分析（process analysis）

Lead-in

There are many ways to structure your argument within a paragraph, for example, by discussing cause and effect, considering comparisons and contrasts, or conducting a process analysis, and so forth. In this lecture, we will focus on **the method of process analysis**.

What is a PROCESS? A process is a series of actions which are carried out in order to achieve a particular result or a series of things that happen naturally and result in a biological, chemical or other form of physical change.

Objectives

- Understand the characteristics of paragraphs using Process Analysis.
- Understand the basic organization of a process analysis and be able to write a process analysis based on the organization of some process.

Tasks

When do we write a paragraph structured to describe a process? Yes, when we need to explain how something is done or how something works. Namely, when we analyze a process.

Can you come up with scenes from college and the workplace in which you are asked to describe or analyze a process?

Examples

1. As part of a chemistry lab report, you are asked to summarize the procedure you followed in conducting an experiment.
2. While working as an engineer at a water treatment plant, you are asked by your supervisor to write a description of how the city's drinking water is tested and treated for contamination.
3. On orientation day, as a senior student, you are asked to write the instructions for freshmen on how to register for classes.

…

We have lots of examples of process analysis in daily life. Now, let's think about: **What do you provide people with in the above scenes?**

Yes, you provide people with practical information. Whatever the purpose, the information in a process analysis must be accurate, clear, and easy to follow.

> 过程分析写作包括两种情形：引导读者完成一件事的全过程(how-to essay)或者让读者了解某事件或事物如何运作(how-it-works essay)。第一种类型的过程分析是为了让读者自己能够重复整个过程；第二种类型的过程分析是让读者了解过程、获取信息，无须亲自动手。

Next, I will lead you through the characteristics of Process Analysis paragraphs.

First, Process Analysis usually includes an explicit thesis statement.

A process analysis usually contains a clear thesis that identifies the process to be discussed and suggests why the process is important or useful to the reader.

Two examples of thesis statements for process analysis:

1. "If you really want to land the job, here are some things to keep in mind."

    Then you may provide readers with detailed information of how to prepare for a job interview.

2. "Switching to a low-fat diet, a recent nutritional trend, can improve weight control dramatically."

    Afterwards, you might describe what is a low-fat diet and how readers can follow that type of diet.

Second, Process Analysis is organized chronologically.

The steps or events in a process analysis are usually organized in chronological order—that is, the order in which the steps are normally completed.

Please read the following paragraph.

How You Do Mouth-to-mouth Resuscitation

First, place the victim on his back and remove any foreign matter from his mouth with your fingers. Then tilt his head backwards, so that his chin is pointing up. Next, pull his mouth open and his jaw forward, pinch his nostrils shut to prevent the air which you blow into his mouth from escaping through his nose. Then place your mouth tightly over the victim's. Blow into his mouth until you see his chest rise. Then turn your head to the side and listen for the outrush of air which indicates an air exchange. Repeat the process.

Now pick up the signal words that indicate the paragraph is developed in a chronological sequence.

Yes, the signal words include "**first, next, then, until, then...**"

注意：过程分析写作通常按照时间顺序展开，但也有例外。如：在一篇题为《如何解决同事争端》的习作中，应根据争端的特点和内部逻辑确定顺序，不可刻板套用时间顺序。

Can you come up with more words and phrases which signal the time sequence in a paragraph developed through process?

Yes, we have: **firstly, until, lastly, before, after, when, while, once, as soon as, at the point, at the same time...**

The third characteristic is: Process Analysis anticipates trouble spots and offers solutions.

You need to anticipate potential trouble spots or areas of confusion and offer advice to the readers on how to avoid or resolve them. You should also warn readers of any difficult, complicated, or critical steps, encouraging them to pay special attention to a difficult step or to take extra care in performing a critical one.

If you are supposed to write a short essay entitled *How to Prepare for a Job Interview*, what would you warn the readers about concerning dress codes?

You might say: "<u>During the summer months, many job applicants sometimes dress casually. Dressing casually, in most cases, can only hurt your chances of landing a job. Always dress appropriately.</u>"

Anticipating and offering help with potential problems is also crucial in process analysis.

✔ Visualizing a Process Analysis

The basic organization of a process analysis can be illustrated by a flowchart. When your main purpose is to explain a process, you should follow this standard format, including a thesis statement, main body, and a conclusion (in some paragraphs, the conclusion might appear in a different position). The main body of the essay should explain the steps of the process in the chronological order. Your conclusion should draw the paragraph to a satisfying close and refer back to the thesis statement.

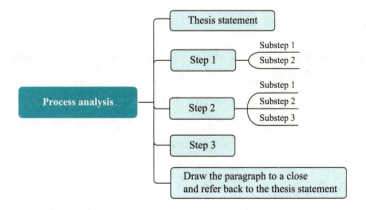

Tasks

✔ Sample

As the day of the exam approaches, there are several things you can do to make life easier. Firstly, you should make sure that you get regular exercise; that way you won't feel tired at night and you won't stay awake worrying. If you can, find someone else who is doing the exam and can share the process of reviewing for the test with you. You can organize little tests and quizzes for each other and this can make the process much more fun than working on your own. Just before the exam, it helps to write short notes about the most important study points on pieces of paper and look at them just before you go to bed. On the day of the exam, don't do any studying. Eat a proper breakfast and take some emergency snacks with you, wear comfortable clothes and take your favorite pen and pencil with you. And don't forget your watch.

After reading this paragraph, I have three questions for you.

Question 1 Does it contain a thesis statement?

Yes. The first sentence (*As the day of the exam approaches, there are several things you can do to make life easier.*) suggests you are going to share with the readers the follow instructions which are so important that they might "make your life easier".

Question 2 How can you tell that the paragraph follows a time sequence?

You must have noticed these signal words: *as the day of the exam approaches, firstly, just before the exam, just before you go to bed, on the day of the exam*... All these words and phrases indicate that the paragraph proceeds in a chronological order.

Question 3 Does the author call the readers' special attention to some critical points?

Yes. At the very beginning, the author encourages readers to take regular exercise so as not to feel tired at night and maintain a healthy mental state in the daytime.

Summary

All right, let's summarize what we've learned today and analyze a sample paragraph to see whether you understand the main points of this lecture.

A process analysis explains in step-by-step fashion how something works or how something is done or made. Process analyses provide people with practical information. Whatever the purpose, the information in a process analysis must be accurate, clear, and easy to follow.

Your main aim in process analysis is to inform readers, therefore, as you develop your essay, keep the following questions in mind:

1. What information does my audience need or want? (thesis statement)
2. How much detail does my audience need or want? (process analysis organized in chronological order)
3. What trouble spots require special attention and explanation?

Ⅲ. 写作练习1

1. Pick up the sequence markers from the box to fill in each blank. Some words might be used more than once.

after	then	now	the last step	next	first

How to Make a Paper Airplane?

1) _____ you need a sheet of paper that is 30cm by 30cm. Fold it in half lengthwise. 2) _____ open the paper and fold one corner toward the center crease. 3) _____ you have

made the final fold, fold the other corner down, in the same way, along the dotted line. 4) _____ fold each side along the diagonal dotted line toward the center. 5) _____, turn the paper over. With the paper turned over, fold one side over along the dotted line. 6) _____, fold the other side along the other dotted line. 7) _____ is to tape the body of the plane together. You now have a paper airplane that is ready for a test flight!

2. There is at least one mistake in each sentence. Locate and correct them.

1) The first step in creating a flower arrangement is to choose an attractive container, the container should not be the focal point of the arrangement.
2) Following signs is one way to navigate a busy airport, looking for a map is another.
3) The firefighters told the third-grade class the procedures to follow if a fire occurring in their school.
4) They emphasized that children should leave the building quickly. Also, move at least 100 feet away from the building.
5) To lower fat consumption in your diet, first learn to read food product labels, next eliminate those products that contain trans-fats or unsaturated fats.
6) Place the pill on the cat's tongue, hold its mouth closed, rubbing its chin until it swallows the pill.

IV. 概述 2

本讲座讲解段落展开的另一种常见方法——分类法。同学们家里的书柜如何整理？超市里的货品如何摆放？答案都是"分类"。想象一下：如果不分类，书柜会凌乱成什么样？超市如何让顾客快速找到他们需要的商品？**分类就是根据某项特征将事物分别归类。以分类法展开段落就是将某一主题分类，再细论其每个部分。**

分类写作有两个特点：1)"标准的一致性"；2)分类标准取决于作者的写作目的和对象。本讲座通过分析、讲解三篇具体例文，帮助大家深刻理解"分类标准一致性"原则的内涵。本讲座的目标是帮助大家了解分类法写作的特点，并且能够基于"标准一致性原则"对写作对象展开分类，进而熟练运用此方法进行段落写作。本讲座还对分类的信号词做了归纳整理。

V. 慕课讲稿 2

讲座 2 分类法 (Classfication)

知识概要 分类法是常见的写作方法之一。分类要遵循"标准一致性"原则。正是因为

WEEK 4

分类的标准具有多元化特征,所以要根据写作目的和对象来确定适用的唯一标准。

关 键 词　分类(classification);"标准一致性"原则(the principle of "ONE-PRINCIPLE")

Lead-in

In our previous session, we learned how to write a paragraph using process analysis. Today, we will focus on another method of paragraph development: **classification**.

Please look at this photograph. What does the photo show?

It shows fruits and vegetables on display at a farmers' market. How are the fruits and vegetables arranged? They are arranged according to types of produce. Can you imagine how difficult it would be to find what you need if all the produce were randomly piled onto a table or shelf, with cucumbers, tomatoes, onions, peppers, and bananas all mixed together?

Whoever arranged the fruits and vegetables in the market used a process called classification—**grouping things into categories based on specific characteristics**. This chapter will show you how to write effective paragraphs based on classification.

As a matter of fact, on a daily basis we use classification to organize things and ideas. Your dresser drawers are probably organized by categories, with socks and sweatshirts in different drawers. Grocery stores, libraries, and even restaurant menus arrange items in groups according to similar characteristics.

> 分类法在写作中有很多重要作用:在涉及内容很广泛的情况下,分类法可使表述的内容条理清晰、层次分明,既反映作者的条理性,也能使读者一目了然、抓住要点。当写作对象是某一主题时,分类法可使同一内容得到多侧面的扩展,使文章更加丰满、具体。当阐明某一理论或观点时,运用分类法可使论述的内容得到多层次的深入呈现。

Objectives

- Understand the characteristics of paragraphs structured to classify objects or ideas.
- Be able to compose such paragraphs successfully based on the method of "ONE-PRINCIPLE".

Key Points

✓ Characteristics of Classification

The first: Classification groups things according to One Principle.

To sort items into groups, a writer needs to decide on what basis to do so. For example, birds could be classified in terms of their size, habitat, or diet. To develop an effective set of categories, a writer needs to choose **ONE** principle of classification at a time.

Tasks

Can you explain why the following classification is not acceptable?

Sports can be classified into jumping, ball games, running, gymnastics and backstroke.

> Because it violates the principle of "ONE-PRINCIPLE", for ball games should be considered a general category, while jumping and running are subcategories of track and field events; gymnastics is also a general category.

Here is a proper example of the use of classification.

One way that sports can be classified is whether they focus on individual athletic ability (gymnastics, track and field events, swimming, golf) or are team sports (basketball, baseball, soccer, etc.) or mainly focus on one-on-one competition (boxing, fencing, tennis).

The second: Classification follows a principle determined by the writer's purpose and audience.

Because several different principles can be used to categorize any group, the writer's purpose and audience should determine the principle of classification. The personnel director of a college might classify professors by age in preparing a financial report for trustees that projects upcoming retirements, whereas a student writing a humor column for the campus newspaper might categorize professors by teaching style.

Sample 1

Indian was an easy way for Europeans to refer to any person living in the mysterious new land across the ocean[1]. But these people never thought of themselves as Indians[2]. Instead they had hundreds of different names, each identifying a separate tribe and culture[3]. Some Indians were hunters, some were farmers, some fishers, some warriors, some slaves, some priests, and some artists[4]. Many groups of Indians lived in one place all their lives; others were almost always traveling, searching for food[5]. Each group had its own language, although some used sign language to communicate with other tribes[6]. Some Indians led a simple life of hunting and gathering; a few groups built great cities and majestic temples[7]. Some were almost always at war with other tribes[8]. But many groups of Indians almost never fought[9]. Each tribe was basically independent[10].

Question 1 What are the principles applied in this paragraph?

> Occupations in [4], ways of life in [5], languages in [6].

Question 2 What effects do these classifications achieve?

> In this paragraph, when the word "Indian" is first mentioned, we have only a general and vague idea of who these particular people are, and may even think that they must be identical to each other in many ways. Then the paragraph begins to classify these people into many recognizable groups by their different characteristics. Thus, we have a much better idea of the Indians as peoples with different cultures, histories, languages and ways of life.

Therefore the usefulness of classification is found in how it gives a clear and in-depth view of a subject and, to a certain extent, produces a feeling of order.

Sample 2

Different people enjoy doing different things. This is certainly reflected in this beach scene. Some like to sit in the shade, watching the splashing waves in the blue sea and listening to the rhythmic sounds. They think that is the most enjoyable thing to do on a beach. Others prefer basking in the sun, not content to leave without an impressive suntan. But primarily the beach is for children. They rush around up and down the sandy beach, in and out of the water. In a quiet corner a few children sit with buckets and spades, building sand-castles. Yet other smaller children step tentatively into the water to try out paddling, making sure that Dad is not too far away.

> In this paragraph, the system of classification is clear. The people on the beach are divided into two major groups, adults and children. Then the adults are further divided into two types, those who like to sit in the shade, watching and listening to the sea, and those who love to stay in the sun to get themselves tanned. The children are also divided into the older ones and the younger ones, interested in doing different things.

Sample 3

There are three kinds of book owners. The first has all the standard sets and best-sellers—unread, untouched. (This deluded individual owns wood pulp and ink, not books.) The second has a great many books—a few of them read through, most of them dipped into, but all of them as clean and shiny as the day they were bought. (This person would probably like to make books his own, but is restrained by a false respect for their physical appearance.) The third has a few books or many—every one of them dog-eared and dilapidated, shaken and loosened by continual use, marked and scribbled in from front to back. (This man owns books.)

> According to the author, book owners can be divided into three kinds: those who do not read their books, those who carelessly read short sections of their books, and those who read closely and carefully every one of their books. In his opinion, only the third kind can be said to own books.

Language Focus

After analyzing the above three examples, I believe you have a better overview of how to write a paragraph using the method of classification. Now, **can you list the signal words and phrases used for classification?**

The signal words include:

◇ many kinds of	◇ differences
◇ kinds of	◇ opposing
◇ basic kinds	◇ opposite
◇ minor	◇ aspects, types, classes, parts, categories, regions, characteristics
◇ primary, secondary	
◇ classify/classifications	◇ fall into…categories
◇ divide/divisions	◇ can be divided into…kinds/types/classes/parts…
◇ similar/similarities	
◇ dissimilar/dissimilarities	

Tasks

Please add items to the following lists.

1. Cities can be classified according to the following criteria:

   1) size

   2) living space for its residents

   Can you come up with more criteria?

   3) _____ (administration ranks)

   4) _____ (population)

   5) _____ (geographic location)

   6) _____ (economic development)

2. Museums can be classified according to the following criteria:

   1) history

   2) popularity

   Any other criteria?

   3) _____ (location)

   4) _____ (theme)

   5) _____ (characteristic)

   6) _____ (size)

Summary

Classification is a process of sorting people, things, or ideas into groups or categories to help make them more understandable. A successful classification should follow ONE PRINCIPLE.

Because several different principles can be used to categorize any group, the writer's purpose and audience should determine the principle of classification. Therefore, you are supposed to choose a principle that will both interest your readers and fulfill your purpose.

Ⅵ. 写作练习 2

1. Write paragraphs of classification by expanding the following outlines. (You can use the signal words of classification like: divide, classify, kinds, types, fall into…categories, can be divided into…types/kinds…)

1) Topic: My Classmates

   Among them are:

   i. their hometowns

   ii. their majors

   iii. their interests and hobbies

   iv. their family backgrounds

2) Topic: The Buildings on Our Campus

   Among them are:

   i. their appearances

   ii. their sizes

   iii. their functions

2. Write a paragraph of classification on each of the following topics. (You can use the signal words of classification like: divide, classify, kinds, types, fall into…categories, can be divided into…types/kinds…)

1) On Movies

2) On Sports

第5周
应用文写作 I(Practical Writing I)

>> I. 概述

本周学习应用文写作，共有五个讲座，讨论了五种商务英语基础写作技巧，内容包括撰写**概要**、**申请信**、**简历**、**商务电子邮件**和**备忘录**。

撰写概要是职场的必备技能之一，在行业调研、研究报告、反馈等环节都可能用到。在讲座中，教师通过案例介绍了两种抓住关键词的技巧：**下划线技巧**和**概要表格技巧**。

撰写申请信是求职时容易被忽略的一项工作，申请信通常与简历一起发送。优秀的申请信可以增加应聘者得到面试的机会，因此撰写申请信是非常重要的求职技能。

撰写简历是求职过程中必不可少的一项技能，然而简历不能一概而论，本周讲座将详细解释应届毕业生和具备一定经验求职者简历的不同之处和撰写技巧。

商务电子邮件随着网络办公而兴起，虽然近年的重要地位有所下降，但仍然是重要的商务沟通方式之一。本周讲座将介绍英文商务电子邮件的各项内容和写作方法。

备忘录或电子备忘录在近年的商务沟通中越来越重要，备忘录通常是请求相关负责人对某一事项或问题进行反馈。本讲座将讲解备忘录各项内容的写作要求和技巧。

本周的讲座彼此独立，任务和学习目标明确，结构清晰。讲座首先提出问题，然后进行技能的培养，最后是练习，最终实现学以致用。课程内容与求职和职场相结合，能为学生今后的求职就业和职场英语运用打下良好的基础。

>> II. 慕课讲稿

讲座1　概要（Summary）

知识概要　概要写作中需要注意正确使用转述动词，有效地传递信息。一句话概要和内容提要需要遵从特定的结构。下划线法和概要表格法可以辅助寻找关键信息，完成

概要的写作。

关 键 词　summary(概要);reporting verb(转述动词);main idea(主旨);
　　　　　　supporting detail(支持细节)

Lead-in

For the following two weeks, we will discuss how to develop your **practical writing skills**.

Objectives

Today, we are going to focus on **summary writing**. After this lecture, you will be able to know what a summary is, recognize and use reporting verbs in summary writing. Finally, you will be able to write a summary.

Business information should be passed on to colleagues, including information about meetings, discussions and reports. Sharing information requires efficiency, too. Therefore, summary writing is an essential skill for a business person.

There are different kinds of summary skills found in the business world: the **one-sentence summary**(一句话概要) or report, the abstract of long reports and the **executive summary**(内容提要/执行概要) which aims to help executives with their decision making.

1. 本讲座的概要写作与学术性摘要写作不同,属于商务英语写作。在工作中,往往需要向上级报告,或向同事传递会议内容等,此时因概要具有简洁、重点突出等特点,在商务英语写作领域中显示出了其重要性。
2. 一句话概要(**One-Sentence Summary**)　一句话概要仅包含主题、作者姓名和文章标题。
3. 内容提要/执行概要(**Executive Summary**)　内容提要/执行概要是对文件细节的描述,如季度财务报告或提案等,主要功能是使读者能够快速查阅信息、掌握重要的事实或要点。

Tasks

Here is an article. Try to summarize this article into one sentence.

General Motors Chooses a Price and Cost Strategy for 2000

In 1990 the big three U.S. auto manufactures—General Motors (GM), Ford and Chrysler—lost $4 billion dollars, and in 1993 they made $5.3 billion. What happened in the meantime?

There are three main answers. First, the American economy moved out of a recession, causing more consumers to buy new cars, especially larger ones, which have better profit margins than do small cars. Second, import quotas were placed on Japanese cars shipped to the United States, thereby increasing sales of Big Three cars. Third, and perhaps most important, the Big Three embarked on massive programs to both cut costs and increase productivity through scrapping old plants and building new automated plants.

The strategy of GM is an example of what the Big Three are planning for 2000. In the past, GM succeeded in making a profit from its bigger, more luxurious cars such as Cadillacs and Oldsmobile Cutlass Supremes. However, the combination of high labor costs per car for GM and its suppliers is about three times those of Japanese auto manufactures for a typical subcompact car.

Because of this, GM must find a strategy to compete in the small car market. It has initiated "Project Saturn" to design a new generation of small cars with two primary strategies.

Price strategy. The Saturns will be priced as low as possible to try to lure into new car showrooms the 1 to 2 million Americans each year who buy used cars.

Cost strategy. Intelligent robots will be paired with teams of workers responsible for whole sub-assemblies or modules, which will then be combined on the final assembly line to produce the wedge-shaped Saturn.

This article was from a long time ago. The Saturn line of cars has been discontinued and GM's long-term strategy proved inadequate. During the 2008 recession GM went bankrupt!

Key Points

◇ In "GM's Price and Cost Strategy for 2000", the author explains why The Big Three lost money and introduces the two primary strategies of GM for recovery.

Read the above-mentioned sample, and try to find out the structure for the one-sentence summary.

One Sentence Summary:

◇ In(title of article), (author's name) describes…(thesis).

The structure only contains **the author's thesis**, **name** and **the title of the article**.

✎ "一句话概要"非常简洁,在句子中体现文章题目、作者姓名与主要内容。

Language Focus

Look at the following sentence patterns of summarizing information you might wish to pass on.

◇ What she was trying to say was…	◇ He(The author) thinks/reckons…
◇ He was talking about…	◇ It has been reported that…
◇ Basically, what she said was…	◇ The company has said/admitted/ promised…
◇ The important point is…	

All those expressions can be used to pass on information in one sentence. They have one thing in common: **the use of reporting words**. They are:

> **Reporting words**
>
> present   describe   state   argue   think   claim   mention
> point out   discuss

✏️ 可根据文章内容使用不同的转述动词,如"表达""描述""声明""驳斥""认为""声称""提到""指出""讨论"。

Now, let's see the full summary.

GM's Price and Cost Strategy for 2000

The year 1993 saw big profit(5.3 billion) because of American economic recovery, import quotas on Japanese cars and massive scrapping and automated plants. Now the GM's strategy is an example of what the Big Three are planning for 2000. In the past, GM made a profit on big and luxurious cars. But the cost of producing a big car is about three times of a Japanese small car. In order to maintain profit, GM has started "Project Saturn" to design a new generation of small cars with two primary strategies:

No. 1 Price strategy. The Saturns will be priced as low as possible to attract 1 to 2 million Americans each year who buy used cars.

No. 2 Cost strategy. Intelligent robots will be used partly for assembling to reduce cost.

✏️ The full summary includes the name of the author, the title of the article, the author's thesis and the main ideas that support it. As you can see, the summary contains only the important information and it is shorter than the original article. It does not copy the information taken from the original article but it paraphrases it.

So far, you have learned what a summary is. Here comes another question: **How to identify the main ideas for a summary?** There are two ways: **underlining ideas** and **using summary grid**.

✏️ 加下划线(Underline) 在词语下面加下划线是为了显示其重要性。
网格(Grid) 一般是交叉或平行的框架,用于总结文章的结构。

Let's talk about **underlining ideas** first.

First, you can underline the key ideas. Sometimes, a paragraph has a key sentence. It might be the first or the last sentence. So while you are reading, you need to pay attention to them.

Second, reread what you have underlined and paraphrase them.

Finally, you can use these paraphrased ideas in your summary. For example, the above-mentioned article could be underlined as this one below.

General Motors Chooses a Price and Cost Strategy for 2000

In 1990 the big three U.S. auto manufactures—General Motors(GM), Ford and

Chrysler—lost $4 billion dollars, and in 1993 they made $5.3 billion. What happened in the meantime?

There are three main answers. First, the American economy moved out of a recession, causing more consumers to buy new cars, especially larger ones, which have better profit margins than do small cars. Second, import quotas were placed on Japanese cars shipped to the United States, thereby increasing sales of Big Three cars. Third, and perhaps most important, the Big Three embarked on massive programs to both cut costs and increase productivity through scrapping old plants and building new automated plants.

The strategy of GM is an example of what the Big Three are planning for 2000. In the past, GM succeeded in making a profit from its bigger, more luxurious cars such as Cadillacs and Oldsmobile Cutlass Supremes. However, the combination of high labor costs per car for GM and its suppliers is about three times those of Japanese auto manufactures for a typical subcompact car.

Because of this, GM must find a strategy to compete in the small car market. It has initiated "Project Saturn" to design a new generation of small cars with two primary strategies.

Price strategy. The Saturns will be priced as low as possible to try to lure into new car showrooms the 1 to 2 million Americans each year who buy used cars.

Cost strategy. Intelligent robots will be paired with teams of workers responsible for whole sub-assemblies or modules, which will then be combined on the final assembly line to produce the wedge-shaped Saturn.

Then, find out what ideas are the main points and what ideas are supporting details that will be presented alongside the main points. Finally, you can rewrite them into a summary.

Using summary grid is another technique that you can apply, especially you are a visual learner. You can create a chart like the one below and organize the information that you need.

Paragraphs	Main ideas	Supporting details
1-2	In 1993, the Big Three made big profits.	American economic recovery, import quotas on Japanese cars and massive scrapping and automated plants.
3	The strategy of GM is an example of what the Big Three are planning for 2000.	In the past, GM made a profit from big and luxurious cars. But the cost per car is about three times those of Japanese small cars.
4-6	GM has initiated "Project Saturn" to design a new generation of small cars with two primary strategies.	Price strategy. Cost strategy.

As you can see, the chart can show ideas clearly and it is easier for us to summarize with the help of it.

Summary

Today, we learned how to write a summary. Hope it can help your both academic and business writing.

Before the end, I would like to say that being concise does not merely mean that the length of your article should be short. Your content should be complete and maintain its original meaning. When you are summarizing an article, always keep two things in mind: Avoid unnecessary repetition and include relevant information only.

讲座2 求职信(Job Application Letters)

知识概述 求职信的内容概括了求职者的职业技能和工作经验。求职信与求职者的简历同样重要，是决定求职者能否赢得面试机会的重要因素。求职信包括开头称呼、主要部分和结束语。求职信需要做到正确用语，避免排印错误，语言专业、正式。

关 键 词 salutation(称呼); main body(主要部分); purpose of writing(写作目的); motivation and reason(动机与原因); closing(结束语)

Lead-in

In this part, we are going to learn **how to write a job application letter**. A job application letter summarizes your qualifications and experience. It is also called a **cover letter** which introduces you and convinces the employer that you are qualified for the position you are applying for. Together, the résumé and job application letter will leave impressions upon your employers, so you should be very careful about writing the letter's salutation, main body and closing.

✎ 求职信(A Cover Letter) 求职信往往要打印在一张纸上，内容包括求职者的工作经历、职业技能、个人兴趣等。

Objectives

After this lecture, you will be able to know **what a job application letter is**, and know **the key points of an application letter**. Finally, you will be able to **write a job application letter**.

Key Points

✓ **How to write a job application letter?**

People will judge you when they read your job application letter and decide whether they will interview you or not. So you need to tailor your letter each time according to the requirements of the particular job.

Make sure your job application letter and résumé support each other. When employers read your application letter, they often would look to a résumé for more information on claims made in the letter. We are going to learn how to write a résumé later.

Besides, your letter should be grammatically correct, free of typos and written in professional and somewhat formal language.

> 求职信一般和简历一起发送给雇主。一封成功的求职信会给雇主留下深刻的印象,让雇主有兴趣打开应聘者的简历。求职信需要根据每次求职的职位专门写成,切忌一信多用。

Example

32 Garfield Ave.
Belford, CT 06100
April 3, 2022

Ms. Maria Castro
Director of Human Resources
The Senior Citizens' Homestead
666 Grand Blvd.
Belford, CT 06100

Dear Ms. Castro,

As an experienced electrician about to graduate from County Community College with an AOS degree in electrical engineering technology, I am applying for the electrician position advertised in the *Daily Herald*.

In college I have maintained a 3.60 grade point average while serving as vice president of the Technology Club and treasurer of the Minority Students' Union. In keeping with my ongoing commitment to community service, last year I joined a group of volunteer workers renovating the Belford Youth Club. Under the supervision of a licensed electrician, I helped rewire the building and acquired a great deal of practical experience during the course of this project. The combination of my academic training and the hands-on knowledge gained at the Youth Club equips me to become a valued member of your staff. Past and current employers, listed on the enclosed résumé, will attest to my strong work ethic. I can provide those individuals' names and phone numbers on request.

Thank you very much for considering my application. Please phone or email me to arrange an interview at your convenience.

Sincerely,
James Carter

Key Points

From the above-mentioned example, you can see the steps to follow when you write a job application letter.

The return address appears at the top of the page. The inside address follows the date.

✎ 写英文信时，需要注意寄信人地址写在前面，收信人地址写在后面。
  寄信人地址(**Return Address**) 寄信人地址是寄方地址，写在信封或包裹上。

At the very beginning, it is the salutation. "Dear Ms. Castro". (Sometimes it is not a person to whom the letter is addressed.)

Then, the author writes, "As an experienced electrician about to graduate from County Community College with an AOS degree in electrical engineering technology, I am applying for the electrician position advertised in the *Daily Herald*."

The opening paragraph identifies the position being applied for and the purpose of writing this letter. It also shows that the author is a confident applicant.

The main body usually contains two or three paragraphs, stating related working experience, education, and skills. Motivations and reasons could be mentioned, too. A job application letter doesn't need to include everything in the résumé, but the contents should be attractive to potential employers. But résumé should be mentioned in the application letter and attached. In the last paragraph, state your willingness of attending the interview and indicate the availability of references.

Finally, write the closing. Here, the letter ends with a standard closing: "Sincerely", followed by the signature.

So far, we know what a job application letter is. Now, pay attention to the format. It is called **standard block style**. You can find double line space between paragraphs and each paragraph starts at the left edge.

✎ 齐头式(**Standard Block Style**) 书写时，每行采用左对齐的格式，这种格式阅读起来清晰明了。

So much for this example. Now, let's see the useful examples of each part.

Language Focus

A job application letter usually starts with salutation. Follow "Dear" with "Mr." or "Ms." and the person's last name, as what we have seen in the previous example. If you don't know whom you should send the job application letter, you may call to find it out, or use other phrases, such as "Dear Sir or Madam" "To whom it may concern".

✎ 如果不知道收件人的名字，即不了解是雇主本人还是人力资源部门的某位员工收信，可以使用"Dear Sir or Madam"或"To whom it may concern"作为称呼。

The purpose of writing is always stated at the beginning of the first paragraph. You may indicate where you learned about the position or where it was posted or listed. For example:

◇ I am writing to apply for the post.
◇ I would like to apply for the position of Account Executive advertised in *the Times Union*.
◇ In response to your ad on *Monster. com*, I am applying for the position of full-time veterinary assistant at Northtown Animal Hospital.
◇ I am writing to apply for the post of…advertised in…on…
◇ With reference to your advertisement in…on…, I would like to apply for the position of…

Useful expressions of **strategies**, **working experiences** and **skills** are listed **below**. Explain what you can bring to the job, describing the particular aspects of your education, job experience, or skills that make you specially qualified.

◇ I am now a postgraduate student in Beijing University of Chemical Technology.
◇ I have been working on Chemistry for the last two years.
◇ I recently completed my Veterinary Technician A. A. S. degree at Copper Mountain Community College and obtained my state certification.
◇ I graduated from college in 2018 with excellent grade in Computer Science.
◇ I obtained the Master's degree in 2017.

When you write the job application letter, you should add **motivations** and **reasons**. For example:

◇ One of the main reasons I am interested in applying for this job is the challenge that it offers me.
◇ I think I am suitable for this position.
◇ As my enclosed résumé indicates, my education and experience working with animals have prepared me well for the opening you have.
◇ I am confident that I am fully qualified for the job.

Indicate that you are available at the employer's convenience, or specify when you are available. Be sure to include **email** and **telephone contact information** so you are easy to reach. For example:

> ◇ I am looking forward to your reply.
> ◇ I will be always available for the interview.
> ◇ I am available for an interview at your convenience and will gladly supply additional references as needed.
> ◇ Please call me at 555-121-1212 or email me at BHuan715@gmail.com.
> ◇ I could be contacted at the address above or on telephone.

You will need to revise your letter for different jobs, depending on what the requirements, responsibilities, and job duties are. This writing skill can be applied to writing your résumé, too.

For example, if the employees are expected to have leadership skills, communication skills and proficiency in Word and PowerPoint, as an applicant, you should tailor your application letter and your résumé to prove your qualifications. Look at this chart.

Desired Qualifications	Proof of Your Qualifications
Leadership skills	Worked as process team leader for FedEX Express. Helped to create and design work process maps. Many of the team's suggestions are being considered and have the potential to greatly impact the safety of employees.
Communication skills	At KT Web Consulting, worked as a web consultant. Served as liaison between team and clients. Communicated directly with vice president on our progress.
Proficiency in Word and PowerPoint	Have used Word for six years. Used PowerPoint to create presentations for KT Web consulting. Using PowerPoint, presented web recommendations to colleagues before submitting formal reports to clients.

✎ 表格内容体现了一封有针对性的求职信需要哪些要点。例如，招聘简章中要求应聘者具备领导力、沟通能力和熟练使用电脑软件的能力。在求职信中，应聘者最好提及上述三种能力。

Complementary close could be "yours truly, yours faithfully, yours sincerely".

Files can be enclosed at the end of an application letter. Here, you can enclose your résumé. For example:

> ◇ I have enclosed my résumé for your reference.
> ◇ Enclosed are my two references and my résumé.

Finally, **your signature**, followed by your printed or typed signature.

Summary

Now you know how to write your job application letter. Let's have a summary.

> ◇ List your address at the top of the page.
> ◇ A job application letter contains salutation, contents and closing. In the main body, purpose of writing, motivations, reasons, strategies, working experiences and skills can be included.
> ◇ Details such as date and position should be listed in the résumé, not in the application letter.
> ◇ You will need to revise your letter for different jobs, depending on what the requirements, responsibilities, and job duties are.

讲座 3 简历(Résumé)

知识概要　一份简历一般包括姓名、联系方式、教育背景、工作经验、技能和证书等。描述工作经历时需要注意动词的使用。简历中的关键词需要与工作要求相匹配。最后，需要检查拼写是否正确、标点符号使用是否合理、大小写是否正确等。

关 键 词　target position(目标职位); job requirements(职位要求);
functional résumé(功能型简历); chronological résumé(时序型简历)

Lead-in

In this lecture, we are going to learn **how to write a résumé**.

When you are hunting for a job, you need to submit your résumé to potential employers. **A résumé** is complete listing of all of your education, training, and work experience, written in an easy-to-read format. The employers will decide whether they will interview you based on your résumé. Therefore, your résumé is of great importance and should be conducted very carefully. You may need to revise it, double check the spellings, change its format into an easy-to-read design. Most importantly, you must tailor your résumé to your target position. So, how to write a good résumé? In the academic world, a résumé is sometimes called a C. V. (curriculum vitae).

> **Résumé 和 C. V. 的区别(The difference between a résumé and a C. V.)**
> 在一些国家和地区，两者可以通用，而区分二者的地区，两种文件有所不同。与 résumé 相比，C. V. 要详细得多，通常以时间顺序列出所获奖项、期刊论文发表等项目。在学术界，C. V. 很常见，申请者可以提供自身的更多信息，C. V. 可能长达几页纸。

Objectives

After this lecture, you will be able to **know the elements of a résumé, know the steps of writing, and learn the useful expressions**. Finally, you will **be able to write one**.

Before we start, there are two key points. Your résumé should be fit into a single page, being concise and clear. Besides, you need to use key words in your résumé.

✎ 简历一般为一页纸,信息准确,言简意赅。如需中英文简历,可以双面打印。

There are several steps when you prepare your résumé. Follow me and at the end of this lecture, you will complete a draft of your own résumé.

Tasks

Let's start with **Name**.

Name should be written at the top of the page. Chinese surnames go first, which is different from English names. In practice, Li Ming could be either written as Li Ming or Ming Li. In order not to cause confusion, you may capitalize your surname. For example, Ming LI or LI Ming. If your name contains three Chinese characters, the last two are put together, such as LI Xiaoming.

✎ 姓氏(Surname) 家族成员具有相同的姓氏,不同家庭成员则用名字来区分。

Then display your **contact information**.

Pay attention to the spelling. Make sure to check that your contact information is correct. For example:

Department of Chemistry
Beijing University of Chemical Technology
No. 15 North 3rd Ring Road, Chaoyang District, Beijing, 100029
People's Republic of China

Email address and phone numbers should be added, too.

Next, list your **education**. Include dates you attended school or received a degree. For example:

Education

- June 2020 Master of Mathematics
  Beijing University of Chemical Technology, China
- July 2017 Bachelor of Mathematics
  Beijing University of Chemical Technology, China

- Will graduate in June 2020 with Master's degree in Mathematics
- Have maintained 3.80 grade point average
- Finance and Accounting, International Finance, Linguistics, Chemical Technology

Here you may find that education is listed in reverse chronological order(按时间顺序排列), which means you put the most recent one first. You may also highlight your grade such as "Have maintained 3.80 grade point average". List course names if necessary, especially the job requirements are closely related to what you have learned in college. For example, Finance and Accounting, International Finance, Linguistics, and Chemical Technology.

> ✎ 时间顺序和倒序排列的区别(The differences between chronological order and reverse chronological order) 时间顺序排列指的是简历中的各项信息按照发生的先后顺序排列,倒序排列则需最先列出最近的经历。

Experience is listed in reverse chronological order, too, starting from the most recent one. The name of the position is followed by the company's name and the details. "Contacted and met with prospective clients, answered client inquires, performed general office duties." What do they have in common? Here is a tip: in a résumé, verbs are usually more powerful when you explain experience details. "Organized conferences" will leave deeper impression than "conference organization".

More examples are listed here; you can replace the underlined words with your own experiences.

> ◇ Organized conferences.
> ◇ Assisted in analyzing market strategies.
> ◇ Collected and analyzed data.
> ◇ Worked as the President of Student Union.

Let's summarize **some useful verbs for describing your experience**.

> maintain, support, develop, establish, organize, manage, create, assist, participate, design, promote, arrange, coordinate, compile, facilitate, write, analyze, install, decide, supervise

The above-mentioned verbs are exactly key words that employers prefer to read.

The experiences listed in your résumé should relate to the job requirements. Tailor your résumé each time when you apply for a new job. Key words listed in the experience part will be used to match words in the employer's electronic job database. It will decide whether some companies are going to interview you or not. So key words related to skills and experiences are of great importance.

> ✎ 简历中的工作经验用词建议选择动词,可表达出求职者过去在这项工作中实际做了什么,能给雇主留下深刻的印象。

Next, you should list **your skills and qualifications** in your résumé. They include foreign language skills, computer skills and communication skills. Here are some examples:

> ◇ Excellent spoken and written <u>English</u>
> ◇ Good command of both <u>English</u> and <u>Chinese</u>
> ◇ Proficiency in <u>computer operation</u>
> ◇ Some reading ability of <u>Japanese</u>

You may change the underlined words into your own skills.

Besides, **your personality** may be listed here, too. For example:

> ◇ hardworking, dynamic, adaptable, cooperative, energetic, motivated…

Key Points

Now, let's have a look at a sample.

Carole A. Greco

61 Stebbins Dr.
Smallville, NY 13323
(315) 555-5555
cagrec@email.net

OBJECTIVE: A permanent position in financial services.

EDUCATION: Associate in Applied Science (Accounting), May 2021
County Community College, Elliston, NY

GPA 3.65, Phi Theta Kappa Honor Society, Phi Beta Lambda Business Club, Ski Club.

EXPERIENCE: Intern (Fall 2020)
Sterling Insurance Company, Elliston, NY
Contacted and met with prospective clients, answered client inquiries, performed general office duties.

Trust Administrative Assistant (Summers 2018-2020)
First City Bank, Elliston, NY

Researched financial investment data, organized trust account information, screened and answered customer inquiries, composed business correspondence.

Student Congress Treasurer (Fall 2019-Spring 2020)
County Community College, Elliston, NY
Maintained $300,000 budget funding 35 campus organizations, approved and verified all disbursements, administered Student Congress payroll.

SERVICE: Volunteer of the Year, 2020
American Red Cross, Elliston, NY

As you can see, all the parts are included and are clearly presented. Contact information is put at the top of the page. Boldfaced headings are used to make the résumé easy to read. We can see there are objective, education, experience and service. When you have a target position, you can add objective like this sample.

You should do research to see what a résumé in your particular field looks like. Résumés can be very different—the résumé of an accountant is very different from that of an industrial designer. Similarly, the résumé of a college graduate or postgraduate is very different from that of a skilled employee. Look at the samples below.

James Carter

32 Garfield Avenue, Belford CT 06100
(203)555-2557 jamcar@email.net

Career Objective
Secure, full-time position as an electrician

Education
County Community College (2018-present)
1101 College Drive, Belford CT

Will graduate in May 2021 with AOS degree in Electrical Engineering Technology. Have maintained 3.60 grade point average while serving as vice-president of Technology Club and treasurer of Minority Students' Union.

Experience
- Counter Clerk (2018-present)
  Quick stop Grocery, 255 Bergen Avenue, Belford CT

  Part-time position to help meet college expenses.

- Warehouse Worker (2015-2018)
  S. Lewis & Sons, 13 North Road, Belford CT
  Full-time job after high school, before deciding to pursue college education.

Community Activities
- Volunteer, Belford Youth Club Renovation Project (Summer 2020)
  Under supervision of licensed electrician, helped rewire building.

- Assistant Baseball Coach, Belford Little League (2019-present)

- Choir Member, First Baptist Church of Belford (2013-present)

Max Benson

666 Street. Southridge, SC.
(555) 555-5555   maxbenson@email.net

Objective	Sales Manager		
Experience	2017–2021	Arbor Shoe	Southridge, SC

National Sales Manager

- Increased sales from $50 million to $100 million.
- Doubled sales per representative from $5 million to $10 million.
- Suggested new products that increased earnings by 23%.

2012–2017   Ferguson and Bardell   Southridge, SC

District Sales Manager

- Increased regional sales from $25 million to $350 million.
- Managed 250 sales representatives in 10 Western states.
- Implemented training course for new recruits—speeding profitability.

2007–2011   Duffy Vineyards   Southridge, SC

Senior Sales Representative

- Expanded sales team from 50 to 100 representatives.
- Tripled division revenues for each sales associate.
- Expanded sales to include mass market accounts.

2002–2007   LitWare, Inc.   Southridge, SC

Sales Representative

- Expanded territorial sales by 400%.
- Received company's highest sales award four years in a row.
- Developed Excellence in Sales training course.

Education   1998–2002   Southridge State University Southridge, SC

- B. A. Business Administration and Computer Science.
- Graduated Summa Cum Laude.

Interests   SR Board of Directors, running, gardening, carpentry, computers.

The first one is a functional résumé, designed for a college graduate or postgraduate. Skills, education are listed before work experience. **The second one is a chronological résumé**, designed for a skilled employee. As you can see, this applicant has a very clear objective, so it is put at the beginning of this résumé. Experience, the longest part of this résumé, are listed chronologically and tailored to the position.

Now adjust your own résumé, making it easy to read.

A final step: you should correct errors of spelling, punctuation, and capitalization. Make sure you have double checked your résumé before you send it.

Summary

Today, we learned how to write your résumé. Starting with your name and contact information, we discussed useful expressions of education, experiences, skills and qualifications. Besides, you now know the importance of key words and format. Remind you: you should always be concise when you write your résumé!

讲座4 商务电子邮件(Business Emails)

知识概要 商务电子邮件包括邮件主题、附件、内容、签名档几个部分。书写邮件主题的时候需要使用与内容相关的词语，以便于他人日后检索。如需添加附件，可在邮件内容中提及。邮件内容需要直奔主题，言简意赅，用语正式，不得使用电子表情或网络用语。

关 键 词 subject(主题); attachment(附件); content(内容); signature file(签名档)

Lead-in

In this lecture, we are going to talk about **how to write business emails**.

Within a company, email is now the most common way to communicate with each other, including colleagues, customers and vendors. Since you apply for a job, you may begin to write emails. Business email writing skills will be important after graduation and you will likely use emails every day in the future. So it is very important for us to master how to write business emails.

Look at the picture below. This is a typical business email. As you can see, what we are going to focus on today will be **business emails' subject, attachment, content and signature file**.

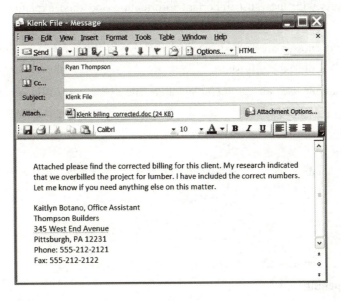

商务电子邮件包括邮件主题、附件、内容和签名档。

We are going to discuss them one by one.

First, let's see the first line "To". This is the name of the person the email is addressed to. If you do not store the receiver's email address in your email software, you must insert his or her email address here.

Next, "Cc" stands for carbon copy, which indicates that this email will be seen by others apart from the receiver. If you want to hide other receivers' email address, you can click "Blind Carbon Copy(密送)". In this way, the receiver will not know there are other receivers of this email letter.

When writing emails, it is important to use a relevant subject line which should be the emails' main point. It is better to refer to a client or a file name so it will be easier for others to locate or retrieve(检索) your business emails.

If relevant files should be attached, you must not forget to actually attach them. Most of the email software service will inform you if you do forget. But you need to be careful. Otherwise, it will cause problems for others and may delay everything. Besides, you should mention the file in the content of your email.

Then comes the body, the content of the business email. Business emails don't need to be as formal as traditional business letters. However, they also correspond to your company's image and reputation. Read **the body part** of our example and summarize its language features.

Attached please find the corrected billing for this client. My research indicated that we overbilled the project for lumber. I have included the correct numbers. Let me know if you need anything else on this matter.

As you can see, the author uses a polite tone and writes directly to the point, being concise and precise. It starts with the most important information and then explains it in the following sentences.

The words and phrases are formal. Do not use emojis(电子表情) or online slang.

The message should be really short.

Finally, the author uses an automatic signature file at the end of this email.

密送(Blind Carbon Copy)　当向多人发送电子邮件且不希望收件者互相看到其他收件人时，可以使用密送。

检索(Retrieve)　提取存储的信息。

电子表情(Emoji)　电子表情是智能手机、平板和其他电子设备上用以传递情感的小图标，表达比文本语句更加生动简洁。

Key Points

Let's have a closer look at each part.

First, the opening.

In the above-mentioned example, the author starts the email with the purpose because the author and the receiver might work in the same company. Emails can be semi-formal in this case so the author does not write the opening. Usually, when we mail senior people or people in other companies, emails should be formal. For example:

> ◇ Dear Sir or Madam
> ◇ Dear Project Managers
> ◇ Dear Mr. Smiths

When your business email is a reply, you may start your email with:

> ◇ Thank you for your email.
> ◇ Thanks for the information.
> ◇ I got your mail yesterday.
> ◇ I failed to reply you soon because…

Then, you can write the purpose sentence.

Just as I said before, the first sentence of business emails usually state the purpose. The purpose of an email may be:

> ◇ To ask for or send information.
> ◇ To ask people to do things.
> ◇ To give instructions or directions.
> ◇ To confirm arrangements that you have discussed by phone.
> ◇ To send longer documents.

Let's see some useful expressions for each purpose.

商务电子邮件的第一句一般都需要说明写信目的，开门见山。商务电子邮件的主要目的有：问询信息、要求回复、做出指导、确认安排等。

To ask for or send information:

> ◇ Could you mail me the report of the sales today?
> ◇ I am writing to tell you about an exciting new offer from Fine-On-Line called FOL High Speed.

To ask people to do things:

> ◇ Please be reminded that all foreign teachers will meet in Room 207 on Monday, May 8, 2020, at 12:30.

To give instructions or directions:

◇ I am writing to inform you about…
◇ I suggest we have a call at 8 a.m. (EST time). Please let me know if the time is okay for you.

To confirm arrangements that you have discussed by phone:

◇ I would like to invite you to…
◇ As we have discussed on the phone…
◇ I am writing to confirm…

To send longer documents:

◇ Attached is the brochure on the new project you asked for.
◇ Please see the attachment.

End the email with a polite statement to maintain the relationship and further communication.

◇ I am looking forward to your reply.
◇ I am looking forward to seeing you in the conference.
◇ We look forward to serving you again in the coming future.

Use a polite closing such as "Sincerely" if necessary.

Finally, an automatic signature should include your name, title, company address, and telephone and fax numbers so that people can contact you easily.

Summary

Today, we learned how to write business emails. It is essential that you learn how to use it professionally and clearly.

Get ready and show your readers how professional you and your company are!

讲座5 备忘录(Memo)

知识概要 每个备忘录一般只有一个话题，如有两个主题，则需考虑另写一个备忘录。写备忘录时需要列出收件人、发送人、日期、备忘录主题。在主要部分的第一句表明书写备忘录的目的。使用标题和项目符号来辅助书写，让备忘录变得简洁易读。

关 键 词 recipient(收件人); sender(发送人); bullet points(项目符号)

Lead-in

In this lecture, we are going to learn **how to write memos**.

The original meaning of a memo is a reminder or a confirmation. Memo is the short form of memorandum originated from the Latin word "memorare" which means to remember, and it is widely used in business communication within one organization. **Memos are characterized by being direct, short and easy to read.** It is a great way to communicate decisions or policy changes to colleagues.

Objectives

In a memo, there is usually one specific topic. If you have to cover two subjects, you might consider writing two separate memos. **The purpose of a memo could be:**

> ◇ To send a report or summary, notes from a meeting.
> ◇ To give information about events or changes.
> ◇ To ask for information (e.g. preferred holiday dates).
> ◇ To give instructions or remind people to take action.
> ◇ To make recommendations.

 备忘录和电子邮件的格式类似，但是更加简洁，篇幅比电子邮件短，一般来说只有一个主题。

Tasks

Let's see an example first.

MEMO

DATE	9th June
TO	All marketing staff
FROM	Alan Stewart, Marketing Manager
SUBJECT	New product launch

I am delighted to inform you that the Finance Committee has approved the new product plans. We need to get moving ASAP on the marketing campaign.

- Could you send me all the present market research data on the identified target?
- I recommend we set up focus groups for more up-to-date data.
- I would like to see a selection of proposed brand names by the end of this week.
- The creative team must have a proposal for a print media and TV campaign by the end of this month.
- We need to finalise and make decisions at the next meeting early next month.

Make this project an urgent priority. The team must meet the above deadlines.

AS

 ASAP 的意思是"尽快"，是 as soon as possible 的首字母缩写。

The above-mentioned sample shows the components of a typical memo and its format. We are going to discuss them one by one.

Key Points

Let's start with **the memo's heading**.

The word "MEMO" or "MEMORANDUM" should be written at the top of the page. This word could be larger. You can either put it in the center on the first line or align（调整）it to the left edge.

Then, write down **the date**. For example "9th June" "January 19, 2019".

Next, you need to **address the recipient**. Although a memo is less formal than a business letter, you should address readers formally, using their full names. Sometimes, their job titles should be mentioned, too. This sample shows it will be sent to all marketing staff. If you include everyone in your organization, you might write, "TO: All Employees."

Sometimes, there is someone who may be informed by a memo but he or she is not the direct recipient of the memo. In this case, you need to add "CC" line after "TO" line. CC means Carbon Copy, which indicates that this memo is going to be sent to other receivers.

Next, the **writer's name with job title** goes on the third line. For example in this case, "Alan Stewart, Marketing Manager".

Finally, on the subject line, you need to write **a concise statement of the topic** of your memo. It usually begins with "**Subject**" but it could also be "RE" which means the memo is a response. Subjects should always be specific. For example:

> ◇ New product launch
> ◇ Use of information resources
> ◇ Financial data required for 2016 Tender
> ◇ Executives, roundtable meeting notice
> ◇ Approval of overseas trips
> ◇ Request for funds: AWP conference

Add a line below the heading so this part will be separated from the body of the memo.

Now, let's move on to **memo's message**.

A memo should start with your **reason** for writing it. The main point should be covered in the first paragraph and sometimes it is stated together with background information, such as a brief summary of a problem. For example:

> ◇ I am delighted to inform you that the Finance Committee has approved the new product plans.
> ◇ Because of the damage the fire caused to the lower level of the building, all employees with first-floor offices temporarily will use the computers in the training room to do their work.

However, if you are giving bad news or you disagree with your supervisor, you need to make your memo's opening more persuasive. It means that the main idea might not be directly mentioned but expressed in a somewhat indirect manner.

The rest of the memo is to explain your reasoning or to offer evidence for your position. Let's read our example together and find out its language features.

> I am delighted to inform you that the Finance Committee has approved the new product plans. We need to get moving ASAP on the marketing campaign.
> ◇ Could you send me all the present market research data on the identified target?
> ◇ I recommend we set up focus groups for more up-to-date data.
> ◇ I would like to see a selection of proposed brand names by the end of this week.
> ◇ The creative team must have a proposal for a print media and TV campaign by the end of this month.
> ◇ We need to finalise and make decisions at the next meeting early next month.
>
> Make this project an urgent priority. The team must meet the above deadlines.
>
> AS

Have you recognized the memo's style?

Styles could vary from organization to organization, depending on cultures of certain company. However, there are some basic rules.

First, it is less formal than a business letter or email. You may have noticed that there are no salutations such as "Dear Sir" or "Madam". Besides, the memo ends with merely the initials of the writer instead of a closing signature. However, you still need to take a professional and formal tone because the audiences may include your boss.

Second, the tone is relatively neutral. As you can see from the example, "I recommend" and "We need to…"

Third, the memo is short and easy to read. There are some bullet points that help audiences to read. In the business world, people are super busy. So the layout of memos should take this into consideration. Sometimes, numbers and subtitles are used, especially when the memo is long. With the help of its subtitles, a long memo is still easy to navigate(导

航/处理).

Fourth, the memo states everything clearly and it concludes with a request for action. Deadlines are listed such as "the end of this week" and "the next meeting early next month". Meanwhile, all the required actions are followed by their subjects, for example, the name of the team. In this way, readers can be clear about what actions they should take.

Language Focus

Here are some sentence patterns that you may find them useful:
To **give information**, you can use:

> ◇ I have the pleasure to announce that…
> ◇ You will be happy to hear…
> ◇ An investigation conducted by…reveals that…
> ◇ I am delighted to inform you…/be able to announce…
> ◇ I would like to remind you that…

To **request information**, you can use:

> ◇ I would like to have…
> ◇ Could you provide me with…
> ◇ The purpose of this memorandum is to ask for…
> ◇ Following the decision of the Board of Directors on November 9, starting January 1 all employees…

To **recommend options**, you can use:

> ◇ It is recommended that…
> ◇ It is in the best interests of…
> ◇ Having considered all the alternatives, we suggest…

To **give instructions**, you can use:

> ◇ Please read…
> ◇ We kindly request…
> ◇ Make sure that…
> ◇ …is permitted only when…
> ◇ Please call no later than…

To **suggest actions**, you can use:

> ◇ The creative team must have a proposal by the end of this month.
> ◇ I would like to see a proposal by the end of this week.
> ◇ Could you send me all the data?
> ◇ All employees must use the new system by July 1, 2019.

The **ending of the message** could be:

> ◇ Should you have anything unclear about the above-mentioned issues, please contact me directly.
> ◇ Further suggestions will be appreciated.
> ◇ Please be punctual so that we have enough time to…
> ◇ Your kind support and cooperation is highly appreciated.

Tasks

Write a memo to tell all employees the following:

1) Your company decided to hold a Christmas party on Friday evening, 24th Dec. 2021.
2) The party will be held in the ballroom of the downtown Marriott Hotel.
3) Every employee can bring a guest with him/her.

You may add information if necessary.

Sample

> **To:** All Employees
> **From:** Desmond Booth, President
> **Date:** December 10, 2021
> **Subject:** Annual Christmas Party
>
> You and a guest are invited to the company's annual Christmas party to be held on Friday, December 24, beginning at 5:30 PM. In recognition of the company's success this past year, we are celebrating in style. The Christmas party will be held in the ballroom of the downtown Marriott Hotel.
>
> We have engaged a ballroom orchestra for the occasion, and plenty of free refreshments will be on hand.
>
> I hope everyone will be able to join the celebration. You have all contributed to our success, and you all deserve to celebrate. I look forward to seeing you there.

With the popularity of emails, memos can be delivered via emails. But effective memo writing remains an essential skill in communications which follows the same professional and

formatting standards as those printed on paper.

Summary

Today, we learned how to write a memo. You need to begin the memo by listing on separate lines the recipient, the sender, the date, and the subject of the memo. State the purpose of the memo in the first line of the main part. Use headings or bulleted or numbered lists, and keep the memo short and concise.

Before the end of this lecture, let's see some **helpful hints**:

- Think of your readers and their needs.
- Be specific when making your points.
- Make your subject line short and descriptive.
- Use bullet points (项目符号) or numbers to clarify points or lists.
- Cover only a single subject.
- Memos should be short and concise; try to keep them to one page.

项目符号(Bullet Points) 每行以一个小印刷符号开始、由单词或短语组成的列表。

Ⅲ. 写作练习

1. Read the sentences from business emails and choose the one that has an appropriate style in each group.

1) A. I am writing to ask whether you could send me the latest conference schedule.
   B. I'm writing to ask you for some information about the conference.

2) A. Send me the necessary information.
   B. Would you please send me the necessary information?

3) A. Thanks for the opportunity.
   B. I want to express my sincere thanks for the opportunity of employment with this university.

4) A. I think your company will benefit from my working experience.
   B. If given the chance, I will be my best in your company.

5) A. Looking forward to seeing you soon.
   B. CU.

2. Read the experience of a student and choose which sentence should be written into his/her résumé.

1) "As a volunteer, I went to a summer camp and helped the doctors remove the bandages

there. Each of the patients was given prescription glasses."

   A. Experience: Assisted in the eye camp

   B. Experience: Volunteered in the summer camp

2) "I spent 3 years in BUCT. There is one year to go. My major is Computer Science."

   A. Education: Bachelor's degree

   B. Education: Candidate for Bachelor in Science degree, June 2021

3) "In the Student Union, everybody works hard. Fresher's Fair is a wonderful time though we have to do many things like promoting."

   A. Experience: Organized Fresher's Fair

   B. Experience: Worked for Student Union

4) "I can speak good English and passed CET-6."

   A. Qualifications: College English Test Band 6(CET6)   Passed
      Skill: Oral English   Excellent

   B. Master of English

5) "I participated in research on genetic engineering."

   A. Research Experience: Participation in research on genetic engineering

   B. Research Experience: Participated in research on genetic engineering

3. Read a job application letter and answer the questions.

From: John Doe
To: staff@buct.co.cn
Subject: re post of research assistant
Attachment: John's CV

I am writting to aply for the position of research assistant. My major is Computer Science and I will graduate from Beijing Univercity next year. I had experience in computer programming and worked for big companys. I participated in my supervisor's research project last semester and form that experience, I learned to be a research assistant.

I am looking for a position of research assistant which will allow me to improve my skills and develop as a researcher.

John

---

1) Correct spelling mistakes for the writer.

   _____ _____ _____ _____

2) Revise the job application letter.

From: John Doe
To: staff@buct.co.cn
Subject: re post of research assistant
Attachment: John's CV

_____

4. **Read the letter below and write a reply.**

From: Jane Doe
To: John Doe
Subject: re application
Attachment: none

_____

Dear Mr. Doe,

Thank you for your letter of application. We were very much impressed by your experience. Can you come for an interview next Monday morning at nine o'clock? Feel free to contact me if you have any questions.

Best regards,
Jane
___

Jane Doe
HR Manager

From:
To:
Subject:
Attachment:

_____

第6周
应用文写作 II (Practical Writing II)

≫ I. 概述

本周的应用文写作主要关注图表写作。图表是数据的呈现方式，图表写作是研究人员撰写研究报告的基础。撰写研究报告时，选择恰当的图表、给出准确的解释，对于学术写作来讲非常重要。图表写作是研究生阶段必须具备的写作技能。本周通过四个独立的讲座，讲解了几种基本图表的类型和图表写作的核心技巧。

- **讲座1** 图表写作概述：归纳学术报告中图表的主要类型及不同图表的优势和特点。
- **讲座2** 线图写作。线图能够反映数据变化的趋势，因此，本讲座重点介绍如何用英语表达趋势。
- **讲座3** 饼图写作。饼图能够反映整体与部分的关系，因此，本讲座重点介绍用英语表达百分比的技巧。
- **讲座4** 柱状图写作。柱状图能够非常清晰地反映数据的对比情况，因此，在本讲座中，用英语表达对比这一概念是重点讲解内容。

本周的四个讲座相互独立，各有侧重。每个讲座首先介绍各类型图表的特点，通过举例帮助学生构建图表写作的技能，最后通过写作任务要求学生举一反三。学习之后，学生也可以将讲座中的写作技巧迁移到其他图表写作中去。

≫ II. 慕课讲稿

讲座1 图表写作的类型 (Essays Based upon Graphs)

知识概要 学术报告中图表的主要类型有表格、线图、饼图和柱状图等。线图能够反

映数据变化的趋势，饼图能够反映整体与部分的关系，柱状图能够非常清晰地反映数据的对比情况。整体介绍图表时，可以使用一般现在时。

关键词 table（表格）；line graph（线图）；pie graph/chart（饼图）；bar graph/chart（柱状图）

Lead-in

As a graduate student, do you need to read academic reports that contain many graphs（图表）? Are you an intern or a recent graduate who is worried about how to describe graphs?

Objectives

Do you want to improve your skills in writing essays based upon graphs? In this lecture, we are going to learn how to think about and use graphs by dividing this topic into different parts. Each part will focus on one skill. Today, we are going to discuss types of essays based upon graphs. In the following ten minutes, I will present you different types of graphs and provide useful expressions for your description of graphs.

In a report, one can always find some graphs which may help the author visualize（使可视化）his or her data. As an English proverb goes, "A graphic is often worth a thousand words." A graph can represent information clearly and readers can have an overall comprehension of what is presented.

Besides, it is important to select a useful graph. Many graphs are poorly designed, for example, with the information presented in a confused fashion or **with the wrong set of color contrasts**, which makes a graph hard to read.

✎ 绘制图表时，建议使用差异较大的颜色表示不同的内容，使读者能够清晰分辨数据之间的差异。

Key Points

First of all, let's get to know **the types of graphs**.

There are different types of graphs. **Table, line graph, bar graph/chart, pie graph/chart, scatter plot, 3D-surface plots, flow chart.** Those graphs with their different features are common devices for representing information visually.

✎ 学术报告中图表的主要类型有表格、线图、柱状图、饼图、散点图、三维曲面图、流程图。

A table is common in reports. It has vertical columns and horizontal rows. Numbers are listed in tables and they are of great significance. In a table, numbers can be demonstrated clearly. One can easily find the data. However, tables are difficult to read at the first sight. It may not leave deep impressions for readers and it requires readers' effort to read.

Item	1994	1995	1996	1997	1998
Food	65%	60%	48%	42%	35%
Clothing	8%	9%	12%	15%	17%
Recreation	3%	5%	7%	8%	10%
Others	24%	26%	33%	35%	38%
Total	100%	100%	100%	100%	100%

Line graphs can show continuing data, especially the trends(趋势). Points are connected in line graphs and they form a continuous line. It can show how one thing is affected by another. The rises and falls can be demonstrated clearly in a line graph. As a result, line graphs can be used to analyze the changes of one thing during certain period of time.

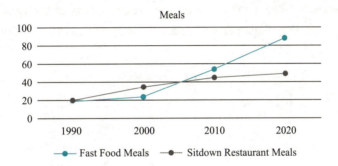

Scatter plots are like line graphs, but, instead of a line, data is indicated by dots or vertical(纵向的) bars to indicate a range of data. This may indicate that the writer does not believe that the data are as closely related as in a line graph. The vertical bars are used when the data point is a range.

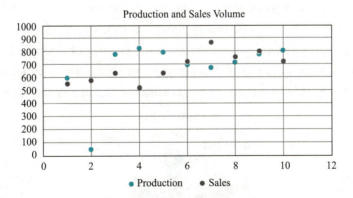

3D-surface plots are used when three dimensions need to be presented, such as in a topographical(地形学的，地质的) chart, where north, south and elevation are shown. But this is also used as a variety of engineering and science applications.

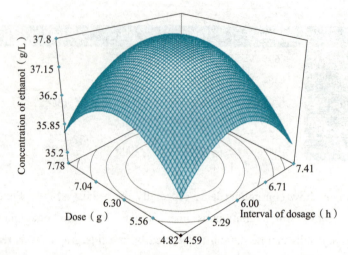

Bar graphs can compare data and show relationships between different items, so they are used to show differences. The length of bars can present trends at the same time. There are horizontal(水平的) bar charts and perpendicular(竖直的) bar charts. Both of them can present differences.

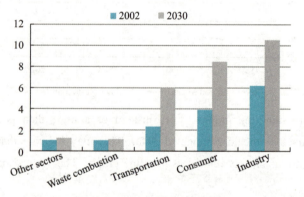

Pie charts can be used to present percentages of different items and their relationships. How part relates to the whole can be clearly shown in a pie chart. In particular, it can show percentages effectively by different colors of the chart. The size of a part indicates the amount. (**However, there is some data which indicates how pie charts are misleading, since humans are not good at being able to see the contrasts between the size of the slices of the pie.**)

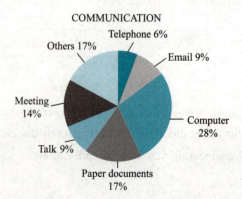

Language Focus

Based on the information from graphs, one can write a report. To begin with, you can ask a question. In this way, it can help you extract information that you need and conduct the first sentence of your essay.

Key Points

✓ What point is the graph making?

The question can be answered by examining **the title** of a graph. It usually tells what kind of information the graph is presenting. In this case, you may only need to rewrite the title as a sentence, telling the readers what information it presents. **If there is no title, you need to look at the labels on the horizontal and vertical axis, which are X and Y axis respectively.** You may find out what categories of information are presented in the graph.

> 如果图表没有标题，需要通过图表的横纵坐标及其关系来找出标题，横轴和纵轴就是 X 轴和 Y 轴。

When you figure them out, you are ready for writing a sentence. The sentence patterns are:

> ◇ The pie chart gives information on the world population figures in 2001.
> ◇ The chart compares the ratio of single males by age group in China.

You may notice that there is **a subject** in each sentence that indicates what we are talking about, and **a verb** that indicates what the graph is illustrating. You may change the verb if necessary. For example, you may also use "show" or "illustrate". It depends on the aim of your report. You may always start your report by writing "The graph shows…" But when you want to compare two items, you may change the sentence into "The graph compares…"

"The world population figures" and "the ratio of single males by age group" are the contents of the graphs. Finally, you may find "in 2001" and "in China". They are time and region respectively, which are of equal importance in graphic writing.

Let's have a look at the following examples:

> ◇ This pie chart represents the average weekly family expenses in Britain in 1977.
> ◇ This table illustrates the economic and social conditions in Japan, Canada and Peru in 1994.
> ◇ This graph shows the number of full-time teachers of regular schools in China between 1960 and 1990.
> ◇ This bar chart describes the participation in higher education by males and females in urban, rural and remote areas in Australia in 1989.

What do they have in common? What are the subjects of the sentences? What is the tense of those sentences?

All of them are charts and graphs. But when you describe them, you need to distinguish them. **"Bar chart" is more specific than "chart"**.

✎ 当描述图表时，具体称其为"柱状图"要明显优于仅仅称之为"图表"。

We usually apply present simple tense in the introduction part of graphic writing because we are now writing a report.

The contents of graphs are usually presented by a noun or a noun phrase, for example, "the average weekly family expenses" and "the economic and social conditions". The modifiers or details could be added by the preposition such as "of" "in" and "by".

Finally, do not forget to add the region or time for your sentence. Otherwise, the introduction might not be clear for readers.

Dear students, have you mastered what we learned today? Let's try to distinguish the types of graphs and try to construct the first sentence of your report. Are you ready?

Tasks

Here is a chart. What kind of chart is it?

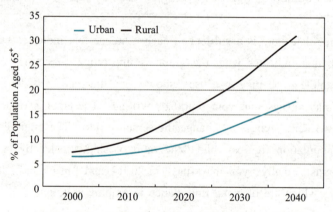

Projected Population 65⁺: Urban and Rural China, 2000-2040

Yes. It is **a line chart/line graph**. So we will start our sentence with "line chart" as the subject. Right?

Then, we are going to decide which verb we will use. There are two lines in this line graph. So we can use "compare". The black line and the grey line signify different things in this chart so we can definitely compare them.

Then, the content of this chart is the title. So we only need to rewrite the title. It says, "Projected Population 65⁺: Urban and Rural China, 2000-2040". So we can be sure that this chart shows the projected population aged over 65 in urban and rural China.

Do not forget the time: 2000-2040.

Then, double check your sentence and read what you've written with me.

The line chart compares the projected population aged over 65 in urban and rural areas in China from 2000 to 2040.

Summary

Let's sum up what we've discussed today.

First, we got to know different types of graphs and their features.

Then, we examined sample sentences and summarized the common features of the first sentence of an essay based on graphs, the general description of graphs.

Next, we tried to write a descriptive sentence.

Are you clear about how to write a report? Or at least know what information to begin with?

Here are some useful expressions to use as a reference.

> ◇ The table/chart/diagram/graph shows(that)…
> ◇ According to the table/chart/diagram/graph…
> ◇ As(is) shown in the table/chart/diagram/graph…
> ◇ As can be seen from the table/chart/diagram/graph/figures…
> ◇ It can be seen from the figures/statistics…
> ◇ We can see from the figures/statistics…
> ◇ It is clear/apparent from the figures/statistics…

讲座2 线图写作：趋势(Line Graph: Trends)

知识概要 线图能够反映事物的变化趋势，需要注意关键点的描述。描述趋势时，需要注意其程度和变化速度，要使用恰当的副词。描述趋势时可以使用动词、名词或名词性结构，增加语言的丰富性。

关 键 词 point(点)；increase(增长)；decline(下降)；degree(程度)；speed(速度)

Lead-in

In the previous lecture, we learned how to write the first sentence of the essay. In this lecture, we are going to consider **how to describe trends** and thus make our essay more sophisticated.

For most kinds of graphs, trends can be seen and described. **Here we take an example of a line graph because it is the most significant one.** Besides, trends can be easily recognized in a line graph or a line chart. As we can see from the chart, a line goes up and down, indicating the trend.

✎ 图表都能够表现数据变化的趋势，但是在线图中，趋势变化表现得更加明显。

Tasks

So, here comes the question for today: **How to describe trends in line graphs?** Before we get down to our task of describing trends, let's do an exercise.

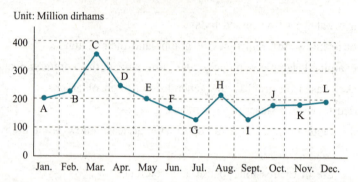

Now have a look at this chart. It is a line graph. From the graph we can see some points. Each of them corresponds to a particular value of the data. **Which data in your opinion needs to be explained?** You may think about it before I tell you how to do our exercise.

Good. Now you know there are trends in this chart. **Main points should be explained, including the biggest and the smallest.** Point C, Point G, Point H, and Point I therefore should be explained. If a trend continues, such as from C to G, from I to L, those points can be explained together.

> 图表中的峰值和谷值都需要描述出来，因此 C、G、H、I 点的数据需要描述。然后，由峰值到谷值/谷值到峰值的数据可以一并描述，如从 C 点到 G 点、从 I 点到 L 点的数据变化趋势。

Let's start with a banked cloze test. There are several blanks. Please choose the correct expressions from the box and fill in the blanks based on the graph. Let me show you the options:

| a low point | declined | doubled | recovered | increased slightly |
| remained | rose sharply | sudden | | |

In Jan., gold sales were 200 million dirhams. In Feb. they 1) _____ to 220 million dirhams and 2) _____ to a peak of 350 million dirhams in Mar. Over the next four months, sales 3) _____ steadily, reaching 4) _____ of 120 million dirhams in Jul. In Aug., there was a(n) 5) _____ increase. Sales almost 6) _____, rising from 120 million dirhams in Jul. to 210 million dirhams in Aug. This was followed by a drop in Sept. to 120 million dirhams. From Sept. to Oct, sales 7) _____ from 120 million dirhams to 180 dirhams. In Oct. and Nov., sales 8) _____ steady, and there was a small increase in Dec. to 190 million dirhams.

When you fill in the blanks, pay attention to what appears before and after each blank. The content could help you. Let's do it together.

✎ In those types of exercises, the first sentence should be a complete one. Otherwise, at the beginning we will have no idea how to interpret what is being presented. "In Jan., gold sales were 200 million dirhams." Dirham is a basic unit of currency in Morocco(摩洛哥) and United Arab Emirates(阿拉伯联合酋长国). The first sentence tells us about the data of Point A, 200 million. Let's go on. The second sentence is about the data in February. From A to B, what happened? Yes, the line rises. So the possible answer could be "doubled" "recovered" "increased slightly" and "rose sharply". They are all about "increase". However, from A to B, it is only a slight increase and there is no comparison with previous data. Therefore, we decided to choose "increased slightly".

Let's move on to the second blank.

"Blank No. 2 to a peak of 350 million dirhams in Mar." Here we can see there is still an increase. But compared to the previous one, this one seems to be more significant. So we can fill in the blank with "rose sharply".

Next, there will be a decline. What are the expressions for describing declines? There is only one. That is "declined". So it is going to be "Over the next four months, sales declined steadily".

At the end of a decline, there should be a low point like what we have here; G, Blank 4 is going to be "reaching a low point of 120 million dirhams in Jul."

"In Aug., there was an increase." It seems that there's no need for us to fill in the blank. So we can add an adjective for the increase, a "sudden" increase. From G to H, there is indeed a sudden increase.

Then, the next sentence is a comment. From 120 to 210, sales almost "doubled", right? Blank 6 can be filled in with "doubled".

"This was followed by a drop in Sept." That is from H to I. How about from I to J? It rises again. So we can say "Sales recovered from 120 million dirhams to 180 million dirhams."

Finally, from J to L, there is a steady increase. So "sales remained steady, and there was a small increase in Dec. to 190 million dirhams."

From this exercise, we understand that trends can be described by mentioning its degree and its speed. In other words, when you describe a trend, you need to explain whether it is an increase or a decrease. Then, you need to explain whether it is a sharp one or a mild one. Here are some useful expressions that you may find it helpful.

For describing an increase, we employ words such as *increase*, *rise*, *grow*, *leap*, *surge*, *soar*, *skyrocket*, *reach*. They are **verbs**. You may also use **phrasal verbs** such as *go up/push up/amount to/move upward*. Besides, you can use **noun phrases** such as *an increase of/a growth/a leap/an upward trend*.

As for describing a decrease, we employ such words as *decrease*, *drop*, *fall*, *slip*, *decline*, *slide*, *shrink*, *trim*, *dwindle*, *cut*, *plunge*, *plummet*, *nosedive*, *slump*, *collapse*, *crash*, *slash*, *slacken*, and *dip*. You may also use **phrasal verbs** such as *move downward/spiral downward/slowdown/be reduced*. Besides, you can use **noun phrases** such as *a decline/a downward trend(movements)*.

There are several ways for us to use the above-mentioned expressions.

The number of aged people over 65 increased significantly from 2000 to 2010.

Or we could use the noun phrase:

There was a significant increase in the number of aged people over 65 from 2000 to 2010.

The period between 2000 and 2010 experienced a significant growth in the number of people over 65.

Apart from the trend, we should also describe the degree of a trend. They can be divided into two groups. *Rapid*, *dramatic*, *significant* and *sharp* are all describing sudden increases while *steady*, *gradual*, *slight* and *stable* are relatively mild. If we use "increase" as a verb, we should use "rapidly" or "steadily" to describe verbs.

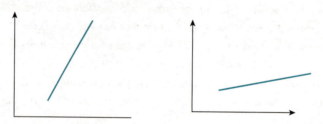

数据的趋势也需要用副词来修饰，根据速度快慢分为两组。在描述时，要根据图表观察是相对急速的上升或下降趋势还是相对缓和的趋势。

I am sure that now you are ready for the task of describing line graphs. Here you are.

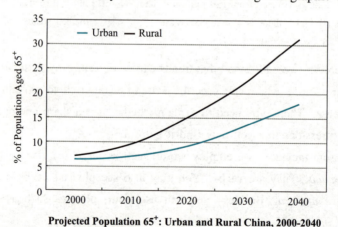

Projected Population 65+: Urban and Rural China, 2000-2040

Please describe the line graph, using what we've learned in this session.

You may notice that there are two lines, so we need to compare and show the differences. At the same time, the highest and the lowest point should be described, too.

Sample

This line graph compares the projected population aged over 65 in urban and rural areas in China from 2000 to 2040.

It is clear that from 2000 to 2040, there will be an increase, mirroring the rise in the number of projected rural and urban population. In 2000, the percentage of 65^+ population in both urban and rural areas in China were relatively the same, which was around 7%. Then the figure of urban projected population rises steadily, reaching at about 18% in 2040. In contrast, the rate of rural 65^+ population increases dramatically to over 31% in 2040.

Overall, the graph shows how the urban and rural population will increase over the period.

The sample uses "rises steadily" and "increases dramatically" to describe the two lines.

Summary

To sum up, we learned how to describe trends in line charts and summarized useful expressions. However, in other types of graphs, there might be trends, too.

讲座3 饼图：百分比(Pie Chart: Percentage)

知识概要 饼图体现了部分与整体的关系，即可视化地体现了部分占整体的百分比。描述时可以遵循一定规律，如从占百分比较大的数据开始描述。在图表描述中，根据数据的特点，需要灵活使用一般现在时和一般过去时，必要时也会使用现在完成时。

关 键 词 percentage(百分比)；category(类别)；proportion(部分)

Lead-in

In this lecture, we are going to learn **how to describe pie charts**.

Objectives

A pie chart contains different parts. It shows how a part relates to the whole, so describing percentages and how to present percentages effectively are what we are going to learn today.

Key Points

First of all, let's read an example and see the sentence patterns used when we talk about percentages.

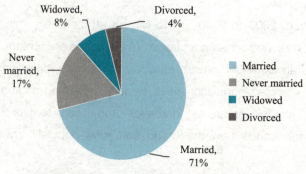

Marital Status of Adult Americans(1970)

This is a pie chart. It shows the marital status of adult Americans in 1970. Each category is presented by a different color. **When we describe a pie chart, we can start with the largest proportion.**

✎ 饼图可以按照所占比例最大到最小的数据顺序进行描述。

Let's read the following example and figure out what are the useful expressions.

This pie chart shows that married people accounted for the greatest proportion of the adult American population in 1970(71%). The American adults who were never married made up 17% of the population. By contrast, people who were widowed represented 8% of the population. It is particularly noticeable that divorced couples only constituted 4% of the American population in 1970.

Just as I said before, we usually begin with the largest proportion(部分), that is the percentage of married people in this example. We may also notice that this example contains four sentences, one for each category(种类). Please pay attention to the phrases used to describe percentages in each sentence and see if you can locate them.

In the first sentence, we can find the phrase "account for".
In the second sentence, we can find the phrase "make up".
In the third sentence, we can find the word "represent".
In the fourth sentence, we can find the word "constitute".

Those are useful expressions for describing percentages in pie charts. Let's have a summary.

In those sentences or clauses, the **subjects** are the categories, for example, "married people" "the American adults who were never married" "people who were widowed", and "divorced couples". "Account for" "make up" "represent" and "constitute" are **predicates**, followed by their percentage respectively.

There are other ways for describing percentages:

When A constitutes exactly 25% of the total amount, we could use the expression "**a quarter**". Meanwhile, we can say that B accounts for three-quarters of the total amount.

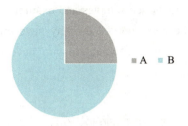
The population of Europe, Latin America, North America and Oceania(大洋洲) accounts for a quarter of the world's population in 2000. "Account for" is what we have already discussed. A quarter means 25%. Almost three-quarters of the world's population live in Asia and Africa. Here, three-quarters means 75%.

When it comprises 50% of the total amount, we can put it as "A comprises half of the total amount." Or simply put it as "The percentage of A is 50%."

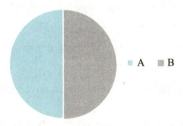

Tasks

Now it is your turn. Can you use what we have just learned and describe a pie chart?

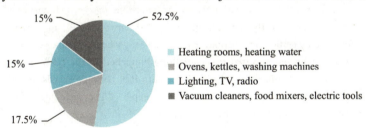

Purposes of Using Electricity

This pie chart presents reasons for using electricity. Based on what we have learned, can you apply those useful expressions in your own essay? Do it right now.

Here is a sample for your reference:

It is clear that the electricity is used for four reasons. Heating rooms and water accounts for the highest proportion(52.5%) of the total amount of electricity used, while the running of ovens, kettles and washing machines constitutes 17.5% of the total consumption of electricity. Lighting, TV and the radio represent the same proportion(15%) of power consumption as vacuum cleaners, food mixers and electric tools do.

The sample starts with the largest proportion which is heating rooms and water. Then, it describes four parts respectively. The last two parts are the same, so the sample compares the two by using "as". We are going to elaborate this point in the next part—describing bar charts.

Now, you must be very clear about how to describe pie charts. Before we move on to the next session, I would like to ask you another question:

Have you noticed the **tenses** that were used in the above-mentioned samples and examples? When did we use the present tense? When did we use the past tense? You may have the same problem when you write essays based on graphs. So today, we would like to have a summary.

Please have a look at the examples listed here:

◇ This pie chart represents average weekly family expenses in Britain in 1977.
◇ This graph shows the number of full-time teachers of regular schools in China between 1960 and 1990.
◇ Oil prices increased from the second quarter of 2000 through to November but then eased, partly because of the global slowdown.
◇ The percentage of American adults who were never married made up 17% of the population.

The first two sentences use present tense as we can see from the predicates, "represents" and "shows". What do they have in common?
Yes, they are overviews of graphs. **The graphs are usually printed on a page or projected on a slide, so they are just in front of their readers. Besides, they are facts. Thus, when we describe the charts, we use present tense.**

The last two sentences use past tense. What do they have in common? Why we have to use past tense here? Let's read them in detail. "Oil prices increased from the second quarter of 2000 through to November but then eased, partly because of the global slowdown." "Increased" and "eased" are predicates, followed by certain time period. As you can see, when the author talked about oil prices, **the data were already collected and that was something happened in the past. So the author used past tense.** Pay attention to the time referred to in the chart. Past tense correlates to the time. Besides, the tense of clause corresponds to the main clause. For example, "The percentage of American adults who were never married made up 17% of the population in 1970."

当图表在读者面前或者图表数据是事实的时候，描述图表时可以使用一般现在时。
当作者讲述之前的数据（或者已经发生的事件的相关数据）时，使用的是一般过去时。

The past perfect tense could be used in graphic essays, too. Let's look at this example:

◇ After that peak, these calls had fallen back to the 1995 figure by 2001.

This example talks about things happened in the past. From "by 2001", we know that the year of 2001 had been passed. **So we are talking about the past of past. Therefore, past perfect tense is applied here.**

当描述的数据发生在过去的过去，使用过去完成时态。

Summary

Today we learned how to describe pie charts. The main feature of writing about pie charts is the expressions of percentages. We read an essay and summarize the useful expressions, in particular, the verbs. They are "account for" "make up" "represent" and "constitute". Next, we did an exercise, describing a pie chart and reading a sample. Finally, we talked about tenses of graphic writing.

讲座 4　柱状图：对比（Bar Chart: Contrast）

知识概要　柱状图能够清晰地表现事物之间的差异，可以是水平的，也可以是垂直的。比较级和最高级的表达法可以帮助描述事物之间的差异，需要注意连词的使用。表达数据时，如果不能从图表中读出精确的数字，可以使用一些表示估计的词汇辅助表达。

关 键 词　difference（差异）；contrast（对比）；conjunction（连词）；estimate（估计）

Lead-in

Today, we are going to focus on **bar charts**. Bar charts can be drawn either vertically or horizontally.

✎ 柱状图可以是柱形，也可以是长条形。

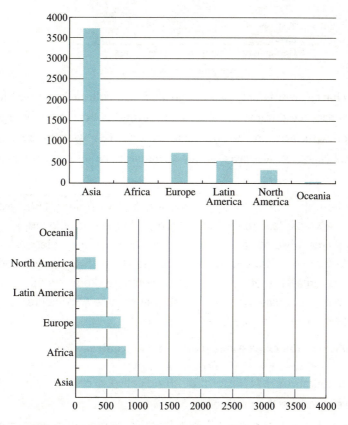

Bar charts can effectively show differences. So when we describe bar charts, we need to pay attention to how to make contrasts.

In order to answer this question, let's have a look at **bar charts** below.

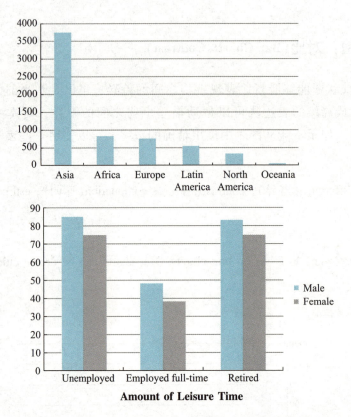

In the first chart, there is only one category of data collected. So we only need to figure out the differences between different items. **In the second chart**, data are organized according to different categories so there are two different columns(柱) with different colors. When we describe the second chart, we also need to pay attention to the differences within each category.

Example

We can see from the bar chart that in the employed full-time, unemployed and retired groups, men enjoyed more leisure time than women. In the unemployed group, men enjoyed 85 hours of leisure time while females only had 75 hours. In the category of retirees, males had 83 hours of leisure time whereas females had less than 75 hours. The gender gap in this group is two hours smaller than that in the full-time workers' group. Women who were employed on a full-time basis had the least leisure time (38 hours), while their male counterparts had 48 hours of leisure time.

Can you underline the expressions used to make contrasts?

> ◇ The comparative(比较级) form of an adjective is one of them: "Men enjoyed more leisure time than women."
> ◇ There is also a superlative(最高级) form: "Women who were employed on a full-time basis had the least leisure time (38 hours), while their male counterparts had 48 hours of leisure time."

Finally, we have seen the **conjunctions** that serve to connect phrases and clauses, such as "whereas" and "while".

Key Points

Here are more examples.

The superlative form helps us to locate the most noticeable data within one group. For example, we could say, "Asia is by far the biggest region, with 3,721 million people." or "Sales stood at the lowest level in March." indicating the highest or the lowest column in one bar chart.

> ◇ The population of China is more than that of Britain.
> ◇ The volume of our branch is approximately twice that of their branch.
> ◇ The sales of TV sets were half as much as the sales of VCD players.
> ◇ The percentage of profit doubled from July to October.
> ◇ In the unemployed group, men enjoyed 85 hours of leisure time while females only had 75 hours.

We need to identify the counterpart when we make contrast. That is why "that" is highlighted here. The sentence pattern is **more/twice/three times + than**. *Double* and *triple* could be verbs when we describe the changes of certain data.

> 在使用英文进行比较的写作中，注意避免受汉语的影响，要分清比较的是哪两个事物。汉语表达为"中国的人口比英国多"，但实际上是在表达"中国的人口比英国的人口多"。因此，英语句子中的"that"指代的是英国的人口，不可以舍弃。

Conjunctions can be used to make contrasts, too. When we use conjunctions, we need to make sure that the subjects should be different in the main clause and the clause. For example, "men" and "ladies" "males" and "females".

Tasks

This bar chart reveals that carbon dioxide emissions will expand to varying degrees in different sectors by 2030. **Please describe this bar chart, using the expressions we've just learned.**

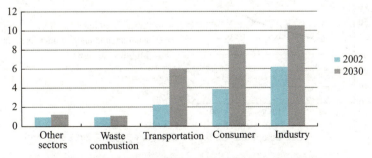

Worldwide Carbon Dioxide Emissions by Sector

Let's read the sample. Find out the expressions used to describe data in the bar chart.

The bar chart reveals that carbon dioxide emissions will expand to varying degrees in different sectors by 2030. Industry will continue to be the major producer of carbon dioxide, rising to more than 10 billion tons in 2030. Next comes the consumer sector, which is projected to more than double its emissions from less than 4 billion to 8 billion or more tons. Transportation, the third largest producer, will see a huge growth to 6 billion tons, triple the amount in 2002. By comparison, waste combustion and other sectors make up a much lower proportion, each producing an estimated 1 billion tons of carbon dioxide.

We can find the expressions such as "the major" "double" "the third largest" "triple" and "lower" that indicate contrasts.

So far we have talked about bar charts. A bar chart can show trends too, especially when the data of its categories are organized according to certain time sequence.

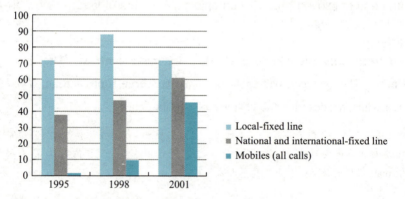

UK Telephone Calls, by Category, 1995–2001

If we change the columns of this bar chart into different points, it turns out to be a line chart.

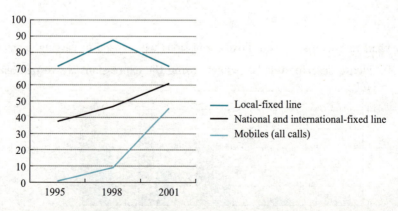

UK Telephone Calls, by Category, 1995–2002

So we could definitely use what we have learned in the previous lesson to describe this graph. And at the same time, we need to make contrasts between different categories.

Let's see the sample.

This bar chart shows the time spent by UK residents on different types of telephone calls between 1995 and 2001.

Local-fixed line calls were the highest throughout the period, rising from 72 billion minutes in 1995 to just under 90 billion in 1998. After that peak, these calls had fallen back to the 1995 figure by 2001. National and international-fixed line calls grew steadily from 38 billion to 61 billion at the end of the period in question. There was a dramatic increase in mobile calls from 2 billion to 46 billion minutes. This rise was particularly noticeable between 1998 and 2001, during which time the use of mobile phones tripled.

To sum up, although local-fixed line calls were still the most popular in 2001, the gap between the three categories had narrowed considerably over the second half of the period in question.

Language Focus

Before we finish this lecture, I would like to talk about numbers. When we write reports, data are first-hand data. In this case, we use exactly these data in our reports. Have you noticed that sometimes it is impossible for us to read the exact number from a chart or a graph? **So when we report second-hand data, we sometimes have to estimate the numbers.** Here are some useful expressions:

> ◇ Over 300 enterprises provided more than 6,000 positions on this employment fair.
> ◇ The automobile travels 150 kilometers in under an hour.
> ◇ It'll take less than an hour to get there.
> ◇ It took more or less a whole day to paint the ceiling.
> ◇ It cost approximately 300 yuan.
> ◇ Some 430 thousand men and women worked on Canadian farms in 1995.

These expressions are handy when you describe a chart or a graph.

📝 如果需要描述的数据是二手资料，无法获取准确的数字，描述时要注意严谨，可使用"大约""左右"等词语。

Summary

In this lecture, we started with the features of bar charts, and then we summarized useful expressions through reading sample charts. Superlative forms, comparative forms and conjunctions are handy for bar chart description. Finally, we compare a bar chart with a line chart and draw the similarities.

Now, we have discussed different types of graphs and their features. We learned about line graph, pie chart, and bar chart. We focused on describing trends, percentages, and contrast. Now you must be very confident about writing an essay about graphs.

Ⅲ. 写作练习

1. Match the title/content with the graphs.

(　　) 1) Glycerol availability in the 2006 – 2017 period and trend predicted till 2024.

(　　) 2) Market size and price of glycerol derivatives.

(　　) 3) Comparison between the profit in the conversion of petroleum into traditional fuels and of vegetable oils into biodiesel.

(　　) 4) Reaction scheme for the transesterification of triglycerides with methanol to yield biodiesel.

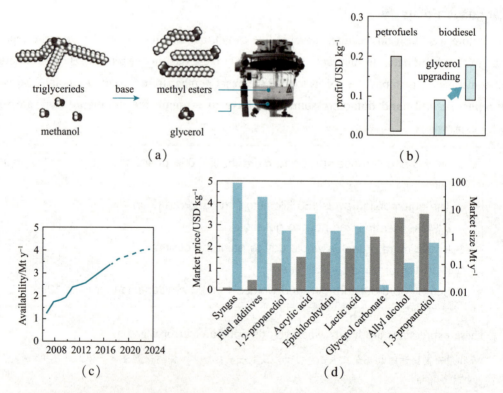

2. Read the chart below and decide which sentence is correctly describing the chart.

1) The population of women who are 45-49 reached over 52,000 in 2018.

2) China's population grew steadily over the years.

3) Compared to the middle-aged group, there were fewer people under the age of 30.

4) There are more women than men in China.

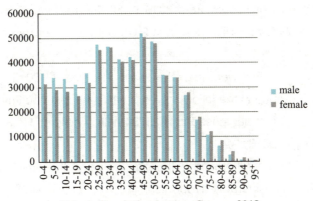

China's Population by Age Group, 2018

3. Read the chart and fill in the blanks.

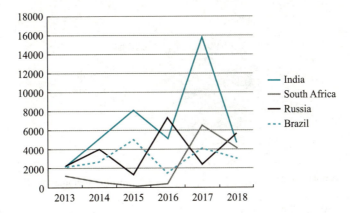

FDI(Foreign Direct Investment) from Other 4 BRICS Countries, 2013–2018

The graph shows the value of FDI, measured in 10 thousand U.S. dollars, from four other BRICS countries between 2013 and 2018.

As we can see from the graph, FDI from four countries had all grown or dropped during the period, but their rates varied.

1) _____ had offered the largest amount of FDI since 2013. The amount almost increased four times from $20.75 million dollars to $80.8 million dollars, and then dropped to $57.58 million dollars in 2016. However, it soared to $157.72 million dollars in 2017. The FDI from 2) _____ was not stable. In 2018, it experienced a downward trend to $47.57 million dollars which was even lower than the year of 2014.

FDI from 3) _____ grew at a similar rate from over $23.04 million dollars to $50.84 million dollars. In 2016, it also decreased to the lowest point and then caught up in 2017.

In comparison, FDI from 4) _____ had been significantly lower in quantity and it went down gradually from 2013 to 2015. From 2015 to 2016, it remained more or less the same level and then increased significantly from 2016 to 2017, reaching $65.18 million dollars. Then, it went back to $41.85 million dollars in 2018 but it had enjoyed over 3 times' growth since 2013.

The trend of 5) _____ FDI went the other way. The year of 2015 witnessed its lowest point and the amount went up in the following year. While the rest countries had reached their peaks in 2017, 6) _____ FDI decreased to $23.84 million dollars. However, it had become the largest FDI country in 2018.

To sum up, despite the differences, the gap between the amounts of FDI from four countries had narrowed considerably by the year of 2018.

4. Using the information from the graphs and write a report describing them.

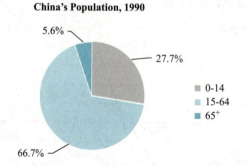

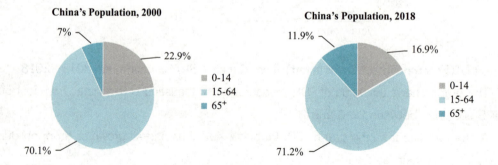

第7周
篇章写作 I (Essay Writing I)

>> I. 概述

在进入不同体裁的篇章写作之前，我们首先需要了解什么样的文章才是好文章，即好文章的评判标准有哪些，这是我们即将学习的内容。简言之，好文章一般都具有独创性，风格独具特色。但是，这并不意味着好文章没有共性。好文章都具有完整性、统一性和连贯性。对于英语写作者来说，一篇好文章通常要采用正确的文稿格式，要体现良好的语言基本技能、娴熟的语言应用能力以及符合英语思维的谋篇布局。

此外，我们还将学习文章开头和结尾的写法。一篇文章的开头会决定读者是否被吸引并愿意读下去。一般文章的开头要实现抓住读者的注意力、交代背景以及表明文章中心思想的目的。有些文章会在开头给出主题句并引出文章中间展开部分的要点。如同好的开头一样，好的结尾对于给读者留下深刻印象也至关重要。文章结尾一般会重申中心思想，但这并不是简单的重复，好的结尾会加深读者的理解，但不会显得冗长多余。通过学习本周的多个例子，相信你将对开头和结尾的写作有更多了解，你的文章的开头和结尾也会更有法可循。

>> II. 慕课讲稿

讲座 1 判断好文章的标准（Features of Good Effective Essays）

知识概要 虽然文章因体裁、风格和写作目的不同很难有统一的标准来评判优劣，但是好文章一般都会表现出内容统一、完整，结构清晰、合乎逻辑，符合写作规范，几乎没有明显的语言使用错误这几个特征。

关 键 词 内容(content)；结构(organization)；语言规范(mechanics)

Lead-in

Have you ever wondered why some students always get high grades for their writing assignments and you seem to make no progress even though you have tried harder and harder each time? Have you ever wanted to improve your writing product and simply do not know how? Have you ever asked what makes a good piece of writing? If one of your answers to these questions is yes, you should probably follow my advice in this lecture.

Objectives

- Tell the elements that make a writing a good one in general.
- Identify the elements that make a writing effective or ineffective.
- Make use of the knowledge acquired to improve on your own writing or give feedback on other people's writing.

Tasks

Some students say they probably cannot write well in English, but if they are asked to judge which essay is better or best they will not make mistakes because they are better at reading and have read a lot since they began learning English. Do you think so, too? Let's do an exercise to get some ideas about effective writing.

Read and compare the two short paragraphs in each question. Pick one that is better from the two given and try to tell in which way the chosen one is better.

Question 1

A. I really don't like baseball because I think it is too boring. Most of the game the players are just standing around doing nothing. I think it is stupid to run around the bases after hitting a ball with a bat.

B. I really like baseball because I think it is fun. My cousin plays on the same team as me. He's got a pet frog at home. We spend a lot of time playing together in the summer.

✎ You've probably found "A" is better because the writer stays focused on the topic or controlling idea, while "B" wanders from the topic.

✎ 很显然，B 段落没有围绕一个主旨思想展开行文，所写内容不聚焦。

Question 2

A. The third little pig was smart because he didn't get eaten. Wolves like to eat pigs. Pigs need to be protected from wolves so they won't get eaten.

B. The third little pig was smart because he built his house out of brick. He knew the straw and sticks were not good enough to build a house. A house made of brick would stand when a wolf came to huff and puff and blow the house down.

✏️ "B" is better because in content "B" is fully and clearly developed.

✏️ 对比这两个段落不难发现，A 段落虽然也是围绕一个中心思想展开的，但是在内容的完整性和逻辑的清晰性方面明显逊色于 B 段落。

Question 3

A. A reason I like to eat pizza is the melted cheese that stretches from your mouth when you take a bite. I like the thick crispy crust at the end of each slice. I like that you can eat it with your fingers.

B. I like pizza because you can pick it up and eat it with your hands. Even more, I like it because of the melted cheese on top that stretches from your mouth when you bite into it. But the best thing about pizza is the crust. I love to munch on the thick crispy crust after eating the rest of the piece.

✏️ "B" is better. "A" and "B" have the same content while "B" is well organized. "B" gives the reasons in a specific and clear order with linking words.

✏️ 这两个段落的内容信息量基本上是一样的，但是 B 段落更具可读性，因为 B 段落在说明原因时，不仅遵循了一定的清晰顺序，而且句子之间恰当地使用了连接词，使段落结构更明了易懂。

Question 4

A. We start the day with two hours of Language Arts, kind of boring but we read some cool stories. After that we get a break from the classroom and go to Special. My favorites are P. E. and Computer Lab. Next we have an hour of either Science or Social Studies. Science is awesome when we get to do experiments. Finally, your favorite or mine, lunch and recess. Last but not least, we end the day with an hour of Math. We do lots of different things in Math, so I think you'll actually like it.

B. First we have two hours of Language Arts. Then we go to Special. Then we have Science or Social Studies for an hour. Then we go to lunch and recess. Then we go to Math. Then we go home.

✏️ "A" is better. Though "B" also uses linking words to organize the content, "A" is rich and precise in word choice and sentence structures, which keeps the audience interested.

✏️ 1. 此部分练习旨在通过段落对比总结好文章具备的基本特征。
2. 两个段落均使用了连接词，但是 A 段落在连接词选取和句子结构运用方面更加丰富、准确，更能够保持读者的兴趣。

Key Points

The task we've just finished may give you some idea about the factors that may influence the quality of your essay. When evaluating an essay, people may place the emphasis on different

aspects, and they may also have different ways to categorize the factors that may affect the effectiveness of the essay. However, generally speaking, we believe the following three aspects determine the quality of the essay to a large extent: **the content**, **the organization** and **the mechanics**.

The content of the essay is the writer's message. Good essays have a single clear central idea, and each paragraph should be closely related to the central idea and have a clear main point or topic sentence. You may have heard people mentioning the "unity" of a piece of writing. Staying focused is what is meant by "unity". Good essays also develop the writer's main points through thorough discussion and provide specific details. Thoroughness gives the reader a sense of completion and satisfaction. General is boring; specific is interesting. A good essay includes specific details to support the writer's explanations.

> 在内容方面，好文章都有一个明确的中心思想，每个段落都与中心思想紧密相关，并且每个段落都有明确的主旨或者主旨句。此外，内容完整、详略得当、提供必要的细节等也是好文章应该具备的特征。

An effective essay is organized with **an introduction**, **main body**, and **conclusion**. **The introduction** should begin in an interesting way that gains the reader's attention; it should then lead the reader to the thesis statement. **The main body** should consist of several well-developed paragraphs. Each paragraph should support or expand the central idea of the paper. The idea of each paragraph should be explained and illustrated through examples, details, and descriptions. **The conclusion** should "wrap it up" by giving the reader a sense of closure.

Each paragraph should also be organized by **following certain logical order**. Many writers give a topic sentence at the beginning of the paragraph, which controls the development of the whole paragraph. The last sentence or sentences often conclude the paragraph and also serve as the transition to the next paragraph.

> 在组织结构方面，好文章一般都有开头、主体和结尾三大部分。一般开头部分吸引读者的注意，介绍背景，并且亮出文章的主题思想。主体部分包含几个方面、多个段落时，可以每个方面回应前文提出的主题思想的一个方面；主体部分通过运用描写、举例、对比等手法围绕全文的主题思想来展开。结尾部分必不可少，可以总结、重申或者升华前文的内容，给读者完整的感觉，并且留下深刻的印象。在组织结构方面，无论是段落与段落之间，还是段落内部，都应遵循一定的逻辑顺序行文，使文章清晰易懂。

Finally, the writer should **use transition words and phrases** to move the reader smoothly from one idea to another within a paragraph or from one paragraph to another. Transition words are a device for increasing coherence, and that's why when people talk about coherence, they usually mention transition words and phrases. But you should know transitions are not the only device you can use to achieve coherence. For example, **synonymous expressions** and **pronouns** are also frequently used to make the writing coherent.

> 为了让段落之间和段落内部结构合理、清晰并具有连贯性，好文章中经常会运用过渡词句、连接

词和短语等。要实现文章的连贯性，还可以运用同义词、代词和句型重复等手段。

A good essay is well written and carefully edited in terms of **mechanics** as well. Some students are familiar with "content" and "organization", but they do not know what "mechanics" refer to. **"Mechanics" is the use of language; "grammar" "punctuation" "word usage" and "spelling" are all mechanics.** Some people may feel it is the easiest to improve an essay's mechanics because they can ask somebody, check in some reference books or on some websites or even use grammar checking software to deal with this category of problems. For example, you may have noticed there are some spelling mistakes or typos in the previous task of comparison, and you can easily correct them.

In simple words, "content" "organization" and "mechanics" are the key elements that determine whether an essay is well written or not. In terms of content, how you present the elements of the essay and, if you are making an argument, how you **back up your propositions** also affects the quality of your essay. In some other segment of this course, the issue of **word choice** is taken up, since proper word choice is often the difference between a good essay and a great one.

1. 这里的"语言规范"指语言使用规范，包括语法、标点符号、词的使用和拼写等。对于英语为外语的学生来说，语言规范更显重要，不规范的写作甚至是错误会导致表达不清、无法使读者保持兴趣和读懂等问题。
2. 虽然在本节课中，我们只强调内容、结构和语言规范这三个方面的标准，但是好文章还具有其他共性特征，例如在议论文写作中，主论点(命题)需要得到强有力的支撑。另外，在所有文章中，选词精准都是很重要的。

Tasks

Now please read and analyze the sample essay.

Parents throughout the world place spend time reading with their offspring to prepare them for school where their literacy skills are further developed; however, recent research suggests that focusing on reading at an early age can be detrimental, and participating in fun activities would be far more beneficial. I am a strong advocate of this approach, and the benefits of it will be covered in this essay.

A fundamental reason for this is that there is no biological age for reading, and pushing infants to acquire this skill before they are ready could have repercussions. For example, in the UK, many boys are reluctant readers, possibly because of being forced to read, and this turned them off reading. By focusing on other activities and developing other skills such as creativity and imagination, when they are ready to read, they usually acquire this skill rapidly. In addition, the importance of encouraging creativity and developing a child's imagination must be acknowledged. Through play, youngsters develop social and cognitive skills, for example, they are more likely to learn vocabulary through context rather than learning it from

a book.

Furthermore, play allows youngsters to mature emotionally, and gain self-confidence. There is no scientific research which suggests reading at a young age is essential for a child's development. Moreover, evidence suggests the reverse is true. In Finland, early years' education focuses on playing. Reading is only encouraged if a child shows an interest in developing this skill. This self-directed approach certainly does not result in Finnish school leavers falling behind their foreign counterparts. In fact, Finland was ranked the sixth best in the world in terms of reading.

Despite being a supporter of this non-reading approach, I strongly recommend incorporating bedtime stories into a child's daily routine. However, reading as a regular daytime activity should be swapped for something which allows the child to develop other skills.

Consider the following questions:

1. Does the essay stay focused on a central idea? What is it? How do you know?
2. Which part is the introduction? The conclusion?
3. Are all the sentences necessary and closely related to its central idea?
4. Is the thesis statement well supported? How many supporting points does the author give? Do you find the examples helpful?
5. How does the author move on from one point to another, from one sentence to another? Can you point out some important transition words or expressions?
6. Do you think the conclusion clear and effective? Why?
7. Is there any mechanical error?
8. Do you think the essay needs to be improved on any aspect?

Summary

Now, do you think you have more awareness about the key ingredients that make an essay good and effective? Do not forget to do the quiz to deepen your understanding.

讲座2 开头和结尾的写法（Effective Introduction and Conclusion）

知识概要 一般来说，文章的开头主要由三个部分组成："钓钩"、文章背景和主题句。开头部分的写作可以看成一个上宽下窄的倒三角形，问题和主题逐步聚焦。结尾的部分则恰好相反，可以看成一个三角形，上窄下宽，因为结尾部分一般先重申主题思想，再概述文中要点，最后把所讨论的问题放置在更大的语境中，启发读者思考，给读者留下深刻的印象。

关 键 词 钓钩(hook)；主题句(thesis statement)；三角形(triangle)；
重申(restatement)

Lead-in

Welcome back to our discussion of essay writing. In this lecture, we will focus on **writing effective introductions and conclusions**.

Introductions and conclusions are the first and last impressions made by your essay. Much like in real life, you always want to leave a good first and last impression. But how? People say "All beginnings are hard", do you agree? Some may think "A conclusion is simply the place where you got tired of thinking". Do you believe it is possible to produce a good piece of writing without giving much thinking to the conclusion? Actually, we can safely say nearly all experienced writers would agree that introductions and conclusions play a special role in essays, and they frequently demand much of our attention as a writer.

Objectives

- Know what important elements make a good introduction.
- Know the organization of the introduction.
- Know what important elements make a good conclusion.
- Know the organization of the conclusion.

Tasks

Task 1 Think about the essays you have read, brainstorm what kind of information can be included in the introduction of an essay and what roles an introduction plays.

Task 2 Read an introduction paragraph and then read the three conclusion paragraphs that follow. Decide which is the best conclusion and tell why you think so.

Introduction: Before I travelled to the UK last year, I thought that British food was just fish and chips, roast beef, apple pie, rice pudding and endless cups of tea. These foods are popular in Britain, but during my travels, I discovered that there is so much more to eat in the UK. People from all over the world have made their home in Britain, and they have brought with them their own food. Even in small towns, you can find Chinese, Indian and Italian restaurants, amongst others. The UK can be divided into different regions that each has its own characteristic foods influenced by the culture of the people who live there.

Conclusion 1: The British eat many different kinds of food, but the typical diet of many people includes eating a lot of fast food and ready-made dishes. The popularity of hamburger and pizza restaurants has increased greatly over the years. As a result of this diet, many British people have food-related health problems. To create a healthier society, people should learn about eating a good diet and should teach their children to do the same.

Conclusion 2: Clearly, it is difficult to say that there is one type of British food. Every part of the country has its own special dishes based on the produce and tastes of that region.

From the Ancient Britons and the Roman, Saxon and Viking invasions to present-day immigrants, the cuisine of the UK continues to change with its changing population.

Conclusion 3: People who have come from other countries to live in the UK have brought their own traditions and customs with them and added them to British culture. It is possible to find restaurants from all different ethnic backgrounds, especially in larger cities around the country. Immigrants may also maintain their traditions by building places to practise their religion, such as mosques, temples and churches. By continuing to follow some of their customs and beliefs, immigrants can stay in touch with their past while also living a new life in a new country.

Key Points

Let's consider how to write the introduction first. The introduction paragraph usually **starts from something broad and it narrows down gradually**, so generally speaking, we can use this **triangle** to show the structure of the introduction. The first few sentences are usually something that tries to get the attention of the reader, which is called a "**hook**" or **the attention grabber**. Having gained your reader's attention, you should lead the reader to the next stage of your introduction, which provides **background information** and continues to **narrow the topic down** until you come to **the thesis statement** you want to make, which is **the main idea or main point** of your essay.

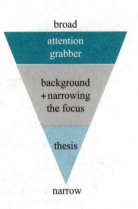

> 文章开头一般从比较宽泛的话题入手，逐步细化聚焦，最后给出文章主题，呈上宽下窄的倒三角形状。这个三角形最宽的层面是"钓钩"，即吸引读者注意的部分；中间的层面提供所涉及话题的背景信息，在最下层三角形的尖角处，作者一般会给出统领全文的主题句或中心句。

Now let's consider some important elements in introduction writing. Just now we mentioned the "hook". The hook attracts and engages the reader, but it does not argue or explain anything. And always remember the hook should not only be engaging and interesting but also always closely relate to the point you want to make. Here are the first few sentences in the Scientific American online article entitled *The False Promise of Fish Oil Supplements* by R. Preston Mason on August 22, 2019.

Every 38 seconds, someone in the U.S. dies from cardiovascular disease. Even more worrisome: deaths from cardiovascular disease have been rising dramatically since 2011 following years of decline. Strokes, heart attacks and other cardiovascular events cause great suffering and are an enormous health care burden.

Without doubt, with the startling statistics and facts, the reader's attention is immediately grabbed and the reader would like to read more.

◈ "钩钩"的作用是吸引读者，因此它不做出辩驳或者解释，需要注意的是"抓眼球"固然重要，但是"钩钩"必须与文章的中心思想紧密相关。

Here are the most frequently used five ways to grab the attention of the reader. **First**, use a quotation or sayings of famous people. **Second**, ask a question that will be answered by your essay or will catch the reader's attention and lead toward your thesis topic. **Third**, tell an anecdote or a surprising fact or statistic. **Next**, describe a problem, dilemma, or controversy associated with your essay. And **last**, challenge a statement of opinion.

◈ 文章开头引起读者兴趣的常用方法：使用引语或名言，提出问题，讲述轶事，运用惊人的事实或数据，描述一个与文章内容相关的问题、困境或者争议，对已有观点提出质疑等。

Many writers give **a theist statement** at the end of the introduction. A thesis statement is the sentence that states the main idea of the essay and helps control the ideas within the paper. It is not merely a topic. It often reflects an opinion or judgment that a writer has made about a reading or personal experience. A strong thesis statement usually is **a road map** for the essay; in other words, it tells the reader what to expect from the rest of the essay.

◈ 很多文章在开头部分的末尾给出统领全文的主题句，表明文章的中心思想，并以此主题句提供后文展开的"路线图"。

Here are two examples of a thesis statement.

> 1. We should wear school uniforms because they would help reduce the need for disciplinary measures, be cheaper than other clothing, and help create school pride.
> 2. C. S. Lewis's *Chronicles of Narnia* series is one of the richest works of the 20th century because it offers an escape from reality, teaches readers to have faith even when they don't understand, and contains a host of vibrant characters.

◈ 主题句例1有明确的中心思想，即"我们应该穿校服"，此句还提供了支持此观点的三个理由，读者很容易预测作者下文将从"穿校服能够减少纪律约束的必要性、校服比其他衣服花费更少、校服能帮助建立学校荣誉感"三方面来展开说明。主题句例2的中心思想是"刘易斯的《纳尼亚传奇》系列是20世纪最丰富的作品之一"，此中心句的后半部分也提供了后文行文的"路线图"，即"它为读者提供了一种逃离现实的方式，它教导读者甚至在不理解的时候也要保持信念，它展现了许多鲜活的人物"。

It is not easy to write an introduction, but you should know you do not have to start your writing from the introduction part. Actually, many successful writers choose not to start the writing by writing about the introduction.

Writing about **the conclusion** is not easy, either. Many students do not know what to put in the conclusion since it seems all the things have been mentioned and all the words have been said. Again we can use a **triangle** to show the general structure of the conclusion; this triangle looks as if it reverse(颠倒) the previous triangle in introduction part because it starts from something narrow or specific, and it goes broader gradually. Usually in an effective conclusion, the writer introduces the end of the essay and **restates the thesis first**, using different words and expressions. A good conclusion draws together the points which readers just read and are fresh in their minds. And with the main points being restated, the writer usually **links the main points to some larger context**, and finally **tries to leave the reader with something to think about**, which can be a question, a resonating fact or statistic, or an action etc.

> 结尾段的架构相当于把开头段的三角形倒置过来，形成一个上窄下宽的三角形，也就是说，结尾段是从具体到一般的写作过程。首先，作者通常用不同于之前的表述重申文章的主题，再次概括总结文章中之前提及的要点，最后把文章的核心要点与更宽泛的语境相连接、拓展和升华，启发读者思考，给读者留下深刻的印象。

There are also a few "**dos**" and "**don'ts**" for a conclusion. A conclusion should stress the importance of the thesis statement, give the essay a sense of completeness, and leave a final impression on the reader. A conclusion should not repeat the introduction, be just a summary of the body paragraphs, or be the place to add new content or new arguments.

> 文章结尾可以强调主题的重大意义，给读者完整感，并留下最后的印象。文章结尾不能简单重复开头部分，不是主体部分的要点总结，不能加入新的内容或者论点。

Tasks

Now let's analyze some introduction and conclusion samples. First, read and analyze the following paragraph about writing a good hook. Mark the "attention grabber", the "background information" and the "thesis statement".

How can a writer expect to get a reader's attention without a good hook? The first sentence of an essay is often overlooked by writers, but readers depend on it to set the tone for the whole essay. Writing a good hook isn't always easy, but it is an important skill to learn if you want to write effectively.

> The writer tries to get the attention of the reader by using a rhetorical question first, and then provides some background information, narrowing down the topic. Finally, the writer clearly airs his or her opinion in the final thesis statement sentence.

Here is a sample conclusion paragraph. Read the paragraph, analyze its structure and label each part of the paragraph. After reading the paragraph carefully, you may have found out how the paragraph was structured. The first sentence restates the thesis or the main idea of the essay, and the last sentence leaves the reader to think further. The rest of the paragraph reviews the main points.

[Restate Thesis & Revisit Value of Essay] It is clear that the only acceptable way of ensuring the safety of airline passengers is to begin a program to issue Safe Traveler Cards or national ID cards to United States citizens. [Review Main Points] These cards would screen out those who are unlikely to be terrorists and would also eliminate the delays that currently characterize air travel. Most important, they would help prevent terrorists from hijacking American planes. At the same time, by making racial profiling unnecessary, these cards would help protect personal and civil liberties of Americans. [Leave Readers Thinking] Only by instituting a national ID card system can the U.S. make certain that the terrorists who attacked the United States did not hijack the liberties that are so precious to us.

Language Focus

✓ Signposting stems for an introduction in an academic paper

> ◇ To understand the role of...(your topic *) this essay aims to provide a discussion of...(the ideas you will develop)
> ◇ This essay seeks to investigate/evaluate/illustrate/discuss the impact of...(your topic) in relation to...(the ideas you will develop)
> ◇ Firstly, this assignment examines...(your topic) and its links with...(your first idea) Next, it closely examines...
> ◇ ...in relation to...(your next idea) Finally, it focuses on...and how this affects...(your next idea)

✓ Transitional expressions in the conclusion part

> finally, in a word, in brief, briefly, in conclusion, in the end, in the final analysis, on the whole, thus, to conclude, to summarize, in sum, to sum up, in summary

Summary

Writing the introduction and conclusion always demands your special effort. But with this lecture, you have probably found that they do not present by any means an impossible mission. With these guiding principles in mind, you should read more, paying special attention to how successful writers write the introductions and the conclusions. You can practise writing your own introductions and conclusions by imitating what you've learned from other writers. Gradually, you will not need to rack your brain when it comes to effective essay introductions and conclusions.

Ⅲ. 写作练习

1. The following sentences speak about the advantages of travelling by train. One is a topic sentence and others are supporting sentences which justify the argument presented in the topic sentence, but they are all jumbled. Arrange them in a logical sequence.

1) Additionally, a few things like pillows, towels, newspapers are provided according to the services promised.
2) Finally, when we travel by train we reach our destination quickly.
3) Travelling by train is very comfortable.
4) First, it is convenient as trains are spacious and have plenty of room to move about.
5) Next, one need not carry food as there are dining cars.
6) Secondly, every train is provided with sleeper cars and baggage cars.

2. Read the following viewpoints and justifications. Match them and develop them into a paragraph.

Viewpoint		Justification
1) Fast food is an easy solution for people with busy lives.	(　)(　)	a) It is high in fat and salt, and is not fresh.
2) Fast food is unhealthy.	(　)	b) Ordering fast food saves time and energy.
3) Fast food is expensive.	(　)	c) People who work long hours can order on phone and take away the parcel.
4) The material used in packing fast food damages the environment.	(　)	d) Money spent on fast food for a week is enough to buy groceries for two weeks.
5) Though it serves the immediate purpose, it damages both the environment and the human body.	(　)	e) People who do not have civic sense throw away the plastic material everywhere around.
		f) Thus, it is easily available tasty food but is equally harmful.

3. Do you think the following paragraph unified and coherent? Why?

The Human Body

1) The human body is a wonderful piece of work that nature has created. 2) It is not beautiful like the body of a butterfly or peacock but it is shaped practically. 3) It can do many types of work which other animals cannot. 4) It is not strong like the body of a tiger. 5) But in place of physical strength it has a big and sharp brain. 6) By using this brain the human

physique has been able to overcome many of its limitations. 7) By sitting in an aeroplane it flies faster than a kite, by riding a motorcycle it travels faster than a leopard, and by firing a machine gun it fights much better than a tiger. 8) In spite of all this, the human body suffers from many diseases because it has a weakness for habits such as smoking, drinking and overeating. 9) When it is healthy the body can give great pleasure but when it is sick it can cause great pain. 10) The wise man would always keep his body fit because a healthy mind can work only in a healthy body.

4. Please identify and point out a paragraph that does not support the thesis "Many people are changing their diets to be healthier" and tell the reasons.

1) People are concerned about pesticides, steroids, and antibiotics in the food they eat. Many now shop for organic foods since they don't have the pesticides used in conventionally grown food. Meat from chicken and cows that are not given steroids or antibiotics are gaining in popularity even though they are much more expensive. More and more people are eliminating pesticides, steroids, and antibiotics from their diets.

2) Eating healthier is also beneficial to the environment since there are less pesticides poisoning the earth. Pesticides getting into the waterways is creating a problem with drinking water. Historically, safe drinking water has been a problem. It is believed the Ancient Egyptians drank beer since the water was not safe to drink. Brewing beer killed the harmful organisms and bacteria in the water from the Nile.

3) There is a growing concern about eating genetically modified foods, and people are opting for non-GMO diets. Some people say there are more allergic reactions and other health problems resulting from these foods. Others are concerned because there are no long-term studies which clearly show no adverse health effects such as cancers or other illnesses. Avoiding GMO food is another way people are eating healthier food.

5. These conclusion sentences are in the incorrect order. Put them in the correct order (restatement of main premise→summary of key points→broad statement).

1) The main causes of student difficulty appear to be that secondary school assessment has a different focus from university expectations and that universities are increasingly attracting mature age students who may require an up-date on their skills. In response, universities invest considerable capital into well-run programs that effectively assist students to overcome their writing problems. 2) All students deserve to be successful in their studies and responsible universities must respond to student needs so that they graduate well-educated students of the highest standard, now and in the future. 3) To conclude, university students who have experienced difficulty with their academic writing skills will require assistance to reach their academic potential.

6. The following sentences are from the introduction and conclusion of the same essay.

Separate them into two groups, introduction and conclusion, and put them in the correct order.

1) Despite these problems, it is possible for teachers to make a positive contribution to learners' knowledge in this important area.

2) The essay which follows gives a brief history of prepositional theory and discusses two major teaching strategies from a cognitive linguistic perspective.

3) The concept of definiteness in relation to articles remains, however, more problematic, and needs further investigation.

4) The evidence presented here suggests that learners do not use articles randomly, but that they choose articles according to whether or not the noun is countable.

5) These small connecting words do not necessarily exist in other languages, or may not have exactly the same meanings.

6) The use of prepositions in English has always been problematic for language learners.

7) In conclusion, it is apparent that the most effective element in teaching of English articles is the reinforcement of the notion of countability.

8) This makes teaching of this area very difficult, and research indicates that no single method has yet proved successful.

7. Read the following introductory paragraphs and see whether you can tell how each author opens the essay respectively.

1) Hands flying, green eyes flashing, and spittle spraying Jenny howled at her younger sister Emma. People walked by gawking at the spectacle as Jenny's grunts emanated through the mall. Emma sucked at her thumb trying to appear nonchalant. Jenny's blond hair stood almost on end. Her hands seemed to fly so fast that her signs could barely be understood. Jenny was angry. Very angry.

2) "People paid more attention to the way I talked than what I said!" exclaimed the woman from Brooklyn, New York in the movie *American Tongues*. This young woman's home dialect interferes with people taking her seriously because they see her as a cartoonist stereotype of a New Yorker. The effects on this woman indicate the widespread judgment that occurs about nonstandard dialects. This type of judgment can even cause some to be ashamed of or try to change their language identity.

3) Is ASL a language? Can ASL be written? Do you have to be born deaf to understand ASL completely? To answer these questions, one must first understand exactly what ASL is. In this paper, I attempt to explain this as well as answer my own questions. (ASL: American Sign Language)

4) Gallaudet University, the only liberal arts college for deaf students in the world, is world-renowned in the field of deafness and education of the deaf. Gallaudet is also

proud of its charter which was signed by President Abraham Lincoln in the year of 1864. All of this happened in Gallaudet's history, an enormous part of Gallaudet's legacy comes from its rich history and the fame to two men: Amos Kendall and Edward Miner Gallaudet.

8. Read the following paragraphs and see how the author concluded the essay in each situation.

1) Without well-qualified teachers, schools are little more than buildings and equipment. If higher-paying careers continue to attract the best and the brightest students, there will not only be a shortage of teachers, but the teachers available may not have the best qualifications. Our youth will suffer. And when youth suffers, the future suffers.

2) Campaign advertisements should help us understand the candidate's qualifications and positions on the issues. Instead, most tell us what a boob or knave the opposing candidate is, or they present general images of the candidate as a family person or God-fearing American. Do such advertisements contribute to creating an informed electorate or a people who choose political leaders the same way they choose soft drinks and soap?

3) American Sign Language is a fast growing language in America. More and more universities and colleges are offering it as part of their curriculum and some are even requiring it as part of their program. This writer suggests that anyone who has a chance to learn this beautiful language should grab that opportunity.

4) Because of a charter signed by President Abraham Lincoln and because of the work of two men, Amos Kendall and Edward Miner Gallaudet, Gallaudet University is what it is today—the place where people from all over the world can find information about deafness and deaf education. Gallaudet and the deaf community truly owe these three men for without them, we might still be "deaf and dumb".

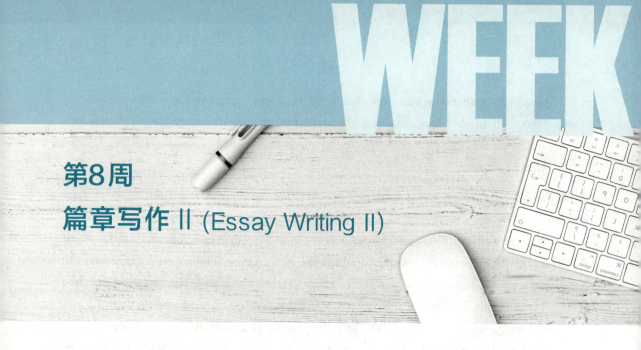

第8周

篇章写作 II (Essay Writing II)

❱❱ I. 概述

本周我们将学习记叙文和描写文的写法。这两种写作很多时候会同时出现在一篇文章中，即记叙的过程中有描写，比如，人物描写、动作描写、心理描写、环境描写等；而描写也通常不是单纯地为了描写，一般情况下，作者用描写来展示一个生动的画面，使读者的头脑中产生意象，如临其境，如闻其声，突出主题和中心思想。画面感一般可以通过对细节的描写来实现，作者可以借助人的五种感官来让读者达到身临其境的目的，也可以运用比喻、拟人、夸张等修辞格。记叙文一般要交代清楚时间、地点、人物、事件，同时也要选择合适的时态和人称以达到突出主题的目的。

❱❱ II. 慕课讲稿

讲座 1　记叙文 (Narrative Essays)

知识概要　英文记叙文写作与中文记叙文写作相似。作者首先要思考的问题是：为什么要把文中的事件或者故事写下来？也就是说，文章的意义很重要。其次，记叙文的可读性在很大程度上依赖细节的选取和描写。再次，人称视角的选取也是作者在动笔前需要仔细思考的。最后，英文记叙文还要注意时态。

关 键 词　人称 (point of view)；时态 (tense)；时间顺序 (chronological order)

Lead-in

Do you believe nearly everyone loves stories—real ones or imaginative ones? How about you? Look at the following pictures and see whether you know something about the stories. You will probably find you love stories more than you know you do.

  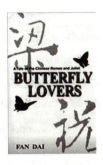 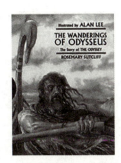

I guess even though you cannot retell the stories, at least you can say something about them. There is no culture worldwide without stories. When there were people, there were stories, and they began telling stories. Stories are part of our life. A native American proverb says, "Those who tell the stories rule the world." How do you understand it? To what extent do you agree to the proverb?

In writing, telling stories is to narrate or to write narrative essays or paragraphs. In this lecture, we are going to understand what a narrative essay is, and to understand the important elements in narratives.

Tasks

First of all, choose one from the two tasks and try to finish a narrative essay.

Task 1 Write a short essay to tell about your most unforgettable travelling experience.

Task 2 Write a short essay to tell about your first experience of doing something.

Before you start writing, think about the following questions.

1. Why do I choose to tell this travelling or experimental experience?
2. When and where did the story take place?
3. Who was involved?
4. What happened first? Next?
5. How did the story end?

Key Points

Probably you've found you love reading or listening to stories, but narrating or writing a story that even happened to you is no fun or easy job. Let's start from the beginning—what is a narrative? Although the four **genres**—narration, description, exposition and argumentation, also known as **the modes of discourse**, have been criticized by some composition scholars, we still "borrow" a definition to give you a clearer idea about such kind of writing tasks. Narrative is a kind of writing that presents events in some kind of time sequence with a distinct beginning, middle, and ending (but not necessarily in strict **chronological order**) and that is **written for the purpose of making a point**. When we talk about narratives, most of the time we refer to

stories. Only under a few very special occasions may it not be set in stories; for example, when your instructor asks you to write a book report, it definitely is not a story. So here we use narratives to mean stories. In organization, a story usually includes an **introduction**, **plot**, **characters**, **setting**, **climax**, and **conclusion**. For students like you, most of the time you will need to write **personal narratives**—things you experienced.

1. genre 表示体裁，与"话语模式（modes of discourse）"同义。有些学者不赞成把文章分成记叙文、描写文、说明文和议论文等。
2. chronological order 表示按照时间顺序叙述，即按照事件发展的先后顺序来展开写作。
3. 记叙文或者故事的叙述都要有明确的目的，也就是用事件来传达某种观点或道理。
4. 记叙文一般包含开篇、情节、人物、背景、高潮和结局等要素。
5. personal narrative 即个人叙事，讲述作者亲身经历的故事或事件。

Here are some essentials to writing a narrative essay:

◇ Some indication of the narrative's significance.
◇ Vivid detail.
◇ **Point of view**[①]: Who is telling the story? First person or third person?
◇ **Tense**[②]: Usually past tense, but not necessarily.

There are different ways to organize a personal narrative. The most common one is chronological order; that is from beginning to end.

Sometimes, some writers begin in the middle of the story and fill in the details afterwards.

A third way is to start telling the end of the story and go back to the beginning afterwards.

An experienced writer always has good reasons for selecting a certain way to organize the narrative essay. Before you write, spend some time thinking through the essential elements and select a way to organize your essay.

Tasks

Read the sample essay and answer the following questions.

Frustration at the Airport

I had never been more anxious in my life. I had just spent the last three endless hours trying to get to the airport so that I could travel home. Now, as I watched the bus driver set

---

① point of view 指人称视角，即采用第一人称还是第三人称来讲述。第一人称写作的好处在于人物心理刻画更细腻，情感也更加动人，增加了文章的真实感。第三人称写作的好处在于不受时间和空间的限制，能够比较自由灵活地反映客观内容，有比较广阔的活动范围，作者可以选择最典型的事例来展开情节。
② tense 表示时态。英语记叙文一般采用过去时。

my luggage on the airport sidewalk, I realized that my frustration had only just begun.

This was my first visit to the international terminal of the airport, and nothing was familiar. I could not make sense of any of the signs. Where was the check-in counter? Where should I take my luggage? I had no idea where the immigration line was. I began to panic. What time was it? Where was my plane? I had to find help because I could not be late!

I tried to ask a passing businessman for help, but my words all came out wrong. He just scowled and walked away. What had happened? I had been in this country for a whole semester, and I could not even remember how to ask for directions. This was awful! Another bus arrived at the terminal, and the passengers came out carrying all sorts of luggage. Here was my chance! I could follow them to the right place, and I would not have to say a word.

I dragged my enormous suitcase behind me and followed the group. We finally reached the elevators. Oh, no! They all fit in it, but there was not enough room for me. I watched in despair as the elevator doors closed. I had no idea what to do next. I got on the elevator when it returned and gazed at all the buttons. Which one could it be? I pressed Button 3. The elevator slowly climbed up to the third floor and jerked to a stop. A high, squeaking noise announced the opening of the doors, and I looked around timidly.

Tears formed in my eyes as I saw the deserted lobby and realized that I would miss my plane. Just then an elderly airport employee shuffled around the corner. He saw that I was lost and asked if he could help. He gave me his handkerchief to dry my eyes as I related my predicament. He smiled kindly, and led me down a long hallway. We walked up some stairs, turned a corner, and, at last, there was customs! He led me past all the lines of people and pushed my luggage to the inspection counter.

When I turned to thank him for all his help, he was gone. I will never know that kind man's name, but I will always remember his unexpected courtesy. He helped me when I needed it the most. I can only hope that one day I will be able to do the same for another traveler who is suffering through a terrible journey.

1. What is the narrative hook?
2. Where is the setting of this story?
3. What is the theme, or the basic idea, of *Frustration at the Airport*?
4. Read the final sentences in Paragraphs 2, 3, 4, and 5. How does each one prepare the reader for the action to come?
5. What do you think the mood of the story is? What feeling or atmosphere does the writer create?
6. What verb tense is used in *Frustration at the Airport*?
7. How is the essay organized?
8. Does the story end with a moral, prediction, or revelation?

Were you engaged in the story? Do you think it is a good piece of writing? Do you think the essay needs some improvement on any aspect?

Language Focus

Chronological Order	Prepositions	Time Words That Begin Clauses
first(second, third, etc.)	after(a moment)	after
next	at(9:00a.m.)	as soon as
finally	by(bedtime, then)	before
later	during(the afternoon)	until
now	from(then on)	when
then	until(five o'clock)	whenever while

Summary

Sometimes narration serves as part of an expository or argumentative essay, and narration is always combined with description as well. Whether it is a narrative essay or narration as part of the essay, the essential elements are the same. So, read more, think more and practise more, you will feel you are better and better at telling stories.

讲座2 描写文(Descriptive Essays)

知识概要 描写可以分为多种：人物、地点、场景、心理、情感等。描写一般与记叙、说明、议论等相结合，帮助作者有效传达中心思想。描写重在生动，让读者仿佛身临其境。

关 键 词 图像(image)；感觉(sense)

Lead-in

Nearly all people have their favorite style of music and songs. Sometimes we fall in love with a song simply because we love the words—the lyrics of the song. What kind of lyrics do you like best? What do you think of the following lyric stanzas?

> Blackbird singing in the dead of night
> Take these broken wings and learn to fly
> All your life
> You were only waiting for this moment to arise
>
> —*Blackbird* by the Beatles

Take me into your loving arms
Kiss me under the light of a thousand stars
Place your head on my beating heart

—Thinking Out Loud by Ed Sheeran

Sittin' in the morning sun
I'll be sittin' when the evening comes
Watching the ships roll in
Then I watch them roll away again

—(*Sittin' on*) *The Dock of the Bay* by Otis Redding

When we were reading the lyrics, were there images or pictures in your mind? I think you saw them just as I did. What makes the readers or listeners see the pictures and feel strongly inside? You have probably found there are some common quality in these lyric stanzas; that is, there is description in all the three. So now you see description does not only appear in stories; there is description in songs as well. Before we come to the question of "how", let's do another exercise to warm up a little bit.

Read the first stanza of the poem. What is the girl like? Can you use your own words to describe her?

She walks in beauty, like the night
Of cloudless climes and starry skies;
And all that's best of dark and bright
Meet in her aspect and her eyes;
Thus mellowed to that tender light
Which heaven to gaudy day denies.

—*She Walks in Beauty* by Lord Byron

She Walks in Beauty 是英国浪漫主义诗人乔治·戈登·拜伦的一首歌颂女性之美的抒情诗，此诗有很多中文翻译版本。以下是周永启的译本。

她在幽美中行走
像静夜——万里无云，满天星斗，
一切明暗交织的美色
都在她那容貌和双眸中汇合，
如此融就的柔和光泽，
艳丽的白天岂能轻得？

Objectives

- Understand what descriptive writing is.
- Know what makes descriptive writings good ones.

Tasks

As usual, we try to achieve these objectives by doing some tasks.

Task 1 Describe your mother or a person whom you know well.

When you describe a person, usually you describe his or her appearance, personalities, mannerism or emotions etc. Of course, a writer usually combines narration with description to let the reader know what kind of person the character is. That is to say, the writer tells what the person did or does, and descriptions are usually mingled(与……结合) in the narration. We should also know we cannot write down all aspects about the person, and we should keep the controlling idea in mind and focus on one or two perspectives of the person.

> 描写一个人时可以写外表、性格、举止、情感等方面，但通常描写应与叙述相结合，即讲述这个人做了什么事情，这样人物形象才鲜活。注意：不能试图写一个人的很多方面，而是应该根据主题思想选取一两个方面来写。

Task 2 Describe the most delicious food you've ever eaten.

When you describe the food, you also think about different aspects of the food. What makes you miss the food so much? It can be its color, smell, taste, texture etc. or the combination of these factors. Think of a logical order of your description.

Here is an easy excise to help you get more ideas about how you can make your food description "yummy". **Compare the following writings and decide which one is better.** Tell why you think so.

A. I could smell the peppers. It was dinner time. I washed my hands.

B. The sweet, burnt scent of roasting peppers hung in the air. I knew dinner was almost ready. I washed my hands, watching the dirt swirl around the sink and disappear.

> I think nobody would choose "A" because simply speaking, as a reader we do not feel a thing after reading the sentences.

Key Points

The previous two tasks are just two examples of descriptive writing assignments. Actually you do not just describe people or food. A descriptive essay is a genre of essay that asks the student to describe something—object, person, place, experience, emotion, situation, etc. This genre encourages the student's ability to **create a written account of a particular experience**. What is more, this genre allows for a great deal of **artistic freedom**(the goal of which is to **paint an image** that is vivid and moving in the mind of the reader). Let me quote from the Purdue Owl: "One might benefit from keeping in mind this simple maxim: If the reader is unable to clearly form an impression of the thing that you are describing, try, try again!"

> 描写文可以描写物件、人物、地方、经历、情感或情景等，它是某种特殊经历的书面记录，因此很多情况下描写和记叙是交织在一起的。这种文体允许有大量的"艺术自由"，即描写的目的是在读者头脑中描绘一幅画或者图景。

In detail, here are the qualities of a descriptive writing. They are also **the tips for writing good descriptions**.

> ◇ Use of Clear and Concise Language: It is necessary to describe things clearly and concisely.
> ◇ Use of Vivid Language: Word choices should be precise.
> ◇ Use of Images: Imagery is used to make things seem real and remarkable.
> ◇ Use of Five Senses: The use of the five senses creates the imagery, or a mental picture for readers.
> ◇ Use of Emotion Words: Describe emotions or feelings related to your topic.

要想成功地在读者头脑中描绘出一幅图，要注意以下几方面：1）使用清晰、简洁的语言；2）使用生动的语言，用词精准；3）使用意象；4）使用调动各种感官的语言；5）使用表达情感的词。

Tasks

Task 1

Read the following excerpt from the essay *My Favorite Place*. **Circle the expressions you like or find useful.**

1. Richmond Beach was my spiritual hangout in my childhood. It is a rocky beach in the city of Richmond Beach, which can be accessed by a long downhill drive (by car or bicycle) from the city of Edmonds. Or, as I did often, took the 30-minute walk from my house to the calm waters through a tranquil stroll through the woods of Woodway. It used to be a place inhabited by Native Americans, but now it is occupied by mostly Caucasian people. However, a totem pole stands in tribute to the tribes that used to call the beach home. It has a vast property, with a beach, a playground, two upper lawns for the view and recreation, myriad "secret" trails along the clay hillsides, picnic areas, and a square where people can walk around, take an outdoor rinse-shower after a swim, and benches for the spectacular view.

2. With the sagebrush, chattering birds, train tracks, the croak of frogs, wind, herons, various shells, a cave along the beach, and a fantastic view of the Olympic Mountains, Richmond Beach is at once ordinary and extraordinary. Being there brings you into another state, in which you want to introspect, be calm, and be positive.

3. In high school, I was not a very social person. I did not have so many friends, and I did not feel like I belonged in a group most of the time. But when I went to Richmond Beach, these worries were left behind. It seemed like a mystical place to me, and in a way, it still does.

Task 2

Read the sample descriptive excerpts from the novels. **Notice how the precise and vivid** words or expressions help you form an image in your mind.

1. "She had pewter-colored hair set in a ruthless permanent, a hard beak, and large moist eyes with the sympathetic expression of wet stones."

—*The High Window* by Raymond Chandler

2. "It was a cold grey day in late November. The weather had changed overnight, when a backing wind brought a granite sky and a mizzling rain with it, and although it was now only a little after two o'clock in the afternoon the pallor of a winter evening seemed to have closed upon the hills, cloaking them in mist."

—*Jamaica Inn* by Daphne du Maurier

Language Focus

When we describe a place, we usually need to follow certain order and make use of phrases that show location relationships. Here are some location phrases for your reference.

◇ in the middle of/in the center of
◇ next to/adjacent to/adjoining/close to/near
◇ opposite/across from/diagonal to
◇ between/sandwiched in between
◇ to the left(of)/toward the left(of)/on the left
◇ to the front of/at the front(of)/in front of
◇ to the rear of/at the rear/behind
◇ inside

Summary

Descriptions are more like art. You need to put your heart and head into them to make creative and beautiful pieces.

Ⅲ. 写作练习

1. Which sentence(s) would not be (a) good hook(s) for a narrative essay?

1) It was freezing on that sad December day.
2) After my brother's accident, I sat alone in the hospital waiting room.
3) My friend and I should not have been walking home alone so late on that dark winter night.
4) She gave her friend a birthday gift.
5) A shot rang out in the silence of the night.

2. Please identify and underline the transitional sentences in the following paragraphs.

This was my first visit to the international terminal of the airport, and nothing was familiar. I could not make sense of any of the signs. Where was the check-in counter? Where should I take my luggage? I had no idea where the immigration line was. I began to panic. What time was it? Where was my plane? I had to find help because I could not be late!

I tried to ask a passing businessman for help, but my words all came out wrong. He just scowled and walked away. What had happened? I had been in this country for a whole semester, and I could not even remember how to ask for directions. This was awful! Another bus arrived at the terminal, and the passengers stepped off carrying all sorts of luggage. Here was my chance! I could follow them to the right place, and I would not have to say a word.

3. Read the following paragraph and answer the questions that follow.

The subway is an assault on your senses. You walk down the steep, smelly staircase onto the subway platform. On the far right wall, a broken clock shows that the time is four-thirty. You wonder how long it has been broken. A mother and her crying child are standing to your left. She is trying to clean dried chocolate syrup off the child's messy face. Farther to the left, two old men are arguing about the most recent tax increase. You hear a little noise and see some paper trash roll by like a soccer ball. The most interesting thing you see while you are waiting for your subway train is a poster. It reads, "Come to Jamaica." Deep blue skies, a lone palm tree, and sapphire waters call you to this exotic place, which is so far from where you actually are.

1) From the information in this paragraph, how do you think the writer feels about the subway?

   _____

2) Which of the five senses does the writer use to describe this place? Give examples from the paragraph to support your answers.

   _____
   _____

4. When you think about possible topics for a narrative essay, try to remember something exciting, difficult, wonderful, or frightening that happened to you. Can this event be developed into an interesting narrative essay? Look at the pairs of topics. Put a tick(√) next to the topic that is the better choice for a narrative essay.

1) _____ Your last year in high school
   _____ Your last day in high school

2) _____ A scary airplane ride to another city
   _____ A scary trip around the world

3) _____ Guidelines for buying a car
   _____ Buying your first car

4) _____ Important academic ceremonies that you have participated in
   _____ Your brother's embarrassing wedding ceremony

5) _____ What I did last New Year's Eve
   _____ What I did last year

5. Adjectives add depth to the story by giving additional information. Underline all the adjectives in the following paragraph.

I walked into the noisy classroom and looked for a place to sit down. In the back of the well-lit room, I saw an old wooden desk and walked toward it. After a few moments, the anxious students quieted down when they observed the prim English teacher enter the room.

6. Read the following paragraph and answer the following questions.

My father constantly teased my mother about the amount of time she spent in her beautiful rose garden. He told her that she treated the garden as if it were human being, perhaps even her best friend. However, Mom ignored his teasing and got up every morning to take care of her special plants. She would walk among the thick green bushes that were covered with huge flowers of every color. While she was walking, she would rip out any weeds that threatened her delicate beauties. She also trimmed the old flowers to make room for their bright replacements. Any unwanted pests were quickly killed. When she was finished, she always returned from the garden with a wonderful smile and an armful of fragrant flowers for us all to enjoy.

1) What does this paragraph describe?
   _____

2) Can any sentences be deleted without changing the paragraph's meaning? If yes, which ones, and why? If no, why not?
   _____

3) The writer's mother treated the roses as if they were human beings. Find two example sentences from the paragraph that show how she protected her roses.
   a. _____
   b. _____

7. These sentences form a narrative of a personal experience with death. Read the sentences and number them from 1 to 7 to indicate the best order.

a. (   ) At 7:18 the next morning, a severe earthquake measuring 8.1 on the Richter scale hit Mexico City. I was asleep, but the violent side-to-side movement of my bed woke me up. Then I could hear the rumble of the building as it was shaking.

b. (   ) As I was trying to stand up, I could hear the stucco walls of the building cracking. I was on the third floor of a six-story building, and I thought the building was going to collapse. I really believed that I was going to die.

c. (   ) I flew to Mexico City on September 17. The first two days were uneventful.

d. (   ) My trip to Mexico City in September 1985 was not my first visit there, but this unforgettable trip helped me realize something about life.

e. (   ) I visited a few friends and did a little sightseeing. On the evening of the eighteenth, I had a late dinner with some friends that I had not seen in several years. After a very peaceful evening, I returned to my hotel and quickly fell asleep.

f. (   ) In the end, approximately 5,000 people died in this terrible tragedy, but I was lucky enough not to be among them. This unexpected disaster taught me that life can be over at any minute, so it is important for us to live every day as if it is our last.

g. (   ) When I looked at my room, I could see that the floor was moving up and down like water in the ocean. Because the doorway is often the strongest part of the building, I tried to stand up in the doorway of the bathroom.

8. Copy the sentences from the previous exercise (Exercise 7) in the best order for narrative paragraph. Add a title of your choice.

_____

Background information
(topic sentence)
_____
_____
_____

Beginning of story
_____
_____
_____
_____

Middle of story
_____
_____
_____

End of story
_____
_____
_____

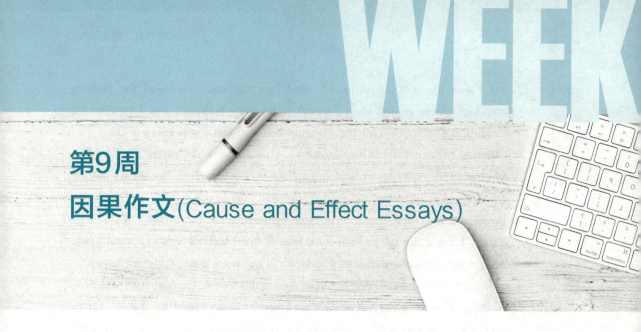

第9周
因果作文(Cause and Effect Essays)

➤➤ Ⅰ. 概述

本周课程将围绕因果作文展开，课程内容由四个板块构成：什么是因果、如何撰写因果作文、范文分析和常用表达。

首先，对原因和结果两个概念进行阐述。在撰写因果作文前，首先要弄清楚与作文主题相关的原因和/或结果：有哪些可能的原因导致了某一事件的发生？某一事件导致了哪些可能的结果？现实世界往往是错综复杂的，在分析事件发生的原因或产生的影响时，切忌把问题简单化、片面化。

然后，讲解如何组织因果作文的内容。与其他类型的说明文一样，因果作文也采用引言、主体、结论三大部分所构成的行文结构。因果作文主体段落一般有两大组织模式。一是板块模式(block organization)，二是因果链模式(chain organization)。两种模式的选择取决于文章所探讨的内容是原因还是结果以及结果之间是否存在因果关系。

此外，基于范文，重点分析因果作文的各个方面。范文分析主要包括：1）文章是属于原因探讨为主型、结果探讨为主型，还是原因结果并重型？2）文章主要阐述了哪些原因或结果？3）引言段组织结构如何，各部分分别承担什么功能？4）主体段落采用了哪种组织模式？5）结论段组织结构如何，各部分分别承担什么功能？

最后，介绍因果作文中常用的表达方式，特别是表达因果关系的过渡性单词和短语，例如 account for, attribute, because, therefore, due to, as a result of, as a consequence 等。

➤➤ Ⅱ. 慕课讲稿

讲座1 什么是因果(What Causes and Effects Are)

知识概要 原因分析(cause analysis)旨在回答由 why 引出的问题，探讨导致某一事件发生的原因；结果分析(effect analysis)则是探讨某一事件产生的影响。在探讨原因时，要找出导致某一事件发生的几个主要、直接原因。当讨论结果时，需要分清楚两类结果，一是连锁反应，二是非连锁反应。

关 键 词 原因(cause)；结果(effect)；连锁反应(chain effect)

During this week, we'll be focused on **cause and effect essays.**

Lead-in

Now, look at the quotation by Carl Sagan, a famous US astronomer.

Every kid starts out as a natural-born scientist, and then we beat it out of them. A few trickle through the system with their wonder and enthusiasm for science intact.

—Carl Sagan

The whole sentence sounds a little sad, but let's focus on the first bit: "Every kid starts out as a natural-born scientist". When we were little, we were as curious as great scientists. Now, think back in time. How curious were you when you were little?

I believe most children would raise some questions whenever they are curious about something. Sometimes they would ask so many questions that their parents would be annoyed. Now, think about your childhood. What kind of question did you often ask your parents?

Did you ever ask these questions? "Daddy, why does the bird fly?" "Mummy, why do stars twinkle?" There could be so many questions like these. Almost in every household there is a curious baby asking "why" questions. Actually, they are **exploring the reason**, or **CAUSE**.

Now, look at this picture. A little baby opens the washing machine and is putting his head into it. Maybe he or she is doing an experiment to test a theory. After watching clothes being washed there a few times, he or she is wondering whether he or she could get the hair washed too. What a "silly" but cute baby! Did you ever do anything like this in your childhood? It looks "silly" in adults' eyes, but it is children's way to **explore what will happen as a result of something, their way to seek the EFFECT**.

Both the CAUSE and EFFECT are the focus during this week.

Objectives

Through this week, we'll be able to understand what causes and effects are. And we'll be able to **find out causes and effects** when reading an article or before writing. We'll also be able to **understand and analyze how cause and effect essays are organized.** In addition, we'll be able to **use the appropriate pattern** when we write our own essays. Last but not least, we'll be able to learn to **use transitional expressions properly** to achieve coherence in cause and effect

essays.

Before writing cause and effect essays, we need first know what causes and effects are and figure them out. Now let's work on some tasks.

Tasks

Task 1 **Think about three possible reasons for childhood obesity.**

It seems that there are more and more overweight children. It is the problem of obesity. It could cause high blood pressure, diabetes and other diseases which were not common in children before. Obesity not only does harm to their physical health but also to their psychological well-being. Overweight children are more likely to be laughed at by their peers and have no friends. They also tend to lack self-confidence. To solve such a problem, we need to find out why they are overweight.

It is rather easy to find out **two factors**: **eat a lot** but **exercise little**. On the one hand, they take in too many calories from food and drinks; on the other hand, there is little activity to metabolize the calories, which accumulate and finally become fat. In addition to these two factors, what could be a third one?

Think a minute. Have you noticed that some people simply cannot lose weight no matter how much exercise they do or how little they eat? They need to consult professionals, like doctors. **There is something wrong with their body**. The problem could be inherited from their parents or grandparents. **There could also be a hormone disorder**, which should be treated with the appropriate medicine. So far, we've got three factors to explain childhood obesity, namely, three causes for childhood obesity. A take-home message here is that **the issues we have are usually complicated and it is NOT wise to simplify causes**.

✎ 儿童肥胖问题除了常见的多吃少动两个原因外, 还应考虑到激素紊乱的生理原因。

Task 2 **Think about what is likely to happen as a result of global warming.**

As we all know, it is getting hotter and hotter along with the increasing emission of the greenhouse gas from factories, cars, etc. Global warming has received lots of attention and concerns. The *Kyoto Protocol*(京都议定书), *Copenhagen Accord*(哥本哈根协议) and *Cancun Agreements*(坎昆协议) are clear indicators of concerted efforts across the world to tackle the issue and prevent the situation from becoming worse and worse. The horrible things that are happening and will happen because of global warming are exactly the reasons why we should fight against it. Then what could be the horrible things as a result of the rising temperature?

Let's think about the North Pole and South Pole first. What will happen to them? When the temperature rises, the glaciers(冰川) and ice will melt, become water, and there will be more and more water going to the sea. Accordingly, the rise in the sea level will pose a risk to seaside cities and the people living there.

Secondly, have you realized that it rains more than before or it becomes drier and drier than before in your own city? Research has found that global warming has shifted the precipitation(降水) patterns, bringing about more floods in some areas but more droughts in other places.

Thirdly, due to the changed climate, animals which used to enjoy their habitat are leaving their home and looking for cooler areas, affecting the biological diversity there. All the three horrible things are the possible effects of global warming.

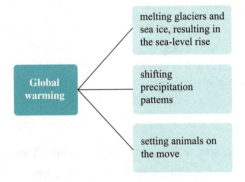

全球变暖带来多方面影响，例如极地温度上升→冰川融化→沿海城市面临威胁，降水规律变化、生物多样性受损等。

Task 3 Think about what is likely to happen in a sequence as a result of a shortage of a certain product on the free market.

It is a familiar topic, isn't it? The invisible hand.

When a product is rather rare and many people want to buy it, the factory increases its price and therefore gains more money, more profits. The other factories notice it, get jealous and start to make the same product. And now more and more are made and offered to the market. At some point, the supply is higher than the demand, which means the factories have to compete fiercely against each other in order to sell their own products. One of the promotion strategies is to lower the price. With the lowered price, the factories gain less money for each product sold, thus the decreased profits. Here we can see a few things can happen because of the shortage of a product on the market. These things are the effects of the shortage on the market.

> 这是大家比较熟悉的一个话题——市场供求关系。一旦某一商品稀缺，就会引发市场一系列波动，包括：竞争厂商加入→商品数量增加→竞争加剧→价格下降→利润下降。

Now, think about Task 2 and Task 3. Both tasks are about effects, but what are the differences?

Let's start with Task 3. Each effect is a result of the previous effect, the effect before it. All the effects do not happen at the same time, but one after another. We can call it the chain effect. However, in Task 2, does melting ice cause shifting precipitation patterns? Maybe not. At least, not directly. They are separate effects. All the effects of global warming here can happen almost at the same time.

> chain effect 指连锁反应。这是比较特殊的一系列结果。在连锁反应中，一个事件会产生多个结果，但除第一个结果外，其他结果都不是由这一事件直接导致的，而是由前一个结果所引发的。全球变暖和供求关系案例均涉及连锁反应。全球变暖对极地的影响是一个连锁反应，供求关系变化的整个案例就是一个连锁反应。

Summary

Now, let's review what we have mainly talked about. **Task 1** is about the reasons for childhood obesity, the causes for childhood obesity. **A cause is a reason why something happened or is happening.** **Task 2** is about the change to glaciers and ice, precipitation patterns and animals because of global warming, the effect of global warming. **Task 3** is about the change to the price, profit, production, and competition because of a shortage of a product, the effect of a shortage of a product. **An effect**, as both tasks show, **is a change as a result of something that happened or is happening.**

讲座 2 如何撰写因果作文 (How to Write Cause and Effect Essays)

知识概要　因果作文一般有三种：原因为主型、结果为主型、原因结果并重型。在文中组织原因和/或结果时，一般有两种组织模式供我们选择。大多数因果作文采用板块模式，而重点探讨连锁反应的文章则采用因果链模式。

关　键　词　板块模式 (block organization)；因果链模式 (chain organization)

Lead-in

In this lecture, we are going to talk about **how to write cause and effect essays**, the key points of Week 9.

Before we go on, let's briefly review what we learned last time. We introduced two concepts: causes and effects. A cause is a reason why something happened or is happening, while an effect is a change as a result of something that happened or is happening. Please note that in many cases making such connections can be difficult or controversial since the issues we have are usually complicated and not all people agree on the causes or effects.

Key Points

Then, what is a cause and effect essay? **The cause and effect essay** is a piece of writing that explores the causes and/or effects of an action or an event. Sometimes, we choose to **focus on causes only** in our writing and we can call it a cause essay. Sometimes, we can also put our sole focus on effects and we can call it an effect essay. In other times, we need to address both causes and effects because they are equally important to us, and we call it a cause and effect essay.

As we talked about last time, we need first figure out the causes and effects before we write the essay. The next step is to put them together in a clear and logical way.

Actually, there are two organization patterns for cause and effect essays. One is the block organization; the other is the chain organization. **A chain organization** examines causes or effects that are directly linked sequentially. In other words, one cause leads to an effect, which leads to another effect, and so on, such as the effects of a shortage of a product on a free market we discussed last time. On the other hand, **a block organization** is for the multiple causes or effects of an action when they are not directly linked. For instance, child obesity could result from three causes, namely, too many calories from food and drinks, little activity and genetic and hormone factors. Calories from food and drinks may not have anything to do with little activity but have a lot to do with a non-balanced diet. Therefore, if you intend to write about child obesity and focus on the three causes, you'd better use the block organization instead of the chain organization.

> 板块模式(chain organization)和因果链模式(block organization)的最大区别在于文中主要探讨的相邻原因/结果之间是否存在因果关系。如果每两个相邻原因/结果不存在因果关系，则采用板块模式；如果每两个相邻原因/结果存在因果关系，则采用因果链模式。

Now, let's look at **the block organization** for a cause essay.

As you have learned in the previous weeks, a typical essay is made up of three major parts: the introduction, body and conclusion. In the introductory paragraph, we introduce the topic of the essay, and more importantly, we present the thesis statement, the main idea of the essay, usually at the end of the paragraph. In each of the body paragraphs, we give the major supporting ideas to further explain the thesis statement. Each body paragraph is centered around one major supporting idea. The concluding paragraph is our last chance to appeal to readers. In this paragraph, we can restate the thesis, express it again in different words, and we can also summarize the body paragraphs. In many cases, we can add a final remark at the end, giving comments on the topic.

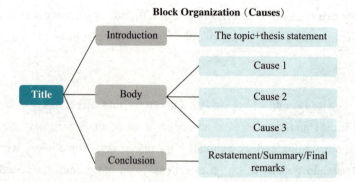

Back to the cause essay, where we follow the same structure. But now we'll focus on introducing the topic and the body part. There are various ways to introduce the topic. One of the most common ways to **start the introduction in a cause essay is to point out why it is important to talk about the topic**. Another common way is to **briefly talk about the effects first, which will naturally lead readers to wonder what causes the effects and therefore bring the thesis statement in**. In the body part, we explain the causes one by one. Usually, we **focus on only one cause in each of the body paragraphs** by telling a clear cause in the topic sentence and supporting it with details. Sometimes, you may read a body paragraph with two causes. It is very likely that these two causes are linked closely and it's a good idea to talk about them in the same paragraph. As for which cause goes first in the body, we'd better follow a logical order. Most of the time, the order of importance is a good choice. We can start with the most important and end with the least important; we can also start with the least important and end with the most important.

> 一个主体段通常聚焦于一个原因/结果，但如果两个或多个原因/结果关系密切，也可以在同一段内说明。比如，当阐述全球变暖对极地的影响时，极地温度上升→冰川融化→沿海城市面临威胁，这些是一系列连锁反应，彼此关系密切，就可以放在同一自然段内详细说明。

Now, what you see here is the block organization for an effect essay. It looks very similar to the organization for the cause essay, doesn't it? The only differences lie in the topic and the body. In the cause essay we usually start the introduction by mentioning the effects, while **in the effect essay, we can start the introduction by mentioning the causes**. In the cause essay we explain the causes one by one in the body while in the effect essay, we discuss the effects one by one. Now, let's move to **the chain organization**.

Here is an organization pattern mostly for explaining chain effects. Like the block organization for an effect essay, the chain organization has a body, where only one major effect is talked about in each paragraph. But pay attention to the two arrows between effects in the chain organization. They indicate sequences; one thing happens after another. Therefore, **when we use a chain organization, we cannot choose any other order but sequence**. In other words, the order of the effects is fixed, and a different order would break the chain. Then the body doesn't make much sense.

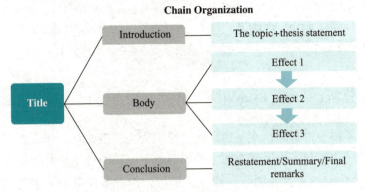

    ✎ 使用因果链模式(chain organization)时，务必注意几个结果的排列顺序。通常我们采用时间先后顺序。

    Besides the organizational patterns, there are also some good suggestions for writing cause and effect essays. **First, don't oversimplify causes or effects**. The issues we deal with are usually complex and people do not always agree on the causes or effects. In writing, we should be aware of alternate views so that we'll not seem to be uninformed or engaged in simplistic reasoning. An essay then might have a sentence like this. "<u>I am aware that modern approaches are often skeptical about simple forms of causation, and that some critics might consider a different range of causes and effects as pertaining to the issue under consideration. But for the purposes of clarity, in this essay I will limit myself to showing how X can be shown to be a plausible explanation for Y.</u>"

    Second, limit the essay to a discussion of major causes or effects. In a short essay, we generally don't have enough space to discuss minor or indirect causes or effects; therefore, we need to concentrate on the most immediate, most important factors. Covering too many causes or effects usually results in insufficient support and readers may feel the essay is not convincing enough.

    Third, use qualifying words when presenting a cause or effect, especially in the thesis statement. Qualifying words are words like *probably, possible, likely, mostly, maybe, might, some of the main reasons*, etc. They are used to make the statement sound less absolute.

    Fourth, convince readers that a causal relationship exists by showing how the relationship works. Many beginning writers are so focused on the cause or effect itself that they forget to explain to readers what the cause leads to or how the effect is caused. For example, when writing about animals on the move as an effect of global warming, don't just state the change in the habitat; it is equally important to show readers how climate change has brought about the change.

✎ 撰写因果类作文时需要注意以下四点：首先，切忌把原因或结果过度简单化；其次，文章重点要放在主要原因或结果上；再次，当提出原因或结果时，最好加上限定词，避免观点绝对化，比如 probably, mostly, maybe, might 等；最后，当说明原因/结果时，不能仅仅停留在原因/结果上，而是要揭示因果关系形成的过程，即某个原因是如何导致某个结果的。

讲座3 范文分析（Sample Essays）

知识概要 本讲座讲解的范文是典型的"原因为主"型文章。作者在引言段结尾处给出了清晰、明确的主旨句，告诉读者两大原因导致了腼腆的性格。在主体段落采用板块模式（block organization）对主要原因——详述。最后，作者不仅重申了主题句，还总结了文章的主要内容，并对文章主题进行了点评。

关 键 词 主旨句（thesis statement）；组织模式（organization pattern）；重申主旨句（restatement）；总结（summary）；文末评语（final remark）

Lead-in

In this lecture, we are going to read a sample essay together and analyze how it is written so that we can have a better idea of how cause and effect essays are constructed. Hopefully, it will benefit you in your own writing.

Before we go on, let's briefly review what we learned last time. We mainly talked about two common organization patterns for cause and effect essays: **the chain organization** and **the block organization**. The first pattern works best for causes or effects that are linked directly in a sequence, while the second one is suitable for causes or effects that are not linked directly.

Tasks

Now, I have provided a 7-paragraph essay for you.

The Biological and Environmental Causes of Shyness

If you suffer from shyness, you are not alone, for shyness is a universal phenomenon. According to recent research, "close to 50 percent of the general population report that they currently experience some degree of shyness in their lives; in addition, close to 80 percent of people report having felt shy at some point in their lives" (Payne, 1999). As shyness is so prevalent in the world, it is not surprising that social scientists are learning more about its causes. They have found that shyness in an individual can result from both biological and environmental factors.

Recent research shows that some individuals are born shy. Indeed, researchers say that between 15 and 20 percent of newborn babies have signs of shyness: they are quieter and more watchful. In fact, researchers have identified physiological differences between sociable and shy babies that show up as early as two months. In one study, two-month-olds who were later identified as shy children reacted with signs of stress to stimuli such as moving mobiles and tape recordings of human voices. These babies had increased heart rates, jumpy movements of arms and legs, and excessive crying. Furthermore, parents and grandparents of shy children more often say that they were shy as children. They report childhood shyness more frequently than grandparents of non-shy children(Henderson and Zimbardo, 1996).

However, environment can, at least in some cases, triumph over biology. A shy child may lose much of his or her shyness. On the other hand, many people who were not shy as children become shy as adults, a fact that points to environmental causes.

The first environmental cause of shyness may be a child's home and family life. Children who grew up with a difficult relationship with parents or older siblings are more likely to be inhibited in social interactions. Another factor is that today's children are growing up in smaller and smaller families, with fewer and fewer relatives living nearby. Growing up in single-parent homes or in homes in which both parents work full time, children may not have frequent visits by neighbours and friends. Because they have less interaction with relatives and other visitors, they may begin to feel shy, when they start school(Henderson and Zimbardo, 1996).

A second environmental cause of shyness in an individual may be one's culture. In a large study conducted in several nations, 40 percent of participants in the United States rated themselves as shy, compared to 57 percent in Japan. Of the countries participating in the study, the lowest percentage of shyness was found in Israel, where the rate was 31 percent. Researchers Henderson and Zimbardo(1996) note the differences in the way each culture deals with attributing credit for success and blame for failure may account in part for the higher rate of shyness reported in Japan than in Israel. In Japan, failure is generally attributed to the individual but success is not, while the reverse is often true in Israel. Therefore, Israelis may be more likely to take risks than Japanese.

In addition to family and culture, technology may play a role. In the United States, the number of young people who report being shy has risen from 40 percent to 50 percent in recent years(Henderson and Zimbardo, 1996). The rising numbers of shy young people may result in part from a growing dependence on technology(Payne, 1999). Watching television, playing video games, and surfing the Web have displaced activities that involve face-to-face interactions for many young people. Adults, too, are becoming more isolated as a result of technology. Face-to-face interactions are no longer necessary because people can use machines to do their banking, fill their gas tanks, order merchandise, take online courses and make friends. As a result, people have less opportunity to socialize in person. Therefore, they become increasingly awkward at it. Eventually they may start avoiding it altogether. In short, they become shy.

To sum up, shyness has both biological and environmental causes. Some people come into the world shy, while others become shy as a result of their experiences in life. It appears

that most people have experienced shyness at some time in their lives, and recent research indicates that the number of shy people is increasing. Therefore, if you are shy, you have lots of company.

While reading this essay, please think about the 7 questions here. I strongly suggest that you take a pause now and spend 8 minutes reading and analyzing the essay.

1. Is it a cause or effect essay?
2. What is the thesis statement?
3. What is talked about before the thesis statement?
4. How many causes or effects are explained?
5. What is Paragraph 3 for?
6. How is the essay concluded?
7. Which pattern is used, the chain organization or the block organization?

Have you finished reading the essay and found answers to all the questions?

Let's start with **Question 1**: Is it a cause or effect essay? I believe this is an easy question because the title of the essay clearly shows it is mainly about causes of shyness.

Question 2 is about the thesis statement. Usually, it is located at the end of the introductory paragraph and it is the central idea of the essay. Now, take a look at the last sentence in the first paragraph. "They have found that shyness in an individual can result from both biological and environmental factors." Relate the sentence to the title. Both of them refer to two types of cause. It sounds like the central idea, doesn't it? We can say the last sentence here is the thesis statement.

> 文章主旨句一般包含两项内容：文章主题和文章大意。这篇范文的主旨句也包含了两项内容。shyness 是文章主题；biological and environmental factors 为文章大意。

Then, **Question 3** is about the sentences before the thesis statement. It is not difficult to find out that this part talks about two things. The first is shyness as a universal phenomenon, a very common one; the second is scientists' interest in analyzing the causes. The prevalence of shyness is the reason why it needs to be talked about. Here the author establishes the importance of this topic and touches upon the causes at the same time.

> 范文开头就指出腼腆是一个普遍现象，值得科学家探讨其原因，这就成功地提出了分析原因的意义。

Now, let's move on to **Question 4**, the number of causes explained. We have already learned there are two types of cause from the title and thesis statement, but how many causes are there in the body? We need to read the body paragraphs one after another. The first body paragraph is Paragraph 2. The author is rather reader-friendly by telling us the main idea of this paragraph in the topic sentence: "Some are born shy, which is a biological cause." The rest of the paragraph supports the topic sentence with various research findings.

Paragraph 3 seems quite different from Paragraph 2. It mentions a new type of cause—environmental causes but doesn't provide support for the idea. So, what is the function of this paragraph? It is **Question 5**, isn't it? Now let's pay attention to two sets of words and expressions here.

"Biology" in Paragraph 3 refers back to "born shy" in Paragraph 2.

"Environment" and "environmental causes" refer forward to "the first environmental cause" in Paragraph 4, which obviously will further explain the cause.

Therefore, Paragraph 3 links both Paragraph 2 and Paragraph 4. We call such a paragraph a transitional paragraph, which is quite common. Sometimes we may not find a transitional paragraph used to link two paragraphs in an essay; instead, we can find a sentence or phrase at the end of a paragraph or one at the beginning of the next paragraph which serves as a transition to link the two paragraphs. You can also see such a transition later in the essay.

✎ 范文第三段没有主题句、支撑句和结论句，并不是一个典型的自然段，而是一个过渡段，起到承上启下的作用。

Now, let's go back to **Question 4**: the number of causes. The topic sentence in Paragraph 4 tells us the first environmental cause: a child's home and family life.

Paragraph 5 also clearly points out the cause in the topic sentence: culture as the second environmental cause.

Once again, another environmental cause is given in the topic sentence in Paragraph 6: technology. So far, how many causes have we found? One biological cause and three environmental causes, four in total. Before we go on, pay attention to the phrase at the beginning of this paragraph, "In addition to family and culture". Have you noticed that "family" refers back to Paragraph 4 and "culture" refers back to Paragraph 5? So, this phrase here serves as a transition.

✎ 虽然范文主旨句只提到两大原因，但从主体段落来看，第二大原因似乎更重要一些。毕竟作者仅仅提出了一个生物学原因，但却阐述了三个环境因素：家庭、文化和技术。

Now, there is only one paragraph left; it must be the conclusion. We can find the answer to **Question 6** here. Let's read through the paragraph one sentence after another. Sentence 1 sounds familiar, doesn't it? Where have we read it? Let's go back to Paragraph 1.

Look at the last sentence in Paragraph 1, which is also the thesis statement. These two sentences are rather similar. Both mean the same thing, related to the two types of cause of shyness. The only difference is that "result from" is used to introduce the causes in the thesis statement, while "has" is used in the conclusion. Obviously, we've got a thesis restatement here.

Now, read Sentence 2. It is still about the causes of shyness, but it is clearer than Sentence 1. "Come into the world shy" explains the biological cause; "as a result of their experiences in

life" explains the environmental causes. It is not a simple restatement, but a summary of the main ideas in the body.

The last two sentences here are not about the causes, are they? Then, what are they about? Expressions like "most people" "increasing" and "lots of company" show that shyness is very common, and they provide a comment on the topic, the final remark. If you can still remember, the essay starts with shyness as a universal phenomenon. The final remark here echoes the beginning. It provides a sense of completeness.

Now, there is only one question left. Is it a chain organization or block organization? To answer the question, we need to look at the body again, especially the causes.

✎ 范文结论段包含三个部分，不仅重申了主旨句，还包含文章主要内容总结和文章主题评论。不是所有结论段都包含这三个部分，但结论段至少应包含其中一个部分。

There is one biological cause and three environmental causes. The biological cause is not directly linked to the environmental causes. Family, culture and technology are three separate factors and they can contribute to shyness at the same time. Therefore, the essay is not a chain organization but a block organization.

✎ 范文主体段落总共探讨了腼腆的四个原因：生理、家庭、文化和技术。由于这四个原因之间没有直接联系，任意两个原因之间也不存在因果关系，因此，作者选择了板块模式(block organization)来有效地组织文章主体内容。

讲座4　常用表达(Useful Expressions)

知识概要　引出原因时，常使用 because, since, as 等连词和 because of, due to, owing to, thanks to 等介词短语。引出结果时，常使用 so 等连词和 accordingly, consequently, eventually, therefore, thereby, thus 等副词以及 as a consequence, as a result 等介词短语。动词和动词短语也常用于体现因果关系，如 result from, account for, be attributed to, play a role in, result in, cause 等。

关　键　词　过渡性单词与短语(transitional words and phrases)

Lead-in

In this lecture, we're going to talk about some useful transitional expressions to achieve coherence in cause and effect essays. Further, we are going to briefly summarize what we've learned in Week 9.

Language Focus

Now, you see two lists of words and expressions.

Transitional Expressions for Causes	Transitional Expressions for Effects
• a key factor • one reason • the first cause • because of • due to • owing to • because/since/as/for	• one effect/outcome • the first effect • as a consequence • as a result • result in • accordingly • consequently • therefore/thereby/thus • so

The left list is about transitional expressions indicating causes; the right list is about transitional expressions indicating effects. Most of them are quite familiar, aren't they?

We'll focus on some of the expressions. Look at the left list first. "**Because of**" "**due to**" and "**owing to**" are interchangeable. They are followed by noun phrases. "**Because**" "**since**" and "**for**" all introduce reasons and they are used to link clauses in a sentence. Then, let's move to the right list. Here "**as a consequence**" and "**as a result**" are the same in usage. "**Result in**" is followed by a noun phrase, which is also an effect. "**Accordingly**" "**consequently**" "**therefore**" "**thereby**" and "**thus**", these adverbs all introduce effects and they are usually used at the beginning of a sentence.

Now, let's work on an exercise. Read the sample essay (pp. 148 – 150) again, *The Biological and Environmental Causes of Shyness*, the article we talked about last time, and identify and circle the transitional expressions used to introduce causes and effects in it. I strongly suggest that you take a pause and spend 5 minutes doing the exercise before coming back.

Have you finished the exercise? It is not difficult to find all the transitional expressions for causes and effects in the essay, is it? Let's look at it together now. This is **Paragraph 1**.

> 1. If you suffer from shyness, you are not alone, for shyness is a universal phenomenon. According to recent research, "close to 50 percent of the general population report that they currently experience some degree of shyness in their lives; in addition, close to 80 percent of people report having felt shy at some point in their lives" (Payne, 1999). As shyness is so prevalent in the world, it is not surprising that social scientists are learning more about its causes. They have found that shyness in an individual can result from both biological and environmental factors.

How many transitional expressions have you found? I've got five. "For" indicates a cause. Different from "because", this word is often used in the middle of a sentence to link two clauses and "," is usually added before it. "As" is also a word to introduce a cause. The word, "cause", definitely is about a cause. "**Result from**" is a verb phrase we frequently use to

introduce both effects and causes. For example, in the sentence, "X results from Y", X is the effect and Y is the cause. However, there is another expression, "result in", which means exactly the opposite. The last word is "**factor**", which refers to a cause, too.

✎ 使用连词 for 引出原因时，for 一般不出现在句首，而是出现在句中。result from 和 result in 这两个短语要区分开来，from 后面接原因，in 后面接结果。

Now, **Paragraph 2**.

> 2. Recent research shows that some individuals are born shy. Indeed, researchers say that between 15 and 20 percent of newborn babies have signs of shyness: they are quieter and more watchful. In fact, researchers have identified physiological differences between sociable and shy babies that show up as early as two months. In one study, two-month-olds who were later identified as shy children reacted with signs of stress to stimuli such as moving mobiles and tape recordings of human voices. These babies had increased heart rates, jumpy movements of arms and legs, and excessive crying. Furthermore, parents and grandparents of shy children more often say that they were shy as children. They report childhood shyness more frequently than grandparents of non-shy children (Henderson and Zimbardo, 1996).

Have you found any? I haven't. But I have found other types of transition, like "indeed" "in fact" "such as" "furthermore" etc.

Let's move on to **Paragraph 3** and **Paragraph 4**.

> 3. However, environment can, at least in some cases, triumph over biology. A shy child may lose much of his or her shyness. On the other hand, many people who were not shy as children become shy as adults, a fact that points to environmental causes.
> 4. The first environmental cause of shyness may be a child's home and family life. Children who grew up with a difficult relationship with parents or older siblings are more likely to be inhibited in social interactions. Another factor is that today's children are growing up in smaller and smaller families, with fewer and fewer relatives living nearby. Growing up in single-parent homes or in homes in which both parents work full time, children may not have frequent visits by neighbours and friends. Because they have less interaction with relatives and other visitors, they may begin to feel shy, when they start school (Henderson and Zimbardo, 1996)

In these two paragraphs, "environmental cause" is used twice. "Another factor" also indicates a cause. The conjunction, "because", introduces a reason or cause.

> 5. A second environmental cause of shyness in an individual may be one's culture. In a large study conducted in several nations, 40 percent of participants in the United States rated themselves as shy, compared to 57 percent in Japan. Of the countries participating in the study, the lowest percentage of shyness was found in Israel, where the rate was 31 percent. Researchers Henderson and Zimbardo (1996) note the differences in the way each culture deals with attributing credit for success and blame for failure may account in part for the higher rate of shyness reported in Japan and than in Israel. In Japan, failure is generally attributed to the individual but success is not, while the reverse is often true in Israel. Therefore, Israelis may be more likely to take risks than Japanese.

Here in **Paragraph 5**, we see "environmental cause" again. And we find two verb phrases, "**account for**" and "**is attributed to**". Both phrases introduce effects and causes at the same time. "Account for" goes after the cause and is followed by the effect. In other words, the idea before it is the cause and the idea after it is the effect. But "is attributed to" goes after the effect and is followed by the cause. So, in this case, failure is the effect, while the individual is the cause. The last word is "**therefore**", which obviously indicates the effect.

✎ 范文中出现的单词 attribute 常常使用被动结构 be attributed to。be 前是结果，to 后是原因。

Now, look at **Paragraph 6**.

> 6. In addition to family and culture, technology may play a role. In the United States, the number of young people who report being shy has risen from 40 percent to 50 percent in recent years (Henderson and Zimbardo, 1996). The rising numbers of shy young people may result in part from a growing dependence on technology (Payne, 1999). Watching television, playing video games, and surfing the Web have displaced activities that involve face-to-face interactions for many young people. Adults, too, are becoming more isolated as a result of technology. Face-to-face interactions are no longer necessary because people can use machines to do their banking, fill their gas tanks, order merchandise, take online courses and make friends. As a result, people have less opportunity to socialize in person. Therefore, they become increasingly awkward at it. Eventually they may start avoiding it altogether. In short, they become shy.

There are quite a few transitional expressions for causes and effects. "**Play a role**" and "**because**" both are about causes. "**As a result**" "**therefore**" and "**eventually**" all indicate effects. The rest introduce both causes and effects, including "**result in part from**" and "**as a result of**". Pay attention to "in part" in "result in part from". Do you remember what I said about qualifying a cause or effect by using words like "possibly"? "In part" here can serve the

same function, meaning that the situation is rather complicated and the cause to be introduced is not the sole or complete cause.

> in part 放在 result from 这个短语中间起限制作用。限定词在学术写作中广泛存在，目的是避免问题、观点的绝对化。

This is **the last paragraph**, conclusion.

> 7. To sum up, shyness has both genetic and environmental causes. Some people come into the world shy, while others become shy as a result of their experiences in life. It appears that most people have experienced shyness at some time in their lives, and recent research indicates that the number of shy people is increasing. Therefore, if you are shy, you have lots of company.

It is easy to find two transitional expressions here, "**cause**" and "**as a result of**". The second one introduces both the cause and the effect. Now, let's make a complete list of the transitional expressions for causes and effects found according to the order of appearance in the sample essay.

This is what we've got.

1. for	1. is attributed to
2. As	2. therefore
3. cause	3. play a role
4. result from	4. result from
5. factor	5. as a result of
6. cause	6. because
7. cause	7. as a result
8. factor	8. therefore
9. because	9. eventually
10. account for	10. cause
11. cause	11. as a result of

Let's classify them into 3 groups: causes, effects, and both causes and effects.

The colored box is for expressions indicating causes, the grey box effects, and the black box both causes and effects. We can do a little math here. There are 12 colored boxes, 4 grey boxes and 6 black boxes. How do we interpret the numbers? It is rather clear that the expressions about causes are much more than the other two categories. Why so? Think about the main idea of the essay: the biological and environmental causes of shyness. It is a cause essay. No wonder most of the transitional expressions are about causes.

> 范文中表示原因的单词或短语多于表示结果和体现因果关系的单词或短语。这一点比较容易理解。范文是一篇"原因为主"型的文章，聚焦于形成腼腆性格的原因，表示原因的单词或短语自然也就多一些。

Summary

OK, now we've talked so much about cause and effect essays. Before calling it a day, we can sum up what we've learned. **First**, we've learned what causes are and what effects are. A cause is the reason why something happened or is happening, while an effect is a change as a result of something that happened or is happening. **Second**, we've learned what a cause and effect essay is. A cause and effect essay is a piece of writing that mainly explains causes, or effects, or both causes and effects. **Third**, we've learned the organization pattern used for these essays. **Cause and effect essays can be organized in two ways. The first** is the block organization pattern; **the second** is the chain organization pattern. The chain organization pattern is used when causes or effect are linked directly in a sequence, with one leading to another and another. However, the block organization is for causes or effects which are not linked directly. Besides, we've learned how to achieve coherence in cause and effect essays by using appropriate transitional expressions. Some expressions are used to introduce causes only, some are used to introduce effects only, and others are used to introduce both causes and effects, such as "result from" "result in" "account for" and "is attributed to". Hope all these ideas will be helpful in your own English writing.

Ⅲ. 写作练习

1. Read the following sentences and circle all the words and phrases introducing a cause.

1) Fortunately, enormous progress has been made in the understanding and treatment of the disorder as a result of research on animals.

2) Its main conclusion is that there have been no measurable radiological effects on the health of local people, and that the only significant problems resulted from psychological factors, notably stress.

3) Highway authorities across the UK may be forced to impose restrictions on the movement of heavy lorries because of serious road damage, according to a confidential study compiled by the Transport and Road Research Laboratory.

4) The government has offered to spend £82 million over the next seven years to make the plant safe, and the headquarters has agreed to train technicians at the plant which suffers from a shortage of skilled workers due to poor working conditions and low pay.

5) The United States announced that it would consider withdrawing from the organization altogether. The reasons behind the decision were thought to be the USA's continuing doubts about the value and cost-effectiveness of the organization's work and its dissatisfaction with the Director-General.

2. Read the following sentences and circle all the words and phrases introducing an effect.

1) These methods enable doctors to detect babies that may have problems with breathing at birth and therefore to be in a position to treat the condition promptly.

2) Some countries lack a suitable economic infrastructure—roads, railways, docks, etc.—and as a consequence are unable to exploit their natural resources.

3) Conservationists in Sri Lanka have launched a successful turtle breeding program which has resulted in 600,000 newly-hatched turtles being released into the Indian Ocean.

4) Economic factors have an important effect on children's smoking habits and evidence from the USA suggests that teenagers are even more responsive to price increases than are adults.

5) Davis is an anthropologist, and, accordingly, his analyses are based on living with people and understanding the locality through close observation and conversations with the indigenous population.

3. Choose an appropriate word or phrase in the box and fill in each of the blanks in the following sentences.

because	caused	consequently	factor
impact	owing to	is attributed to	resulting from

1) Much of Australia's farmlands are threatened with salination, _____ in part by the consequences of farmers cutting down trees to clear land for wheat and other crops.

2) An international study, published in *the US New England Journal of Medicine*, showed that the death rate among Iraqi children under the age of five had tripled after the Gulf War _____ a dramatic increase in disease and malnutrition and reduced access to health care.

3) Before this point, whenever IBM had developed a new computer, it used a completely different architecture from previous models and _____ existing software and hardware were discarded.

4) The council claims that potential investors are leaving _____ the city has hardly any land for industrial purposes, no suitable sites for an out-of-center business park and insufficient land for housing.

5) A key _____ in current video-conferencing developments is the compression of data so that complex multimedia information can be transmitted in reduced form and decompressed on arrival at its destination.

6) A report by the Department of the Environment admits that the practice of planting large stands of conifers on British uplands has worsened the effects of acid rain, _____ the deaths of salmon, trout and frogs, and the pollution of upland streams.

7) The total area lost between 1981 and 1990 was 154 million hectares, with 1,750 million hectares of tropical forest remaining. Most of the loss _____ population growth and rural poverty, leading to land clearance for agriculture.

8) On the basis of tests carried out in the North Sea, Bayne believes that organic pollutants may be having a greater _____ on marine life than heavy metals such as lead, mercury and cadmium, which had hitherto been widely blamed for most of the damage.

4. **Read the following introductory paragraph and answer the questions after it.**

The British voted to leave the European Union. Even at only 52%, Brexit couldn't have been imagined 10 years ago. This fragmentation has been evident throughout Europe, but it's the first case of a nation actually deciding to leave. I doubt that it's the last. Now we should try to understand why the majority of Brits favored an exit from the EU and learn lessons. There are three main factors that led to this outpouring of votes to leave.

1) How many parts are there in the introduction?
2) What function does each of the parts serve?

5. **Read the following body paragraphs and add a topic sentence for either of them.**

1) _____.

There's a growing distrust of multinational financial, trade, and defense organizations created after World War II, such as the EU, IMF, and NATO. Many who oppose the EU believe these institutions no longer serve a purpose. Not only that, these organizations take control away from individual nations. Mistrust and fear of losing control made Brexit a reasonable solution to them. The immigration crisis in Europe was a trigger. Some EU leaders argued that aiding the refugees was a moral obligation. But EU opponents saw immigration as a national issue, as it affected the internal life of the country. Steering clear of this issue was an important driver for the "leave" vote. The EU doesn't understand the power of nationalism. It attempts to retain nationality as a cultural right. On the other hand, it deprives individual nations of the power to make many decisions.

2) _____.

Brexit would eliminate Britain's tariff-free trade status with the other EU members. Tariffs would raise the cost of exports. That would hurt U.K. exporters as their goods become more expensive in Europe. Some of that pain would be offset by a weaker pound. Tariffs would also increase the prices of imports into the U.K. More than one-third of its imports comes from the EU. Higher import prices would create inflation and lower the standard of living for U.K. residents. The U.K. is already vulnerable because heat waves and droughts caused by global warming have reduced local food production.

第10 周
对照与对比作文
(Comparison and Contrast Essays)

>> I. 概述

本周课程将围绕对照与对比作文展开，课程内容由四个板块构成：理解对照与对比、如何撰写比较类作文、如何避免"无意义主旨句"和常用表达。

首先，对比较的概念进行说明。在对两个对象进行比较分析时，通常是讨论两个对象之间的相同点和不同点。有些文章聚焦于两个对象的相同点，通常称之为对照作文（comparison essay）；有些文章聚焦于两个对象的不同点，通常称之为对比作文（contrast essay）；还有些文章既关注两个对象的相同点，也关注两个对象的不同点。

其次，讲解如何组织对照与对比作文，特别是如何组织主体段落。对照与对比作文主体段落一般有两大组织模式。一是按照比较点组织（point-by-point pattern），二是按照比较对象组织（subject-by-subject pattern）。两种模式的选择往往取决于文章的长度、比较点的数量以及比较的目的。同时，基于范文，重点分析其主体段落组织模式，讨论范文采用了哪种模式来组织主体段落以及这种模式是否恰当等问题。

此外还重点介绍了避免"无意义主旨句（so-what thesis statement）"的常用方法。"无意义主旨句"是撰写对照与对比作文时比较容易出现的一个问题。不少初学者容易出现为了比较而比较的问题，这样的作文缺少比较的目的或意义。

最后，介绍对照与对比作文中常用的句型，如 X and Y are similar/different in three aspects, namely, A, B and C, 以及体现比较关系的过渡性单词和短语，如 also, likewise, in the same way, unlike, yet, by contrast 等。

>> II. 慕课讲稿

讲座 1　理解对照与对比（Understanding Comparison and Contrast）

知识概要　虽然 comparison 包含"对照"和"对比"两层含义，但为了严格区分，此处

comparison 专指"对照",聚焦于相似点,而 contrast 专指"对比",聚焦于不同点。当挖掘相似点和不同点时,韦恩图是一种常用的思绪整理方式。不管对照还是对比,都只是一种手段,而不是目的,因此赋予比较以目的是非常重要的。

关 键 词 对照(comparison);对比(contrast);韦恩图(Venn Diagram)

Lead-in

During this week, we'll focus on **comparison and contrast essays**.

Now, take a look at the picture here. In daily life, we are sometimes given two options. It is impossible or unrealistic to have both of them; then we have to make a painful and time-consuming decision. Have you ever been caught up between two choices? What was it about?

Was it about two electronic devices, like mobile phones? Quite a lot of mobile phone users in China are puzzled about two brands, Huawei and Apple. Apple has enjoyed the world reputation as an innovation icon for many years but its mobile phone costs lots of money. In recent years, Huawei's products have been upgraded relentlessly(持续不断地) in both functions and appearance and they have even outshined iPhones in quite a few aspects, therefore winning a large crowd of fans across the world. Despite its superb quality, Huawei's mobile phone is still a lot cheaper than the iPhone. Many loyal users of Apple have started to consider using Huawei's phones but are still hesitating because of their long-established loyalty to Apple. Are you one of the Apple fans going through the dilemma?

Or was it about two men? Both of the gentlemen expressed their affection for you. What's worse, you liked both of them somehow. But who would you accept as your boyfriend? Obviously, you couldn't have both. It must have been a big headache to you.

If you have been involved in a difficult situation like those, how did you finally make a decision? To relieve oneself of the self-imposed "torture", a person in a rational state of mind would try this routine: **pros and cons**. Usually we find a piece of paper, draw two lists. One is the positive qualities for both options and the other is the negative qualities for both options. Then we cross the qualities shared by both of them and carefully analyze the qualities left. If Option A has more positive qualities but fewer negative qualities than Option B, Option A wins. In the whole process, we basically analyze the differences but ignore the similarities.

Both **SIMILARITIES** and **DIFFERENCES** are the focus in Week 10.

Objectives

Through this week, we'll be able to **understand what similarities and differences are and**

accordingly identify them when reading essays or before writing our own. We'll be able to understand how comparison and contrast essays are organized, analyze the organization pattern used in articles and use the pattern properly in our own essays. We'll also be able to write an appropriate thesis statement for comparison and contrast essays and avoid producing "so-what" thesis statements. Furthermore, we'll be able to **use proper sentence patterns to present similarities and differences**. Last but not least, we'll be able to **use proper transitional expressions** to achieve coherence in the essays.

Tasks

Now, let's move on to a task. **Think about the similarities and differences between a dog and a cat.**

When it comes to pets, most people would think of dogs and cats. Look at the cat and dog in the picture. How cute they are! Wouldn't you want to take both of them home? But if you could only have one pet, which one would you choose, the dog or the cat? Another dilemma, isn't it? But we can always try the list of pros and cons to help ourselves to make a decision.

Instead of drawing simple lists, we can also try using **the Venn Diagram**. There are two circles here.

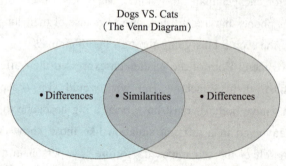

Dogs VS. Cats
(The Venn Diagram)

The left one is for dogs, while the right one is for cats. You can see an overlapping area of the two circles here. Both circles share this area; let's save it for the similarities between the animals and the remaining areas are for the differences. Now think about the similarities first.

It is quite easy to find a few similarities, isn't it? First, both of them are cute. Second, they have similar life expectancies. In other words, dogs live as long as cats. Some of them can live up to 20 years and even 30 years. Third, owners of dogs and cats have to pay similar medical and other costs, like food. Similarities cannot lead us to a decision; therefore, let's spend more time on the differences. Now take a small pause and think about the differences for 3 minutes. Are you ready to go on?

Dogs bark, and it is usually loud and therefore noisy. By contrast, cats are quiet. Even though sometimes they mew, the noise is much softer. Do you agree?

Dogs need more space at home because they don't like to stay at a spot for long and they like to run once in a while. However, cats can live in smaller areas. They are often seen to sleep on the sofa, under the bed and even on the window sill. They just stretch their legs occasionally when staying at the same place for a long time.

Dogs cannot be restricted indoors. We need to walk them outdoors every day. But we don't need to take cats out and it is perfectly fine for them to stay indoors.

Dogs need attention. They scratch at doors; they chew up items; they circle around your legs; they jump to your arms whenever they see you come back home. They do all of these things to get your attention. Cats are completely different in this area. They seldom do such things but only mind their own business.

Dogs please the owner. Many dog owners have reported that their dog can sense their moods and that they would wiggle their tail or lick the owner's face to cheer them up. On the contrary, cats seem to be aloof(冷淡的) and they do not interact with their owners. They only please themselves.

✎ 借助韦恩图，可以很好地梳理猫狗之间的相似点和不同点。

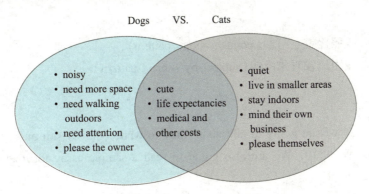

Now, we have got some of the common similarities and differences between dogs and cats, would it be easier for you to decide which animal to keep as a pet? It is surely helpful to me to make a quick decision now. Based on the differences, keeping a dog sounds like more responsibility and effort. For me, keeping a cat would be an easier choice in a busy life.

Summary

So far, we have got a clear understanding of similarities and differences. Similarities and differences are what comparison and contrast essays are mainly about. **If an essay concentrates on similarities, we usually say it is a comparison essay.** **If it focuses on differences, we often call it a contrast essay.** Besides, we can also find essays covering both similarities and differences.

What are comparison and contrast essays for? One of the purposes could be clarifying something unknown or not well understood. By analyzing the similarities and differences between an unknown idea and a learned idea, we can **figure out what the unknown idea is**. Another purpose is to **bring one or both of the subjects into sharper focus in order to catch readers' attention**. A third purpose is to **show that one subject is better than the other** so that we can make a better judgment through comparison and contrast.

> 对照和/或对比的目的一般有三个：一是通过分析相似点和不同点，让读者对比较对象中相对陌生的一个有更清楚的认识；二是突出比较对象中的一个或两个；三是说明哪个比较对象优于另一个。例如，对猫、狗两种宠物的比较就是为了突出猫和狗分别适合不同的人群——第二个比较目的。

讲座 2　如何撰写比较类作文（How to Write Comparison and Contrast Essays）

知识概要　当撰写比较类作文主体段落时，一般有两种组织模式。一是按照比较点组织，二是按照比较对象组织。按照比较点组织更利于突出两个比较对象在各个方面的相同点和不同点；按照比较对象组织则便于突出两个比较对象在整体上的相似和差异。

关　键　词　按照比较点组织（point-by-point pattern）；
　　　　　　　按照比较对象组织（subject-by-subject pattern）

Lead-in

In this lecture, we are going to talk about **how to write comparison and contrast essays**, the key points of Week 10. We are also going to read a sample essay together and analyze it paragraph by paragraph.

Key Points

Before we go on, let's briefly review what we learned last time. We talked about comparison and contrast essays. **A comparison essay focuses on similarities between two subjects, while a contrast essay mainly deals with differences.** We can also find essays that cover both similarities and differences.

How do we organize the ideas in comparison and contrast essays? There are two common patterns. One is the point-by-point pattern; the other is the subject-by-subject pattern.

Let's look at **the point-by-point pattern** first.

Point-by-point Pattern

- Title
  - Introduction — Topic+Thesis
  - Body
    - Point 1: Subject A+Subject B
    - Point 2: Subject A+Subject B
    - Point 3: Subject A+Subject B
  - Conclusion — Summary/Restatement of thesis/Final remarks

The pattern follows the typical essay structure: the introduction, body and conclusion. Our focus here is placed on the most important part in an essay: the body. Suppose there are three body paragraphs; **each of the body paragraphs focuses on one similarity or difference**. In the paragraph, we need to explain in what way the two subjects are similar or in what way they are different. There are two things we need to be careful about. The first is to **maintain the order of the two subjects explained in each body paragraph**. If we explain Subject A and then Subject B in the first body paragraph, we should follow the same order in the other body paragraphs, too. The second is to **strike a balance between the two subjects** when explaining them in each body paragraph. What do I mean by balance? If 100 words are devoted to Subject A but only 15 words to Subject B, there is no balance. Readers will feel that Subject B is not given a fair treatment.

> 使用 the point-by-point pattern 时，有两点需要注意：一是要保持两个比较对象的先后顺序。如果在第一个主体段先说明比较对象一后说明比较对象二，在后面的所有主体段都应该遵照这样的说明顺序；二是确保两个比较对象的平衡。所谓平衡，就是在每个主体段对两个比较对象的阐述，篇幅要均衡。

Now, let's take a look at an example of **the point-by-point pattern**.

Point-by-point Pattern

Thesis: Mom's Hamburger Haven is a better family restaurant than McPhony's because of its superior food, service, and atmosphere.

Point 1: Food
    A. Mom's
    B. Mcphony's

Point 2: Service
    A. Mom's
    B. Mcphony's

Point 3: Atmosphere
    A. Mom's
    B. Mcphony's

Conclusion

From the outline here, we can tell that it is a contrast essay, talking about the differences between two restaurants, Mom's Hamburger Haven and McPhony's. There are three points under discussion, three differences. When each point is introduced, Mom's is explained first and then Mcphony's. In the discussion of all the three points, the same order is followed.

We've seen the point-by-point pattern; now let's move on to the second pattern: the subject-by-subject pattern.

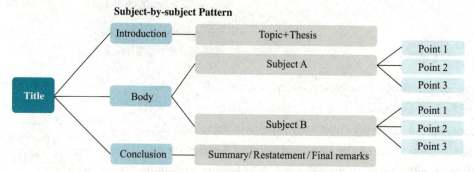

Again, let's focus on the body part. **In the point-by-point pattern ideas are organized according to similarities or differences**, while in the subject-by-subject pattern ideas are organized according to subjects. Suppose there are three similarities or differences under discussion. The body part can be divided into two sections. The first section is for Subject A and the second section is for Subject B. First, we explain all the points about Subject A. When it is done, we continue to explain all the points about Subject B. There are also two things we need to bear in mind. **First, pay attention to the order of the points explained**. The first point of Subject A and the first point of Subject B should be of the same similarity or difference. The rest of the points should be like this, too. **Second, there should also be a balance between the two subjects in terms of content and length**.

✎ 使用 the subject-by-subject pattern 时，也有两点要注意：一是要保持比较点的先后顺序。如果说明比较对象一时分别是比较点一、二、三，在说明比较对象二时，也必须按照相应的比较点顺序来阐述；二是确保两个比较对象平衡，每个对象的阐述篇幅要相当。

To have a better understanding of the pattern, we can look at this outline.

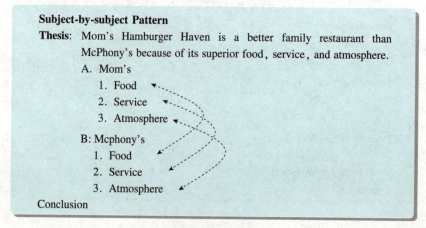

It still has the same topic, the differences between two family restaurants. But there are only two parts in the body, Mom's and McPhony's. When Mom's is talked about, food is first explained, and then service, and then atmosphere. When McPhony's is talked about, the same order is followed.

We've got two patterns for comparison and contrast essays, but which pattern to choose in our writing? It depends on the length of the essay but more importantly the purpose of our writing. **If the essay is long and involves quite a few similarities or differences, the point-by-point pattern would be a better choice**. If we choose the subject-by-subject pattern in this case, it would put too much burden on readers' memory. After reading a long discussion of Subject A, readers might have already forgotten what's written about Subject A when they start reading about Subject B. Therefore, **the subject-by-subject pattern, in general, works better in shorter essays, where a few similarities or differences are included**.

In addition to the length, we also have to consider the purpose of writing when choosing the appropriate pattern. **If the similarities or differences are connected to each other and our interest is in the whole, the subject-by-subject pattern is a better choice. If we tend to bring the two subjects into sharp contrast, the point-by-point pattern is more effective to bring about the effect.**

Tasks

Now, let's read a sample essay to have a better understanding of comparison and contrast essays.

John and Paul

My boyfriend, Paul and I got to know each other this summer at a friend's gathering, and we've been getting along well. Compared with the short relationship I've been with John, my ex-boyfriend, in which I always got myself exhausted and fatigued, now I bask in happiness and satisfaction whenever I am with Paul. In terms of gentleness, romanticism, and attitudes toward life, Paul does way better than John.

There is no comparison between John and Paul in terms of gentleness. When John and I dined out, he complained from beginning to end. The spaghetti was greasy; those stupid cooks in the Pavilion Restaurant never knew how to use peppers; withered vegetables were picked out for salad every time. Everything just made the dinner an infliction. I'd never been shopping with him for over an hour. Looking at his watch constantly, he would immediately have an important appointment to go to if I failed to meet the one-hour deadline, as if Mr. Obama had been waiting for him to resolve problems of world peace at the U.N. If I was out of touch with him for a week, believe me, he would still feel utterly free of worry without even a phone call. However, if I was concerned about what he had been doing, he would say I was nosy and bossy and would go crazy and play Robinson Crusoe, totally evaporating from the world to show his anger.

Yet Paul would never do that. It seems whatever restaurant we go to is the Hilton in his eyes as long as we are together. Even if I tried on and off new clothes for a whole afternoon, he would still patiently give advice to every piece I put on. "The red jacket looks good on you." "The blue pants match the shoes." While crossing a street, he automatically comes to the side closer to the traffic, preventing me from any potential harm. Every day he sends text messages or gives me a call simply to ask if I'm O.K. And, all the information he provides like "X likes animals, and Y has a crush on the teacher" helps me to be more involved in his life.

Unlike Paul who usually creates romance unexpectedly, John was always insensitive like a mummy. It troubled John all the time to remember whether my birthday is December 13 or 31, let alone any surprise that would be expected on that day. Talking on the phone, he was good at creating silence while I had to tell jokes and change topics to please him. The Christmas present he gave me was a book on physics. I knew he meant well, to help me with my weak subject, but I believe no one would want to think about Einstein on Christmas. As for Paul, one minute he does voices to mimic Donald Duck, and the next minute he is explaining how light travels in hot air so we sometimes see mirages in a desert. A delicate pair of soft lamb-skin gloves suddenly coming into my view on a bitterly cold winter afternoon and with his face beaming brightly, he told me he was thinking of me when he saw the gloves. Sometimes when he sees a frustrating look on my face, he may clutch my hand across busy streets and through the bustling crowds, leaving all my boredom or fury behind. Paul is simply so sweet.

Paul also outshines John in his positive attitude toward life. John usually went to a party all night long out of an impulse, despite the work waiting for him the next day. Dragging him out of the sports ground was harder than stuffing Yao Ming into a QQ chatroom. When I was with him, it was like living with a zombie, powerless as if trapped in a marsh. However, always knowing what to do at a certain time, Paul fills his day with work. Seven to nine at night is his regular self-study time during which even I cannot disturb him. Sunday mornings are his favourite time—he makes my phone ring like hell urging me to get out of cosy bed to jog. When I was with him, I'm brimming over with health and vigour, feeling energetic and alive. I'm so much in love with the "me" together with him.

Gentle, romantic, disciplined, and optimistic, Paul surpasses John in all three aspects. The experiences with John made me firmly believe that chivalry was dead, whereas Paul holds my hand helping me recapture the fantasy of love—I have every reason to believe it.

While you read the essay, please think about the following questions.

- What is the thesis statement?
- Is the essay mainly about similarities, differences or both?
- How many similarities or differences are explained?
- Which organization pattern is used? Do you think it is a good choice?

I strongly suggest that you take a pause and spend 8 minutes looking for the answers before coming back.

I believe you have finished reading the essay. It is an easy one, isn't it? The title is *John and Paul*. From it, we know the two subjects, but we cannot tell whether it is about similarities, differences or both. One of the ways to tell that is to look for the thesis statement.

The thesis statement, as usual, appears at the end of the introductory paragraph, the first paragraph here. "Paul does way better than John" shows it is about differences. At the same time, we can tell there are three differences: "gentleness, romanticism and attitudes towards life". So, we've answered the first three questions, haven't we? To further confirm our answer to Question 3, the number of differences, still let's go on to read the body paragraphs. Pay more attention to the topic sentence.

The topic sentence in Paragraph 2 tells us the first difference: gentleness. The rest of this paragraph is all about John, Subject A. It is about how not gentle he is.

Paragraph 3 is all about Subject B, Paul, a gentle boyfriend. And we can see that there are two paragraphs for the first difference; it must be an important point in the writer's mind.

Let's read on. Paragraph 4 is about the second difference, romanticism, as the topic sentence shows. Subject A, John, is introduced first before Subject B, Paul.

In Paragraph 5, we can find the third difference, attitudes toward life. John is negative while Paul is positive. Again, John is presented earlier than Paul.

So far, we've answered three questions. The only one left is Question 4, the organization pattern used. Is the subject-by-subject pattern or the point-by-point pattern used? Let's go through the body again.

The body can be divided into three sections according to the differences. In each section, John, Subject A, is always introduced earlier than Paul, Subject B. Therefore, we can arrive at the conclusion that the essay follows the point-by-point pattern.

Do you think it is a good choice? The choice between the two patterns depends on the length and purpose. The purpose is the more important factor. Let's focus on it. What is the purpose of this essay? Do you remember the thesis statement? "<u>In terms of gentleness, romanticism, and attitudes toward life, Paul does way better than John.</u>" The purpose is to show who is better than the other. The author intends to bring John and Paul to sharp contrast in order to highlight how good Paul is as a boyfriend. Isn't it the strength of the point-by-point pattern? Therefore, the point-by-point pattern is a brilliant choice to achieve the purpose.

> 范文为什么采用 the point-by-point pattern，而不是 the subject-by-subject pattern？范文是为了说明 Paul 是一个更合格的男朋友。为了达到这一目的，作者分别从 gentleness, romanticism 和 attitudes toward life 这三个方面阐述，突出 Paul 比 John 做得更好。相对于 the subject-by-subject pattern 而言，the point-by-point pattern 能更好地突出两个比较对象在各个方面的差异，从而形成强烈的反差。

讲座 3　如何避免"无意义主旨句"（How to Avoid So-what Thesis Statements）

知识概要　什么是"无意义主旨句"？"无意义主旨句"指缺乏写作目的的主旨句。具体到比较类文章，"无意义主旨句"仅告诉读者两个比较对象之间存在的相似点或不同点而已。修正"无意义主旨句"的一条原则就是赋予主旨句意义或目的。

关　键　词　主旨句（thesis statement）；无意义主旨句（so-what thesis statement）；目的（purpose）

Lead-in

In this lecture, we are going to talk about **how to avoid a "so-what" thesis statement**, another key point in Week 10. In a so-what thesis statement, it is unclear for what purpose a comparison is being made.

Key Points

Before we talk about the key points, we can first review what we learned last time. We talked about two common organization patterns for comparison and contrast essays, the point-by-point pattern and the subject-by-subject pattern. The first pattern works better in longer essays with many similarities or differences to cover, and it is mostly used to make the writing more effective through sharp contrasts. On the other hand, the second pattern can function well in shorter essays with fewer similarities or differences in them, and it is suitable for explaining similarities or differences that are connected closely and when the writer's interest is in the whole.

Now, let's move on to the focus in Lecture 3, thesis statements. There are four thesis statements.

- The two family restaurants, Mom's Hamburger Haven and McPhony's, are very different.
- In *Huckleberry Finn*, Mark Twain develops a contrast between life on the river and life on the shore.
- Although Stella's Sweatateria and the Fitness Fanatics Gym are similar in their low student-membership prices and excellent instructors, they have more differences.
- There are many similarities in the character and plot between the movie *Riot of the Killer Snails* and Mary Sheeley's novel *Salt on the Sidewalk*.

What do you think of them? Do they fulfill the requirements of good thesis statements? Think about the criteria of a good thesis statement you've learned in the previous weeks.

Look at **Statement 1**. We can see the two subjects, Mom's Hamburger Haven and McPhony's, and we can also tell that it is from a contrast essay. But what are the differences? We don't know. **Statement 2**. It is clear that there are two subjects: life on the river and life on the shore in Mark Twain's book and it is a contrast essay. Again, what are the differences? Not specific enough. Now, **Statement 3**. Two subjects, Stella's Sweatateria and the Fitness Fanatics Gym, two gyms are contrasted. What are the differences? No idea. The last statement is a comparison essay. It is about the similarities between a movie and a novel. Do we know what the similarities are? Yes, two similarities, the character and the plot. So far, **the last statement** sounds the best, being both clear and specific.

But now, I'd like you to read the four thesis statements again, from readers' perspective this time. What is your response to each of the statements? How do you feel about them? Do you feel like something is missing here? Yes, the two restaurants are different. Yes, life on the river and life on the shore are different. Yes, Stella's Sweatateria and the Fitness Fanatics Gym are different. Yes, the movie and the novel are similar.

But so what? Does this question come to mind when you read them? The writer is telling us there are differences or similarities, but what's the point of telling us these facts? Why should we care about them? Why is it important to know them? We, as readers, couldn't possibly know the answer; only the writers know it. This is exactly the problem the four thesis statements have in common. Such thesis statements are usually called "so-what" thesis statements.

✎ 这四个主旨句都存在同一个问题——比较的意义不清。读者的第一反应很可能是:"然后呢?我知道了这些不同点/相似点又能怎样?!"

So, what is a "so-what" thesis statement? A "so-what" thesis statement contains **no apparent reason** in comparison or contrast, which is a waste of the reader's valuable time. In other words, we don't know what the point is in doing comparison or contrast. Such an essay leaves readers with the impression that the writer is doing comparison or contrast for the sake of comparison and contrast and **there is no sense of purpose to it**. It could be a waste of readers' valuable time. Then, what can we do to avoid such thesis statements?

One of the ways is to **tell one subject is better than the other**. Do you remember the article we've read and analyzed, *John and Paul*? It is written to bring the two subjects into sharp contrast so as to show Paul makes a better boyfriend than John. So, we can revise this thesis statement by adding the point that Mom's Hamburger Haven is a better family restaurant than McPhony's.

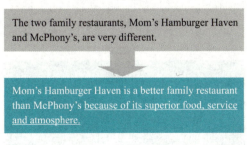

From the new thesis statement, we not only know the two subjects and the differences, but also the purpose of explaining the three differences.

✎ 修正"无意义主旨句"的第一种方法就是直接指出哪个比较对象更好。

Another way to avoid a "so-what" thesis statement is to **find a purpose that will draw in the audience in general**.

> In *Huckleberry Finn*, Mark Twain develops a contrast between life on the river and life on the shore.

> Through its contrasting river and shore scenes, <u>Mark Twain's *Huckleberry Finn* suggests that to find the true expression of American democratic ideals, one must leave "civilized" society and go back to nature.</u>

In the revised version, we can grasp the subjects, river scenes and shore scenes, and we can also tell it is a contrast essay through the word "contrasting". In addition, we can find the purpose added—to find the true expression of American democratic ideals, one must leave "civilized" society and go back to nature. Those who have read this book might have a different interpretation of what Mark Twain suggests in the book, and their interest could be triggered and drive them to read this essay to find out how such an interpretation is achieved. Those who have got the same interpretation might be interested in the essay in order to find out whether they might arrive at such an interpretation based on the same arguments. Those who haven't read the book could get some ideas from the essay first, which could help them understand the book later. You see, with a purpose which attracts those people, the thesis statement has become very meaningful.

✎ 修正"无意义主旨句"的第二种方法就是建立一个针对大众读者的意义，也就是说这些相似点或不同点对读者有何意义。

A third way of avoiding a "so-what" thesis statement is to **direct the thesis statement to a particular audience instead of the audience in general**.

> Although Stella's Sweatateria and the Fitness Fanatics Gym are similar in their low student-membership prices and excellent instructors, they have more differences.

> Although Stella's Sweatateria and the Fitness Fanatics Gym are similar in their low student-membership prices and excellent instructors, <u>Stella's is the place to go for those seeking a variety of exercise classes rather than hard-core bodybuilding machines.</u>

Compare the original version and the revised version here. The difference between the two versions lies in the new idea that Stella's is the place to go for those seeking a variety of exercise classes rather than only being able to use hard-core bodybuilding machines. The added point implies contrast. Stella's provides a variety of exercise classes, while the Fitness Fanatics Gym is equipped with hard-core bodybuilding machines. Therefore, the two gyms serve different customers. Such a thesis statement does not tell which gym is better; instead, it helps gym lovers in the local area, a particular audience, to choose the one which is more suitable to them.

> 修正"无意义主旨句"的第三种方法就是建立一个针对某一读者群的意义。例如，通过对两家健身房的比较，发现一家健身房更适合那些需要多样化锻炼课程的人群，而另一家健身房更适合硬核健身人士。

A fourth way of avoiding a "so-what" thesis statement is to **show a particular relationship between two subjects**.

> There are many similarities in the character and plot between the movie *Riot of the Killer Snails* and Mary Sheeley's novel *Salt on the Sidewalk*.
>
> ⬇
>
> The many similarities in the character and plot clearly suggest that the movie director was greatly influenced by—if not actually guilty of stealing—parts of Mary Sheeley's novel.

The revised version here is better than the original thesis statement because it shows the point of analyzing the similarities between the movie and the novel. The movie director was greatly influenced by—if not actually guilty of stealing—parts of Mary Sheeley's novel. This is the major idea of the essay; doing comparison is just a means for the end.

> 修正"无意义主旨句"的第四种方法就是建立两个比较对象的某种关系，即文中探讨的相似点或不同点能反映、支撑两个比较对象之间存在的关系。比如，通过梳理一部电影和一本小说的相似点，可以说明这部电影很可能受到了这本小说的影响。

Summary

In this lecture, we've talked about a few ways to avoid a "so what" thesis statement. We can tell one subject is better than the other. And we can find a purpose that will draw in the audience in general. We can also direct the thesis statement to a particular audience. Besides, we can show a particular relationship between two subjects. There could be other ways, too. But the golden rule is to tell readers the major point and then use comparison and contrast to support the idea. Don't just compare or contrast two subjects for the sake of comparison or contrast.

高级综合英语写作教程（慕课版）

讲座 4　常用表达（Useful Expressions）

知识概要　表达相似点的常用句型有 X is similar to Y, X is as...as Y, X and Y are similar in terms of... 等；表达不同点的常用句型有 X is different from Y, X and Y are different in terms of... 等。引出相似点的单词或短语有 both, like, as, too, also, similarly, likewise, the same as, in the same way 等；引出不同点的单词或短语有 unlike, whereas, while, but, yet, however, nevertheless, instead, in contrast, on the one hand...on the other hand, on the contrary 等。

关 键 词　表达相似点和不同点的句型（sentence patterns for similarities and differences）；引出相似点和不同点的过渡性单词和短语（transitional words and phrases for similarities and differences）

Lead-in

In this lecture, we're going to talk about some useful sentence patterns to present similarities or differences. We're also going to talk about some useful transitional expressions to achieve coherence in comparison and contrast essays. Finally, we are going to briefly summarize what we've learned in Week 10.

Language Focus

Here we can see a sentence pattern used to present similarities when X, one of the two things in a comparison, serves as the subject of the sentence. Pay special attention to the second column with many adverbial words and phrases. All of them are used to emphasize the degree of commonality, how similar the two things are. They can be classified into three groups. They are listed in the descending order according to the degree of commonality. In the first group, "exactly" "precisely" and "just" describe a perfect commonality. "Virtually" and "practically" indicate a near perfect commonality. The rest of the words and expressions tell us that they are quite similar, but not completely similar.

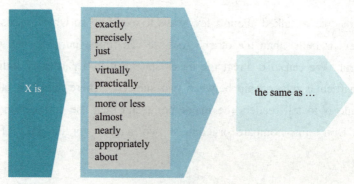

✎ 有三类副词可以修饰 similar, 表示两个比较对象的相似程度。exactly, precisely, just 表示完全相似; virtually 和 practically 表示近乎完全相似; more or less, almost, nearly 等表示不完全相似。

The sentence pattern above only tells us how similar X and Y are; it does not show what the similarity is specifically. The sentence pattern here can do the job through the column in the middle.

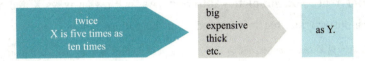

The adjectives in this column can tell us in what aspect X and Y are different. Furthermore, this pattern gives additional information by adding words before the first "as" to show the multiple, such as twice, five times or ten times. But keep in mind that the sentence pattern now is not about similarities, but differences.

✎ 在"as + 形容词/副词 + as"这个结构前加上 twice, three times, six times 等表示倍数的词, 表达一个比较对象是另一个比较对象在某个方面的几倍。例如: X is twice as expensive as Y.

The sentence patterns mentioned all have X as the subject of the sentence. The sentence patterns here have both X and Y as the subject.

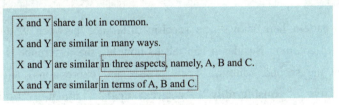

If we simply want to mean there are similarities between X and Y, we can use the first two sentence patterns. If we want to specify what the similarities are, we can choose the last two sentence patterns. In many cases, **we use expressions like "in terms of" or "in…aspects" to introduce specific similarities**. So far, we've seen some sentence patterns for similarities; now let's move on to sentence patterns for differences.

✎ 可以用 in terms of 和 in…aspects 等介词短语引出两个比较对象在几个方面存在相似点或不同点, 也可以简明扼要地指出有哪些方面的相似点或不同点。例如, X and Y are similar in three aspects, 或 X and Y are similar in terms of A, B, and C。同样的句型还可以用来表达不同点, 只需要将 similar 替换为 different。

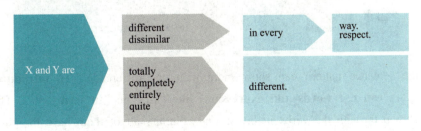

This sentence pattern shows two pieces of information about X and Y. First, X and Y are different. Second, it also tells how different they are, as the adverbs listed in the middle column show. The words in this column fall into two categories. The first three, "totally" "completely" and "entirely" are all about a 100% difference, but the last word, "quite", **means that X and Y are not completely different**. As for in what ways X and Y are different, such a pattern cannot provide that information, but the pattern below can.

✎ 有两类副词可以修饰 different, 表示两个比较对象的差异程度。totally, completely 和 entirely 表示完全不同; quite 表示有一些差别, 但并非完全不同。

The sentence pattern here shows one specific difference between X and Y by using an adjective in the third column. Besides it can tell us how big the difference is through the words and expressions in the second column. These words and expressions can be put into three groups. The first five, **"considerably" "a great deal" "much" "(quite) a lot" and "rather", indicate a big difference**. The second group, **"somewhat" "a little" and "slightly", show a small difference**. The last three, **"scarcely" "hardly" and "only just" tell that there is almost no difference**.

✎ 有三类副词和副词短语可以修饰形容词和副词比较级, 表示两个比较对象的差异程度。considerably, a great deal, much 等表示差异程度比较大; somewhat, a little, slightly 表示差异程度小; scarcely, hardly, only just 表示基本上没有差异。

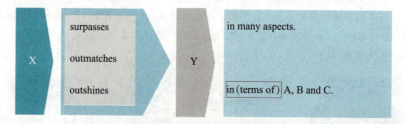

Here the sentence pattern can show more than one difference. **To introduce specific differences, we can use words and expressions like "in" or "in terms of"**. The idea of contrast is shown through the verbs in the second column; all of them have the basic idea of "being better than".

Unlike the sentence patterns for differences we've seen, the sentence pattern here has both X and Y as the subject of the sentence. It shows that there exists a difference and how big it is. To introduce specific differences, as we've seen before, we can also add expressions like "in terms of".

Now, let's work on an exercise to get some hands-on experiences of the sentence patterns. Study the table below, which shows the income of top 10 clubs in European football, and then read the comparisons. **Each sentence contains one error. Find and correct it.**

Income of Leading European Football Clubs 2012 – 2013

Club	Revenue (million)
Real Madrid	518
FC Barcelona	482
Bayern Munich	431
Manchester United	423
Paris Saint Germain	398
Manchester City	316
Chelsea	303
Arsenal	284
Juventus	272
AC Milan	263

(a) Real Madrid was the richest football club.
(b) Real Madrid's income was almost twice much as AC Milan's.
(c) FC Barcelona earned marginally more than Manchester City.
(d) Juventus had less revenue Arsenal.
(e) Chelsea's income was slightly lower than Bayern Munich's.
(f) Manchester United earned approximately same as Bayern Munich.

Look at Sentence A. Real Madrid was the richest football club. It sounds perfect grammatically. Then what's wrong with it? Try reading the sentence again out of context, without looking at the table above. Does it make perfect sense? Not really, "richest" is the superlative and indicates contrast. But what is contrasted with Real Madrid? In other words, in what region was it the richest? We cannot tell it from the sentence alone. Without it, the sentence doesn't make much sense. Therefore, we need to add some information. Like "in Europe". Now, we know **it was the richest football club in Europe**, not in Spain, not in the world. (As for the rest of the exercise, you can finish them in the quiz section.)

Now, let's get to know some transitional words and expressions for similarities and differences.

Transitional Expressions for Similarities	Transitional Expressions for Differences
• both • like • as • the same as • too/also • similarly • likewise • in like manner • in the same way • in similar fashion	• unlike • whereas/while • but • yet • however • nevertheless • instead • in contrast • on the one hand…on the other hand • on the contrary • to the contrary • the opposite of • conversely

The first list is about similarities; the second list is about differences. Most of the words are not new, are they?

Look at the first list now. We'll focus on some of them. **"Similarly" and "likewise" are interchangeable.** Both of them are usually used before we introduce the second subject in comparison. **"In like manner" "in the same way" and "in similar fashion" are also interchangeable.** They are also often used to introduce the second subject in comparison. They can be used before the second subject, or after it, usually at the end of the sentence.

Among the words and expressions to indicate differences, **pay attention to words like "however" "nevertheless" and "instead"**. They are adverbs and can be used to link two sentences. If they are used to link two clauses in a sentence, we should add ";" instead of "," before them.

> 有一类引出不同点的单词需要注意，如 however, nevertheless, instead。这些词常用于两个分句中间，但它们不是连词而是副词，不能承担连接两个分句的作用，因此需要在这些单词前加上分号来连接两个分句，而不能用逗号来连接。

Summary

So far, we've talked so much about comparison and contrast essays. Before calling it a day, we can wrap up what we've learned. **First**, a comparison and contrast essay is a piece of writing which explains mostly similarities or differences between two subjects. But some essays also deal with both similarities and differences. **Second**, there are two organization patterns for comparison and contrast essays. One is the point-by-point pattern; the other is the subject-by-subject pattern. The first works better in bringing out the effective sharp contrast; the second is a better choice if the writer is interested in the whole. **Third**, we should avoid a "so-what" thesis statement. Although there are various ways to avoid it, we'd better keep in mind this rule of thumb: tell readers the point of comparison or contrast and use comparison or contrast as a means to support the point. **Fourth**, we've learned quite a few sentence patterns to present similarities and differences. What pattern to use depends on how similar or different two subjects are and how many similarities or differences there are. Furthermore, we've learned useful transitional words and expressions to achieve coherence in the essay. Hope all these points will be helpful in your writing.

Ⅲ. 写作练习

1. Read the following sentences and circle all the words or phrases indicating a similarity/difference between the two subjects under discussion.

1) Unlike the greenhouse gases, which spread evenly across the globe, sulphur dioxide's effects are short-lived and regional.
2) As one child recently remarked, "If you don't ride a bike fast enough, you fall off." Likewise, if the reader does not recognize words quickly enough, the meaning will be lost.
3) Older people in the U.S. and France are more likely than younger people to say trade destroys jobs. Similarly, lower-income Americans and French are more fearful that trade will decrease employment than are their fellow countrymen with upper incomes.
4) Free-ranged chickens without access to grass do not show any nutritional improvement over conventional eggs, whereas pasturing hens on green grass produces eggs higher in healthy omega-3 fatty acids and vitamin E.
5) The students that are book-smart are generally those who thrive academically—able to memorize endless math formulas or analyze passages of the most advanced literary works. Conversely, the kids with street smarts are able to approach real life problems, take a step back, and adapt to come up with the best solution to have them come out on top.
6) In emerging markets, 52% say global business ties create jobs and 45% hold the view that it improves wages. Americans, on the other hand, are among the least likely to say trade creates jobs (20%) or improves wages (17%), exhibiting notably less faith in the benefits of trade than others in advanced economies.
7) In their study, Almond and Verba found that the Americans and the British "tend to be consistently most positive about the safety and responsiveness of the human environment". The Germans and the Italians, by contrast, were found to be more negative, and the Mexicans inconsistent.
8) In the statement that "She is a difficult person to work with; she is too feminine",

"feminine" implies hysterical, illogical and unreasonable. "Masculine" on the contrary never carries these negative implications; it simply implies strong, sometimes powerful and not effeminate.

9) A conclusion that can be drawn from all these treatment studies is that when dealing with patients who do not require inpatient care, treatment by well-trained non-medical staff (social workers and nurses in particular) is at least as effective as treatment given by psychiatrists.

10) The American writers Ralph Waldo Emerson and Walt Whitman seemed to give the most enthusiastic tribute to the industrialized version of the pastoral landscape idyll. Whitman, especially, was able to assimilate the forces of the machine into the natural landscape. Emerson, too, had an enthusiasm for technological progress as well as a love of nature.

2. Read the following paragraphs and add a topic sentence for both of them.

1) _____.

SARS' symptoms typically began with a high fever and dry cough, followed by shortness of breath and diarrhea. Severe cases often progressed rapidly to pneumonia, requiring hospitalization and, often, intensive care. COVID-19 symptoms are the same, but also may include loss of taste or smell, fatigue, muscle aches, headaches, congestion or runny nose, nausea, and sore throat. More severe instances may include bluish lips or face, the inability to wake or to stay awake, persistent chest pain, trouble breathing, or confusion.

2) _____.

Both COVID-19 and flu can spread from person-to-person, between people who are in close contact with one another (within about 6 feet). Both are spread mainly by droplets made when people with the illness (COVID-19 or flu) cough, sneeze, or talk. These droplets can land in the mouths or noses of people who are nearby or possibly be inhaled into the lungs. It may be possible that a person can get infected by physical human contact (e.g. shaking hands) or by touching a surface or object that has a virus on it and then touching his or her own mouth, nose, or possibly their eyes. Both the flu virus and the virus that causes COVID-19 may be spread to others by people before they begin showing symptoms, with very mild symptoms or who never develop symptoms (asymptomatic).

3. Read the following introductory paragraph and answer the questions after it.

Now that there's rapid growth in virtual reality (VR) and augmented reality (AR), there is increased confusion about the differences between the technologies. While both technologies integrate virtual and real-world elements and have similarities, there are differences. To clear up the confusion, the article aims to distinguish VR from AR by explaining the different experience that they bring about with the help of different devices.

1) Where is the thesis statement?

2) Do you think it is a so-what thesis statement? And why?

4. Read the following concluding paragraph and answer the questions after it.

To conclude, virtual reality and augmented reality accomplish two very different things in two very different ways, despite the similar designs of the devices themselves. VR replaces reality, taking you somewhere else; however, AR adds to reality, projecting information on top of what you're already seeing. They're both powerful technologies that have yet to make their mark with consumers, but show a lot of promise. They can completely change how we use computers in the future, but whether one or both will succeed is anyone's guess right now.

1) How many parts are there in the conclusion?

_____

_____

_____

2) What function does each of the parts serve?

_____

_____

_____

5. Read the following body paragraphs from an article entitled *Democrats vs. Republicans: A Tale of Two Convention Styles* and answer the questions after them.

The look and feel of either convention in many ways reflects the messaging of either party. The Democrats presented a Hollywood production, professionally hosted, with jokes and asides, greenscreen backgrounds, videos, and chats between the hosts. Colors were bright and TV-friendly. The convention could have easily substituted for a pandemic era awards show, with Joe Biden receiving the lifetime achievement award. The Republicans chose more of a *White House After Dark* look, essentially extending the work day, even throwing in some homework that Trump didn't get around to like pardoning felons and inducting immigrants. The look and feel was the familiar White House settings that we see daily in the news. More interesting might be why Republicans felt the need to rely on the White House as its main backdrop. Pundits chimed in with theories from a desire to appear authoritarian to a simple lack of imagination for making a midstream switch when it became clear that a convention as usual would not be possible due to the pandemic.

The way either party treated the pandemic was instructive. For the Democrats, the pandemic was the star. Biden has said: "We cannot get the country moving until we control the virus." Voter polling has consistently shown that the pandemic and the resulting recession are the most important things on voters' minds, and that the Trump administration's response to it has been enormously unpopular. So, Democrats featured Joe Biden and Kamala Harris in masks, socially distancing, and a drive-in celebration and fireworks show on the final night. Their message was that the pandemic has changed everything. In contrast, it was nearly business as usual for Republicans. Their speeches featured maskless speakers, onlookers and audiences. When they referred to the pandemic at all, it was either in the past tense, or, as it is typical with Trump supporters, as another great achievement by an exalted leader. There was no nod to the way day-to-day life was upended due to the lackluster response of the government.

Both parties tried to target women, minorities and youth. A significant difference was the Democratic outreach to disaffected Republican leaders and active encouragement to their opponents to defect and join the big tent coalition they were putting together. While the Republicans offered the usual strange scene of a Democratic legislator eschewing his own party's message, it was more focused on his own story rather than a broad attempt at outreach.

1) Compose an outline for the body paragraphs.
2) Identify the organization pattern.

第11周
定义型作文（Writing a Definition Essay）

⯈ I．概述

定义型作文（Definition Essays）是用来解释某个特定术语含义的文章。

本周课程主要介绍了定义型作文的写作方法，共分为四次讲座。

第一、二次讲座介绍了定义的分类、构成，适合用定义法写作的话题，以及下定义可以采用的方法。通常来说，定义可以分为"词典定义"和"延伸定义"。定义型作文不应只是从词典或网上复制某术语的含义，而应以作者的个人理解为基础，它可以基于某术语的不同用法或特定背景来展开，由作者决定从何种角度来展开对该术语的解释。

一般说来，需要下定义的事物通常具有以下特征：概念抽象、意思模糊或者具有争议性，或是需要用较长篇幅详细描述。标准的定义通常由三部分组成：需要定义的术语＋所属类别＋具有区分度的特征。作者可以采用多种方法对事物进行定义，如查阅词典释义、从语言学角度分析、列举/举例法、分类法、比较法、反向定义法、词源法、效果/用途定义法以及混合法等。

第三、四次讲座阐述了定义型作文的写作以及定义型作文中的常用表达。

首先，在写作准备阶段，要选择合适的主题；搜集与主题相关的素材：词典、网络、文献等；之后，可对这些素材的异同进行比较，从而提出自己的解释，确定定义型作文的论点。

其次，定义型作文一般包括三个部分：起始段、主体部分和结论。一篇好的定义型作文，应该在开头向读者明确表达所定义的术语，给出的定义应简单易懂；主体部分应尽可能地尝试用不同方法说明术语的含义；结尾则要做到首尾呼应，有始有终。

此外，要写出一篇好的定义型作文，还需要对语言进行润色。通过使用一系列表示解释说明的过渡性词语，使读者明确作者在特定语境中对某术语的阐述。

高级综合英语写作教程（慕课版）

Ⅱ. 慕课讲稿

讲座 1　什么是定义（What a Definition Is）

知识概要　本讲座首先对本周的讲解内容做了简要概括，之后阐述了什么是"定义"、定义的结构以及定义法作文的适用话题。主要内容：1. 定义的类别；2. 定义的三个重要组成部分："术语（Term）""类别（Class）"以及"区分性典型特征（Distinguishing Features）"；3. 定义型作文适用的话题：抽象且容易引起歧义的观点、看法、现象等是定义型作文适用的话题；已经达成共识、有确定释义的术语则不需要用定义型作文来阐释。

关 键 词　定义的类别（types of definition）；定义的基本结构（standard structure of a definition）；合适的主题（proper topic）

Lead-in

During Week 11, we'll focus on **writing a definition essay**. We're going to cover the following subtopics: What is a definition? How to make a definition? How do we brainstorm and organize a definition essay? What are some useful transitional expressions in a definition essay? Here in Lecture 1, we're going to deal with the first topic: **What is a definition?**

In this ever-changing society, there are lots of new things emerging every day, which may arouse our desire to know more about them. For instance, in a science class, a five-year old may ask: what is the meaning of "galaxy"? You may think it's easy to answer this question, because we can turn to a dictionary for definitions of unknown terms.

Yes, we can, but how about this question: what does "success" mean to you? This is more difficult to find an answer, since the term "success" is very abstract. Though people may consult a dictionary for a definition, they may have quite different interpretations of it owing to their individual background.

Objectives

After Lecture 1, we'll have a general understanding of what a definition is. We'll cover three topics: 1) **the main types of definition**, 2) **the standard structure of a definition** and 3) **the proper topics for an extended definition**.

Tasks

Task 1　To understand the main types of definition.

Read the following definitions, and try to identify the differences between them:

A galaxy is an extremely large group of stars and planets that extends over many billions of light years.

✎ **No. 1** is the definition of "galaxy" given by a dictionary; it explains that "galaxy" is an extremely large group of stars and planets that extends over many billions of light years.

Reading is far more than recognition of the graphic symbols. It is much more than the mere ability to pronounce the words on the printed page; it is even more than the gain of meaning from printed materials. The reader is stimulated by the writer's words, but in turn vests these words with his own meaning. Reading typically is the bringing of meaning to rather than the gaining of meaning from the printed page.

✎ **No. 2** is an informal personal definition of the term "reading". According to the author, reading involves the reader's bringing meaning to the printed page rather than getting meaning from it.

From these two examples, we may identify the two commonly existing types of definition:

The first one is **the Formal Definition**, which actually refers to the dictionary definition.

The second one is **the Extended Definition**, which explains what something or someone is and requires a paragraph, an essay, or even a whole book.

In this week's learning, we will focus on **the writing of an extended definition**.

✎ the Formal Definition 主要指的是"词典定义"；而 the Extended Definition（"延伸定义"）在此处指的是基于对某术语、某事物的不同用法或特定背景来展开的表述。

Task 2 **Try to find out the standard structure of a definition.**

Read the following definitions and distinguish the three-part structure for each of them.

1. *Behaviorism* is a theory *that* regards the objective facts of a subject's actions as the only valid basis for psychological study.

2. Personally, I think *love* is a unique feeling of respect, adoration, desire for a given individual or "object" *which* eventually makes the person to become one whole entity and at the same time reveals the dependence on the object of love as a carrier of a unique combination of the proportion of certain qualities or peculiarities.

The first one is the definition of "behaviorism", while the second one is a definition of "love". Please look at the words in color. Can you find something in common between these two terms?

If we rearrange the structure of the definitions of these two terms and put them in the table, we may realize that both of them have **a standard three-part structure: Term**(which refers to "behaviorism" and "love"), **Class** (the first term belongs to "a theory" while the second one falls into "a feeling") and **Distinguishing Features** (the first term is explained by a "that" clause, while the second term is illustrated by a "which" clause.)

Term	Class	Distinguishing Feature(s)
Behaviorism	is a theory	that regards the objective facts of a subject's actions as the only valid basis for psychological study.
Love	is a unique feeling of respect, adoration, desire for a given individual or "object"	which eventually makes the person to become one whole entity and at the same time reveals the dependence on the object of love as a carrier of a unique combination of the proportion of certain qualities or peculiarities.

This three-part structure of definition can be very useful for beginners who may need to do some writing practice before they start composing their own definitions in their future writing.

Task 3 Try to identify the proper topics for definition essays.

Compare the two groups of terms below. How different are they?

Material Terms
- a cell
- a plant
- a printer
- a modem
...

Conceptual Terms
- friendship
- love
- honor
- pride
...

In the left column, the words are: a cell/a plant/a printer/a modem. These terms have **definite, concrete meanings**; they are improper topics for a long essay since the readers won't think of them as controversial.

The terms on the right are friendship/love/honor/pride. These terms are **abstract and depend more on the particular point of view of a person**, culture, religion, political system and so forth, and are proper topics for a definition essay.

Key Points

With the analysis of the terms above, let's draw a conclusion of the proper topics for an extended definition.

There are plenty of terms we use every day. Many of them are clear to almost everybody, but still there is a vast body of abstract or scientific terms that can become a topic of discussion. To make things even more complicated, many difficult social and political issues are due to the fact that citizens can define terms in very different ways.

Briefly speaking, if a term has the following characteristics, it can be **a proper topic for a definition essay**.

1) **Abstract terms** (such as feelings, values or other abstract qualities), for example, the word "love";
2) **Ambiguous terms** (for example, those terms which have more than one meaning due to context), for example, the definition of the word "fine";
3) **Controversial terms** (the terms such as "democracy" which can be a topic for one to develop a long essay) and
4) **Complicated terms** which may require exhaustive description, for example, the definition of "quantum tunneling".

Here I would like to provide more of the possible terms that could be chosen as a topic for an extended definition, for example, the term "laziness" "marriage" and so on. You may choose one to have some practice.

- laziness
- success
- marriage
- family
- real estate
- attitude
- love
- religion
- christianity
- endurance
- love
- hatred
- beauty
- morale
- good and evil
- enlightenment
- happiness
- confidence

Summary

Before we finish the first lecture, let's review what we have mainly talked about.

First, we have learned the two main types of definition: the formal definition and the extended definition.

Second, we have identified the standard three-part structure of a definition, which consists of the term, class and distinguishing features.

Finally, we have learned what topics can be proper for us to start an extended definition essay.

讲座2 如何下定义(How to Make a Definition)

知识概要 本讲座主要介绍下定义时可以遵循的基本原则以及针对不同主题可以选择的不同下定义方法。主要内容：1. 下定义时，要牢记以下几个原则：要避免循环定义、避免用抽象的同义词来下定义；给社会政治领域的术语下定义时，要保持中立，避免主观情感的介入。2. 针对不同主题，可以采取以下不同方法来下定义：查阅词典释义、从语言学角度分析、列举/举例法、分类法、比较法、反向定义法、词源法、效果/用途定义法以及混合法等。

关 键 词 定义原则(principles of making a definition);
定义方法(methods of making a definition)

Lead-in

In this lecture, we are going to learn about how to make a definition.

Having become familiar with the types of definition and the standard structure of a definition, the question arises concerning how to make a definition. There are so many different methods of making a definition. How do we use these methods to develop our definition essay? Can we just copy the definition from a dictionary, a famous person, or are there some other sources that we can use to make our own definition more persuasive to the readers?

Objectives

In order to find out answers to this question, we will pursue the following objectives in Lecture 2: 1) to understand the basic principles of making a definition; 2) to become acquainted with various methods of defining a term.

Tasks

Now, let's try to deal with the first task, which is to **identify the basic principles of making a definition**.

Read the following definitions and try to think whether the definitions are proper or not.

1. Democracy is the democratic process.
2. An astronomer is one who studies astronomy.
3. By imagination I mean the power to form mental images of objects, the power to form new ideas, the gift of employing images in writing, and the tendency to attribute reality to unreal things, situations and states.
4. By state enterprises I mean one of the great blessings of democratic planning.
5. By state enterprises I mean high cost and poor efficiency.

In Sentence 1, "Democracy is the democratic process", we notice that the word "democratic" is used to define "democracy", which is improper because these two words are of the same root, and if they are used to define each other, then a **circular definition** (循环定义) is formed.

The same mistake occurs in Sentence 2 when the writer tries to define "astronomer" by the same-rooted word "astronomy".

In Sentence 3, the author is trying to define "imagination" by presenting a long list of abstract synonyms of this word, such as "the power to form mental images" "the power to form new ideas" "the gift of employing images" and "the tendency to attribute reality". The readers may be confused with the meaning of these abstract terms such as "power" "gift" and "tendency" themselves, so they won't be clear with the author's definition of "imagination" either.

Coming to the 4th and 5th sentences, we notice that the writer's definitions are either loaded with favorable emotional **connotations** (隐含意义) or loaded with pejorative (贬义的)

emotional connotations when making a definition for the term "state enterprises".

Having analyzed the mistakes in these definitions, we can clearly identify **the principle for making a proper definition**. **First**, when we define a term, try to avoid **circular definitions**; **second**, we should try to avoid **a long list of synonyms if the term is an abstract one**; instead, we may use some concrete examples to make our description clearer; **finally**, when defining some social or political concepts, we are supposed to **be objective and try to avoid definitions loaded with our preferences**.

> ✎ the principle for making a proper definition 下定义时，要牢记以下几个原则：要避免循环定义、避免用抽象的同义词来下定义；给社会政治领域的术语下定义时，要保持中立，避免所给出的定义带有主观情感。

Key Points

Now, let's come to the key points of Lecture 2: the methods to define a term.

Before we start to give an extended definition, try to ask ourselves these two questions:

1) What is **our purpose in giving the definition**?

2) Who might be **our audience**?

Our main purpose is to explain to readers our understanding of a key term or concept, and consequently, to persuade the readers that our definition is a legitimate(合情合理的) one. We should therefore pay special attention to our audience. For instance, if we are to define the term "patriotism" to a group of college students and a group of war veterans(老兵), our methods of definition should be different.

> ✎ 下定义时应采取何种方法？回答这个问题之前，需要明确以下两个问题：1)我们下定义的目的是什么？2)我们的读者是谁？明确这两个问题，是我们写定义型作文的前提和基础。

Generally speaking, there are more than ten different methods of making a definition, which I have listed here for your reference:

---

1) A dictionary definition or a definition by certain informed people;

2) Linguistic analysis of the formation;

3) Enumeration(列举事实) and analysis of features generally associated with the object;

4) Exemplification;

5) Classification;

6) Comparison;

7) Negation;

8) Origins and causes;

9) Effects and usages;

10) Any combination of the above methods.

Now, let's try to have a detailed explanation of these methods.

1. **A dictionary definition** or a definition by certain informed people.

I have provided two examples here:

Example 1　According to *the Oxford Dictionary*, justice is a noun, and it means: the quality of being just; righteousness, equitableness, or moral rightness.

Example 2　Aristotle defines the imagination as "the movement which results upon an actual sensation".

The first one is the dictionary definition of the term "justice", while the second one is Aristotle's definition on "imagination".

Remember that in a definition essay, this method is only proper to introduce the topic and to hook the reader. We are not suggesting that we develop our definition essay by applying this method only, since that will leave our readers completely bored.

2. **Linguistic analysis of the formation.**

We can separate the term into different parts and define each part separately; the explanation of the divided part may make the reader have a better understanding of the term. For example, when giving definition to "philosophy", we can divide this term into philo (which means "love") and sophy (from "sophia, which means 'knowledge'"), and then define these two parts separately.

3. **Enumeration and analysis of the features generally associated with the object.**

Using "microwave oven" as an example, we can define this term by describing its physical features, functions or uses.

4. **Exemplification.**

For example, in a definition essay about "kindness", we can write about someone we know about (e.g. Mother Teresa) whose benevolence to others to illustrate what kindness is.

5. **Classification.**

Sometimes, it is easier for us to define a term by classifying or dividing it into different sub-types. For example, in defining the word "love", we can classify love to be many different types: parental love, brotherly love, patriotic love, and love of pets, beauty and so forth.

6. **Comparison.**

To define a term, we can compare it to other members of its class and then illustrate the similarities and differences. These differences are special characteristics that make the term stand out. For example, to describe a Siberian husky, you can compare it to other dogs, such as lap dogs, mutts, or sporting dogs. Analogy can also be used when you hope to explain something abstract and unfamiliar to the readers by comparing it to something more concrete and familiar.

7. **Negation**.

Apart from explaining what something is, we can also use negation to mention what it is not to clear the ground for what it is. For example, when defining the abstract feeling of "love", we can define it like this: "Love is not a gourmet dish, a domesticated animal, or a latest trend. Love is not a strategic defense mechanism nor the best kept secret at the Pentagon."

8. **Origins and causes**.

We can describe the origin, the background information, and the historical development of the term to discuss its meaning. For example, the word "Quisling" which means "A traitor(叛徒, 卖国贼) who works for enemies", derives from the name of Major Vidkun Quisling, a Norwegian general who controlled Norway when it was occupied by Germany during World War II.

9. **Discuss the results, effects and uses of the subject in question**.

For example, what is "Sharing Economy"? Sharing Economy is a system in which people rent, borrow, or share commodities, services, and resources owned by individuals, usually with the aid of online technology, in an effort to save money, cut costs, and reduce waste.

Of course, **any combination of the above mentioned methods** can be of great help if we put in mind what is our purpose of definition and who are the readers.

✎ 定义型作文可以根据定义的目的以及针对的读者采取以下方法：词典释义、语言学分析、列举/举例法、分类法、比较法、反向定义法、词源法、效果/用途定义法以及混合法等。

Having been introduced to methods for making a definition, now consider some important tips concerning what we can do and what we can't do when making a definition.

First, let's look at **the things we can do**:

> 1) We should follow a determined structure.
> 2) We should choose terms we understand to make our definitions, or ones that have impacted our own personal experience.
> 3) If we cannot define a new meaning for some concept on our own, then use the definition that already exists, but we should give our own interpretation of it.

Then, let's come to **the things we should try to avoid**:

> 1) We shouldn't stray from the term we are defining.
> 2) We should avoid defining a term that is too broad in scope for the essay.
> 3) It's not necessary to define terms that are well-known and without conflicting interpretations.
> 4) We shouldn't forget that examples are very useful.
> 5) We shouldn't copy the existing definition word-by-word without any reinterpretation.
> 6) We shouldn't make definitions that seem biased.

Summary

Before we finish Lecture 2, let's make a quick summary of today's key points.

By analyzing some common mistakes when making a definition, we have identified the basic principles of making a definition; we then discussed the various methods of making a definition.

讲座 3 如何撰写定义型作文 I (Writing a Definition Essay I)

知识概要 本讲座主要介绍定义型作文准备阶段需要注意的问题：选题；组材以及定义型作文的基本结构。主要内容：1. 在定义型作文的准备阶段，首先应该选择合适的主题；2. 就选定主题搜集各种素材，为选定主题的构思谋篇做好准备：如查阅词典、上网搜索、就选定话题开展问卷调查等；3. 对所搜集信息进行遴选、分类，提出作者对该主题的解释，确定论点，并在此基础上构建定义型作文的基本结构：起始段、正文部分和结论部分。

关 键 词 准备阶段（preparation stage）；论点（thesis statement）；
"三段式"论文提纲（the three-part outline）

Objectives

In this lecture, we are going to consider the pre-writing stage of a definition essay.

We'll need some useful instruction before we start to brainstorm a definition essay. Then we'll learn how to craft the thesis statement. Finally, we'll begin to draft the outline of a definition essay.

Tasks

Before writing a definition essay, please keep in mind the following questions.

1) What is a definition essay?
2) What can be done to develop ideas and details before writing about the chosen topic?

Let's answer the first question.

A definition essay defines a word, term, or concept in depth by providing a formal commentary on what the specific subject means.

The definition essay provides the author's thought out; it is an extended illustration of the term by linking or comparing it to a previous definition and by illustrating how that term should be applied.

> 定义型作文是作者针对特定的术语或事物进行的扩展说明，作者通过与先前定义的比较来对该术语或事物进行说明。

Being aware that a definition essay illustrates our thinking process, we should **accumulate enough materials** to make our writing more supportive and persuasive; therefore, some important items are needed for the brainstorming process.

First, we need to choose a topic. Next, we should gather all possible sources for the definition of the chosen topic: we can look up dictionary definitions; we can surf the Internet for on-line sources; we can also prepare questions in order to interview a variety of people for their understanding of the chosen topic and we may also post questions concerning our topic on social media to gather even more interpretations.

After gathering all possible sources for making a definition, read them all through and analyze them. Try to look for similarities and group the answers into categories for writing our own definition essay.

> 写定义型作文时，首先应该积累足够的材料，使写作更具说服力：可以通过查找词典定义、上网搜索术语来源，或者开展问卷调查等方式来收集关于该术语或事物的更多解释。在此基础上，对不同定义进行比对分析，试着寻找相似、相异之处，以便给出作者关于该术语或事物的定义。

Next, let's come to the thesis statement of a definition essay. **The thesis statement usually identifies the term being defined and provides a brief, basic definition.**

Love is something that means very different things to different people. For some, love can be purely romantic, or even purely sexual. For others, real love is utterly unconditional and only truly exists between family members, or between people and a deity. And for some people, love is fluid, ever-changing, and everywhere, and is felt for family, friends, partners, pets, and even inanimate objects, dead artists, and fictional characters. None of these people would be right or wrong, but one thing is certain: *love is the most powerful force in the entire universe*.

Just like the example definition of "love", we can very easily identify the thesis statement: "love is the most powerful force in the entire universe", for, in the essay, the author has put forth one usage after another of "love", which allows a brief and basic understanding of the term to emerge. As the term "love" has been repeated many times until finally a brief and basic understanding has been provided.

Let's look at another example: the definition of "maturity".

Before you read this essay, please bear the following questions in mind:

1. **Where is the thesis statement?** Is it at the very beginning of the paragraph?
2. **How is the thesis statement set out?** Is it in a question or a complete sentence?
3. **Are there any subtopics?** If yes, what are they?

The Meaning of Maturity

Being a mature student does not mean being an old-timer. Maturity is not measured by

the number of years a person has lived. Instead, the yardstick of maturity is marked by the qualities of self-denial, determination, and dependability.

Self-denial is an important quality in the mature student. The things we want is always more than the things we can achieve and few people has the ability to realize all his dreams. So for most ordinary students, self-denial is necessary. Not only because of our limited abilities, but also self-denial can help us reach our most important goals as well.

Determination is another characteristic of a mature student. Bill Gates gave up the excellent opportunity to study in Harvard and focused on the IT industry; later he became the co-founder chairman of Microsoft Corp. The story tells us that fortune knocks at least once at every man's gate. As the door to success, a mature individual should be equipped with the capacity of deciding things manfully and properly.

Although self-denial and determination are both vital, probably the most important measure of maturity is dependability. It gives people a signal that you are responsible and can be trusted. Dependability shows a grown-up's duty and credit; it's the best understanding of maturity.

In conclusion, maturity is not judged by appearance; it depends on one's inner development. To be a strong-heart person, it's the true significance of growing up.

It is not difficult for us to identify the thesis statement, which is "the yardstick(衡量标准) of maturity is marked by the qualities of self-denial, determination, and dependability".

1. 定义型作文的核心陈述点或论点(thesis statement)通常是关于该术语或事物的特定观点或陈述。当分析一篇定义型作文的时候,首先需要明确以下问题:1)作者是如何提出核心陈述点或论点的?这些核心陈述点或论点位于文中何处?2)核心陈述点或论点是以问句形式还是以直接阐述的形式被提出的?3)核心陈述点或论点是否有其他副标题?

2. 在这篇文章中,作者在第一段中给出了自己对"成熟"的定义:"成熟"应该用自我否定、决心和可靠性等品质来衡量,接着分别用三个不同的段落来对这三个标志"成熟"的品质进行论述,从而使读者从三个维度对"成熟"有了更进一步的理解。

After identifying the thesis statement, let's make a further analysis of the thesis statement to answer the questions given prior to our reading.

1. The thesis statement is put at the end of the introduction paragraph.
2. The thesis statement is expressed in a complete sentence instead of questions or fragments of words.
3. There are subtopics listed in the thesis statement which may be a very effective way to develop the main body of the essay.

With the analysis of this sample essay, we may easily identify some key features of the thesis statement:

1. The thesis statement of a definition essay is usually a complete sentence, not in a question.
2. The thesis statement is usually at the end of an introduction.
3. The thesis statement states an opinion or attitude of a topic. It doesn't just state the topic itself.
4. The thesis statement often lists subtopics.
5. Usually writers won't directly announce the thesis statement.

定义型作文的核心陈述点或论点通常具有以下特征：1)定义型作文的核心陈述点或论点通常是一个完整的陈述，而不是一个问句。2)定义型作文的核心陈述点或论点通常在引言的结尾。3)定义型作文的核心陈述点或论点是对某一术语或事物的观点或态度。4)核心陈述点或论点经常会若干有副标题。5)作者通常不会直接表明核心陈述点或论点。

Key Points

Having learned some useful tips for developing the thesis statement, we then can start to brainstorm the outline of a definition essay.

The Meaning of Maturity

Being a mature student does not mean being an old-timer. Maturity is not measured by the number of years a person has lived. Instead, the yardstick of maturity is marked by the qualities of self-denial, determination, and dependability.

Self-denial is an important quality in the mature student. The things we want is always more than the things we can achieve and few people has the ability to realize all his dreams. So for most ordinary students, self-denial is necessary. Not only because of our limited abilities, but also because self-denial can help us reach our most important goals as well.

Determination is another characteristic of a mature student. Bill Gates gave up the excellent opportunity to study in Harvard and focused on the IT industry; later he became the co-founder chairman of Microsoft Corp. The story tells us that fortune knocks at least once at every man's gate. As the door to success, a mature individual should be equipped with the capacity of deciding things manfully and properly.

Although self-denial and determination are both vital, probably the most important measure of maturity is dependability. It gives people a signal that you are responsible and can be trusted. Dependability shows a grown-up's duty and credit; it's the best understanding of maturity.

In conclusion, maturity is not judged by appearance; it depends on one's inner development. To be a strong-heart person, it's the true significance of growing up.

It is quite easy to identify the outline of this essay, the first paragraph is the introduction part; the second, third and fourth paragraphs form the main body, which explains the subtopics listed in the thesis statement, while the last paragraph is the conclusion.

Our sample essay makes it clear that, like other types of essays, a definition essay mainly comprises three parts, namely: the introduction, the main body and the conclusion.

First, the introduction usually provides the dictionary definition and the author's definition which serves as the thesis statement.

Second, the main body usually consists of three to four paragraphs, and each will analyze a point or subtopic revealed in the author's definition of the term.

Finally, the conclusion usually analyzes the importance and uniqueness of the definition provided by the author, and often restates or echoes the thesis statement.

Summary

In Lecture 3, we have provided some pre-writing instructions which are useful for the preparation stage. We also gained some effective tips to produce the thesis statement. Finally, we made an analysis of the three-part outline for a definition essay.

讲座 4　如何撰写定义型作文 II (Writing a Definition Essay II)

知识概要　本讲座介绍定义型作文开头、主体部分以及结尾部分的写作方法。同时，还会介绍定义型作文写作时常用的词汇、表达方法和过渡词。主要内容：1. 定义型作文的开头应该向读者明确所定义的术语，给出的定义应简单易懂。主体部分应尽可能地尝试采用不同方法说明术语的含义。结尾则要做到首尾呼应，有始有终。2. 要写出一篇好的定义型作文，还需要对语言进行润色。要学会使用一些下定义的常见语汇和信号词，例如define, explain, be known as, refer to, describe 等。

关 键 词　各部分写作(the writing of each part);
　　　　　　过渡性单词与短语(transitional words and phrases)

Lead-in

In this lecture, we are going to come to the central task of Week 11, **the writing stage of a definition essay**.

Objectives

We are going to talk about the writing of each part of a definition essay; meanwhile, we will also cover some useful transitional expressions to achieve coherence(连贯性) in a definition essay.

Now, as we write, we should pay special attention to the delicate skills needed to combine each of the three parts in a definition essay.

Key Points

First, let's start with **writing of the introduction**.

In order to arouse the readers' attention, in the introduction part,

1) we may want to include the traditional or dictionary definition to provide a basis for our personal definition;

2) we may want to open with a contradictory image to illustrate what that term is not.

✎ 为了吸引读者的注意，定义型作文可以从词典释义入手，为所定义的事物提供一个基础含义，还可以从反面入手，从该事物不具备的特征来展开。

So, it is very important for us to put forward our thesis statement properly, which should include the following information:

A. The term to be defined.

B. A sentence which defines the term.

C. Reason(s) for giving a more detailed definition.

D. The kinds of additional information that will be used to extend the definition.

After composing the introduction, **the main body** of the essay comes next.

In the paragraphs of the main body, the author needs to provide his readers with information about the term by using various methods to create a definition observed in Lecture 2.

Paragraph 1—(**Analyzes the first point** presented in the author's definition of the term. It is absolutely necessary to support the definition with examples.)

Paragraph 2—(**Analyzes the second point** presented in the author's definition of the term. The author must provide an example in order to illustrate how his point is correct in terms of the definition.)

Paragraph 3—(**Analyzes the third point** presented in the author's definition of the term. It is absolutely necessary to support the definition with examples.)

✎ 定义型作文的主体部分，需要通过不同方法来展示作者关于该术语或事物的核心陈述点或论点，作者还可以把核心陈述点或论点分成若干个子论点来进行详细陈述。

Finally, what can we write in **the conclusion**?

In the conclusion, we can review our definition's main points and provide a closing attention-getter.

We may also follow these suggestions:

> 1. Sometimes **a reference** back to the opening attention-getter is a good way of unifying the entire essay.
> 2. We may want to close with an explanation of **how our definition has affected us**.
> 3. The definition essay might end with **a description**, **a comparison/contrast**, a process analysis, etc. However, **a comment** about the term or a summarizing statement may often be included.

✎ 定义型作文的结尾部分通常会对核心陈述点或论点进行回顾或重述。

Tasks

Let's try to analyze a sample definition essay on the topic of "Love" to enhance the things we have acquired this week.

What Is This Thing Called Love?

A wise man once said that love is a wonderful thing. Although this statement leaves sparse room for argument, it does little to define what love is beyond the vague realm of "wonderful". It is my duty as a devout romantic to embark upon the seemingly difficult task of defining love by looking at the history, explaining what love is not, and examining the uses of love and the results of that usage.

The origin of the word is probably the most logical place to start. As with many words in the English language, love is a derivative of the Latin word "causemajoraproblemus" which means "You're miserable when you got it and miserable when you don't". The word was created to explain the biological phenomenon that existed when certain individuals came into contact with each other and either remained together or went about their lives separately. Regardless of the outcome, the relationship was usually characteristic of throat lumps, knotted stomaches, weak knees, temporary loss of language, sweaty palms, dizziness, sneezing, and occasional nausea. Belligerent insanity also resulted. History clearly illustrates this. Can we ever forget the face that launched a thousand ships? Federally expressing Van Gogh's ear? The construction of Le Tour Eiffel? All of these were results of love and love lost.

Star-crossed lovers have stated that love is not hand nor foot nor any part belonging to a man. Matrimonial ceremonies also claim that love is not jealous or boastful. Let it be stated here that love also is not a gourmet dish, a domesticated animal, or a latest trend. Love is not a strategic defense mechanism nor the best kept secret at the Pentagon. Love is not another seasoning to bottle and stick on the dust-lined shelves of the spice rack. Love is not to be confused with adhesive tape.

Instead, love is a great counterpart to late, evening thunder storms on hot July nights. Love goes well with cold pizza on picnic blankets. Love is cold, wet sand between bare toes. Love is a capitalistic sell-all for novels, Top-40 pop songs, summer movies, and greeting cards.

In its simplest terms, love is a four-letter word. Much like other words of similar letter make-up, when expressed it can evoke laughter, pleasure, pain, anger, and virtually any wave of reaction. Love also can be confused with feelings of indigestion and gas. Houses have been built, burned, and banished because of love.

Read the sample essay and answer the following questions.

1. What does the essay define?
2. What is the thesis statement?
3. What other definitions are offered before the thesis statement?
4. How is the essay organized?
5. What methods of definition are used in this essay?

In order to detect the answers to these questions, let's look at the sample writing of *What Is This Thing Called Love?*

In the first paragraph, the author leads in the topic by using another's definition of love, and then points out his purpose of writing this essay: "to embark upon the seemingly difficult task of defining love by looking at the history, explaining what love is not, and examining the uses of love and the results of that usage."

In the second paragraph, the author tries to detect the origin and causes of love.

In the following paragraph, the author tries to define love through the technique of negation, by pointing what love is not, giving readers a clearer understanding of the author's viewpoint.

Then, quite naturally, after all his analysis, the author puts forward his own definition of WHAT LOVE IS in the last two paragraphs.

Language Focus

After the analysis of the structure of the sample essay, let's move to the final part of this lesson: the useful transitional expressions in a definition essay. Here is a list of them for your reference:

1. be defined as…
2. be considered to…
3. be explained in this way…
4. the definition of X is…
5. the explanation of X is…
6. the term X is called/is known as…

7. X is a kind/form/species of...which...
8. The term X has come to be used to refer to...
9. The term X is generally understood to mean...
10. The broad use of the term X is sometimes equated with...
11. The term disease refers to a biological event characterised by...
12. X can be defined as...; it encompasses...
13. The term X is a relatively new name for a Y, commonly referred to...
14. X can be loosely described as a correlation to...

While reading these expressions, it is a good idea to remember some key words which can be used as the most obvious signal words in a definition essay; such words are for the word "definition", such as "define, explain, be known as, refer to, describe" and so forth.

✎ 写定义型作文时，可适当使用以下与"定义"相关的过渡或派生词：define, explain, be known as, refer to, describe 等。

Now, let's work on an exercise. Read the first two paragraphs of the sample essay: *What Is This Thing Called Love*, and identify the transitional expressions used to make definitions.

What Is This Thing Called Love?

A wise man once said that **love is** a wonderful thing. Although this statement leaves sparse room for argument, it does little **to define** what love is beyond the vague realm of "wonderful". It is my duty as a devout romantic to embark upon the seemingly difficult task of **defining** love by looking at the history, **explaining** what love is not, and examining the uses of love and the results of that usage.

The origin of the word is probably the most logical place to start. As with many words in the English language, love is a derivative of the Latin word "causemajoraproblemus" **which means** "You're miserable when you got it and miserable when you don't". The word was created to **explain** the biological phenomenon that existed when certain individuals came into contact with each other and either remained together or went about their lives separately. Regardless of the outcome, the relationship was usually **characteristic** of throat lumps, knotted stomachs, weak knees, temporary loss of language, sweaty palms, dizziness, sneezing, and occasional nausea. Belligerent insanity also resulted. History clearly **illustrates** this. Can we ever forget the face that launched a thousand ships? Federally expressing Van Gogh's ear? The construction of Le Tour Eiffel? All of these were results of love and love lost.

Have you finished the exercise? Let's look at it together now. In Paragraph 1, how many transitional expressions have you found? I've found 4. The first one is "is", next "to define", the third one "defining", and the last one is "explaining".

Let's come to the second paragraph, how many have you found? I've found 4 again: they are "means" "explain" "characteristic" and "illustrates".

Summary

OK, now we've talked so much about definition essays. Before we finish this week's discussion, let's sum up what we've learned. First, we've obtained an overview of what a definition is; we have learned the main types of definition and the standard structure of a definition. We then have learned various methods for defining terms; after that, we have analyzed the organization of definition essays. We finished our Week 11's learning with an analysis of the transitional expressions used in definition essays. Hope all these will be helpful in your own writing practice of the definition essays.

Ⅲ. 写作练习

1. Which of the following topics are suitable for a definition essay?

A. Love   B. Wind   C. Smart Phone   D. Maturity

2. Which of the following definitions are proper?

1) Love is a strong feeling from our parents.

2) Famine is extreme scarcity of food in a region.

3) Gambling is a way to make money without working.

4) A proof is a particular piece of evidence.

5) Neutrality is a state between war and peace.

6) Psychology can be defined as the branch of biological science which studies the phenomenon of conscious life and behavior.

7) To walk is to move each foot forward in turn.

8) Women are the weaker sex in the society.

3. Study the following sample and answer the questions.

Luck

Luck refers to moments of good fortune that happen in everyday life. Luck is putting $0.80 into a vending machine and getting the money back with your snacks. It is a teacher's decision to give a retest on a test where you first scored 30. Luck is finding a used car for sale at a good price at exactly the time when your car rolls its last mile. It is being late for work on a day when your boss arrives later than you do. It is having a new checkout aisle at the supermarket open up just as your cart arrives. The best kind of luck is winning a new TV set on a chance for which you paid only a quarter.

1) How is the term "luck" defined in the first sentence? What's the function of the sentence?

2) How does this paragraph develop its definition?

3) What order(time, space, emphatic) does this paragraph follow?

4. Complete the following paragraph by providing supporting details for the topic sentence.

Rudeness

Rudeness is any behavior exhibited by an individual that is offensive or distasteful to others.

Members of all social classes and people of all ages consider rude behaviors to be socially unacceptable, but the standard has changed over the years. _____
_____
_____
_____.

Today rudeness is not just a matter of forgetting small courtesies. Rudeness is also being impatient and pushy. When people cut into my lane or shove in front of me in line, I get angry.

第12周
议论文写作
（Writing an Argumentative Essay）

≫ I．概述

本周介绍了英语议论文的写作，主要探讨了以下主题：什么是议论文？好的论证有什么特点？如何提出有说服力的论据？如何构思不同类型的议论文？议论文中有哪些常用的过渡词？

首先，议论文是围绕一个有争议的观点来展开的，对于那些无可辩驳、为大众所接受的事实，以及某些个人偏好，写一篇议论文是没有意义的。其次，要有充足的论据，可以被用作论据的事物多种多样，如统计数据、先例、专家意见等，我们可以根据不同的语境挑选，但务必记住证据必须充分、相关和具有代表性。最后，议论文应具有合乎逻辑的论证。作者应尽量避免各种逻辑谬误，努力使用演绎或归纳等推理方法一步步推导、论证自己的论点。

第二次讲座介绍了论证时可以采用的一些方法：比较/对比法、数据引用法、举例/列举法、因果法等。此外，还介绍了两种展开论证的模式：传统的论证模式和罗杰斯模式。其区别主要体现在对相反观点的处理上，是先论证自己的观点还是先提出反对观点。在实践中，我们可以根据不同的话题来决定采用何种模式。

第三、四次讲座主要介绍议论文的实战写作阶段。议论文写作首先要确立论点，推荐使用以下三种方式来提出论点：解决问题式、反驳异议式以及思维路线式。

其次，议论文的典型结构通常包括引论部分、论证主体部分以及结论部分。在引论部分，我们可以先介绍关于主题的各种观点，然后阐明自己的论点。根据文章的不同读者和写作目的，论证部分的结构可以有所不同。可以在论证主体部分提出若干分论点，并对每一个分论点展开论述。在文章的结尾部分，应该呼应引论、重申自己的论点，以起到首尾呼应的效果。

最后，议论文写作中也应该积累一些常用的过渡词，通过这些表示比较、转折、顺序等的关联词汇，使我们的语句过渡更为自然，论证更为有力。

Ⅱ. 慕课讲稿

讲座 1 什么是论证(What Argumentation Is)

知识概要 本讲座首先对本周的讲解内容做了简要的概括，之后阐述了什么是论证以及好的论证所具有的特征。主要内容：1. 论证是一个证明某有争议主题所持观点正确的过程。2. 好的论证通常具有以下特征：首先论证必须围绕一个有争议的观点来展开，对那些无可辩驳、为大众所接受的事实展开论辩毫无意义。其次，论证需要充分的论据来支持所持的观点。最后，论证应采用合乎逻辑的推理，避免各种逻辑谬误。

关 键 词 论证(argumentation)；论点(a debatable point)；论据(evidence)；
逻辑(logic)

Lead-in

During this week, we'll focus on the writing of argumentative essays, and we're going to cover the following subtopics: What is argumentation? What features does good argumentation have? How to make cogent arguments? How to brainstorm and organize different types of argumentative essays? What are some useful transitional expressions in an argumentative essay?

Here in Lecture 1, we're going to deal with the first topic: **What is argumentation?**

Now, take a look at the picture here. In our daily life, we are always faced with controversial situations or dilemmas. Issues such as whether we should ban animal testing or not always lead to arguments, since either the answer "Yes" or "No" may have many proponents who can support their opinions with substantial reasons. What is your own perspective and how can you successfully argue your case?

Similarly, we may also encounter many troublesome problems, so we must analyze and propose solutions for them. For instance, the Internet has become so common in our daily lives that we can hardly imagine a day without it. Yet we are faced with possible problems or even hazards associated with increasing Internet use. What might these problems be, and can we find feasible solutions for them?

All the above situations require us to put forth sound and compelling arguments, either to argue or defend our opinions. How can we make our arguments sound and persuasive?

Objectives

Through Lecture 1, we'll gain a general understanding of argumentation. We'll cover the following two topics: 1) **What is argumentation?** 2) **What are the features of good argumentation?**

Tasks

Let's start with the first topic: What is argumentation?

Argumentation is a process of asserting the soundness of an opinion on a controversial topic.

★ Argumentation always **assumes controversy** and involves **the need to address conflicting viewpoints**.

★ In an argumentative essay, **certain ideas should be made clear and sufficient evidence should be presented**.

★ In an argumentative essay, the writer uses **clear thinking and logic** to convince readers of the soundness of a particular viewpoint.

★ In an argumentative essay, the writer should **demonstrate respect for contrasting viewpoints** and those who hold them.

✎ 论证(Argumentation)论证是证明作者就一个有争议的话题所持的主张或观点正确的过程。论证的基础是存在争议的观点，在论证的过程中，要有明确的观点，并提出充分的证据来支持此观点。

Having an understanding of what argumentation is, we will find it is much easier to identify the main purposes of our argument.

We need to make an argument when we want to assert our opinions, or to find solutions to a problem under discussion; when our opinions are attacked, we will make arguments to defend our own viewpoints, to fight against opposing perspectives, or convince our opponents of the value of our opinions.

Now, on to the second topic: what are **the features of good argumentation**? Generally speaking, good argumentation should consist of the following items:

1. a debatable point;
2. sufficient evidence;
3. good logic;
4. tactful, courteous language.

We are going to explain the items above one by one.

✎ 好的论证通常包含以下几个方面：1)有争议的观点；2)充分的论据；3)好的逻辑；4)礼貌、得体的语言。

Key Points

Let's come to the first item: **a debatable point**.

Please read the following statements and try to think whether they can be used to initiate an argument.

1. Donald Trump was president of the United States.
2. Ba Jin is my favorite author.
3. The ancient Chinese invented papermaking.

It is impossible for anyone to argue with the first statement as it is completely based on verifiable fact. For such a statement, there are no reasonable differing opinions, thus making it pointless to write an argumentative essay about it.

Similarly, the second statement is a personal preference and the third one is a general belief. Neither of them can be regarded as a debatable point; therefore, it would be unnecessary to develop any argument concerning them.

By contrast, if we make some change to these statements, things will be different.

Please read the three statements.

The first one "Donald Trump is the best president the United States has ever had." This statement takes a stance on a highly controversial issue and we will need to persuade readers who disagree with us.

If we change the second and third statements in a similar fashion, we will make them arguable, and thus they would become proper initiators of arguments.

Now, let's look at **evidence**; various items can be used as evidence, ranging from statistics, examples, expert opinions, anecdotes to observations, which we can choose to use in our argumentation within different contexts. The most important thing is that evidence must be sufficient, relevant and representative.

The next item we need to consider is **the proper use of logic**.

The organization of our argumentation should display logical reasoning, using either deductive(演绎的) or inductive(归纳的) methods of reasoning.

Induction is the process of reasoning **from the particular details to the general conclusion. It involves examining particular details such as specific cases, facts, or examples. The conclusion is made based on the evidence coming from the specific details.**

For example, if we have bought a bunch of grapes, when we taste the first grape, it is sour; then we taste the second one, sour too; so is the third one. We then draw this conclusion: The rest of the grapes are probably sour. This reasoning method is induction.

There is another famous example of the inductive reasoning:

To compose his *Politics*, Aristotle studied dozens of constitutions, and from them induced some general principles of political science.

Now, let's talk about **deductive reasoning—the process of reasoning from the general to** the specific.

For example: When we have a major premise like this: No dogs have feathers. We also have a minor premise: Snowball is a dog. Then we can draw a conclusion: Snowball does not have feathers.

In our own practice, we should try to make our writing logically acceptable.

> 推理方法分为两种：归纳推理和演绎推理。归纳推理是指从个别性的前提出发，通过推理，得出一个具有概括性结论的过程；演绎推理则是从一般性的前提出发，通过推导即"演绎"，得出具体陈述或个别结论的过程。

At the same time, we should try to avoid various kinds of logical fallacies and errors; here I have provided several examples of logical fallacies:

1) The Ad Hominem Argument（人身攻击）, which means making personal attacks on individuals instead of refuting their viewpoints.
2) The Strawman Argument（稻草人谬误）, which means you misrepresented someone's argument to make it easier to attack.
   Example: After Will said that we should put more money into health and education, Warren responded by saying that he was surprised that Will hates our country so much that he wants to leave it defenceless by cutting military spending.
3) Argument from Ignorance or a Non-testable Hypothesis（无知或不可检验的谬误）, for example, there is no evidence that ghosts do not exist, so it is concluded that ghosts exist.
4) False Dilemma or Fallacy of the Excluded Middle（排中谬误）, for example, if I prove you wrong, I must be right.
5) Argument from Authority or Tradition（诉诸权威谬误）, for example, it is true because our forefathers declare it is true.
6) Circular Reasoning（循环论证）, for example, people are evil because to be a person is to be evil.
7) Argumentum ad Populum（诉诸群众）, which refers to arguments such as "Everybody knows that…"

There are also many other examples of logical errors, which requires us to be careful as we craft our arguments.

Finally, we need to pay attention to the language. We should be aware that:

To argue is not to quarrel. The force of an argument does not come from abuse, sarcasm or fierce attacks, but arises from the presentation of solid evidence, logical reasoning and careful analysis. Therefore, we shouldn't anger our readers by referring to them or their opinions in

rude or belittling terms. Don't write "Everybody knows that…" or "Only morons (笨蛋) believe that…"

We should neither overstate nor understate matters, and avoid using words like "perhaps" "sometimes" "I think" which invariably weaken the force of our argument.

Summary

Before we finish Lecture 1, let's review what we have mainly talked about.

First, we have learned what argumentation is.

Then, we have identified the features that make for good argumentation.

讲座2 论证方法 (Methods to Present Argumentation)

知识概要 本讲座主要阐述了常见的论证方法以及两种不同的论证模式。**主要内容：**1. 根据不同的辩论主题，论证时可以采用不同的论证方法：比较/对比法、数据引用法、举例/列举法、因果法等。2. 论证过程中通常采用两种不同的论证模式：传统的论证模式及罗杰斯论证模式。其区别主要体现在对相反观点的处理上，是先论证自己的观点还是先提出反对观点。

关 键 词 论证方法 (argumentation method)；传统的论证模式 (classical model of argumentation)；罗杰斯论证模式 (Rogerian model of argumentation)

Lead-in

In this lecture, we are going to discuss **how to present our argument**.

As argument assumes controversy, and that we have to work especially hard to convince our readers of the validity of our position. There are different ways of argument, but it is difficult to identify which ways might be more effective concerning our particular topics. Let's take the example of Animal Testing in Lecture 1 again.

After taking a stance on this controversial issue, we are supposed to find proper ways to support our viewpoints. Suppose our position is: Animal testing is necessary, but should be restricted.

Now comes the hard part. What methods can we use for more effective argumentation? Can we use some examples? Can we cite some data? Can we compare the advantages and disadvantages of animal testing? Can we cite the opinions of well-known philosophers or religious leaders? Or should we argue by a combination of these methods?

Objectives

The objectives of Lecture 2 will help answer this question. They are: 1) **to understand** various methods of presenting argumentation; 2) **to be familiar with two commonly applied models of addressing opposing viewpoints**.

Tasks

Let's read the following essay entitled *Should Animal Testing Be Banned*, and **try to answer the following questions**.

1. What is the issue discussed in the essay?
2. What are the controversial viewpoints surrounding the issue?
3. What is the author's thesis statement? Where does he put it?
4. What methods does the author use to present his argument?

Should Animal Testing Be Banned?

Every year, millions of animals undergo painful suffering or death as a result of scientific research into the effects of drugs, cosmetics and other chemical products. The issue of animal testing has aroused wide-spread concern from the public. While most people think animal testing is necessary, others are upset by what they see as needless suffering. This essay will look at some of the positive and negative aspects of animal testing.

According to a survey made by an animal protecting organization, as many as 46% medical treatments have been developed from experiments on animals. Since animals share many features with humans, scientists use animals to test the safety and effectiveness of newly developed drugs before testing on small groups of patients. Medical teams practise new operation techniques such as transplants on animals, too. Without animal testing, many new drugs would be extremely unsafe.

However, many people are concerned that animals are suffering unnecessarily and cruelly. They do not believe that every new drug needs to be tested on animals, especially with the huge database of knowledge and modern computer models. They are also worried that many animal tests are ineffective, pointing out that some drugs had to be withdrawn from the market despite extensive testing. They particularly feel that animal testing should not be used for non-essential products such as cosmetics, shampoos, soaps, and cleaning products. Furthermore, some people would like to see certain tests replaced and more humane methods used.

We need to make sure that millions of animals who are used for testing new products are treated with the minimum of suffering. Although some animal testing may be unavoidable at present, treating our fellow creatures as mercifully as possible will demonstrate our humanity.

✎ [解析] 本文属于阐述利弊/优缺点的议论文，主要探讨"动物实验是否应该被禁止"这一话题。文章开篇描述了一个社会现象：每年都有许多动物死于新药测试实验，从而引出关于"动物实验"的两种不同观点以及本文的写作目的：探寻"动物实验"的积极影响和消极影响。主体部分分为两段，作者对关于"动物实验"的两种观点进行了论述。首先，作者指出了"动物实验"的必要性；其次，作者指出了"实验动物"遭受的残忍对待，探讨了是否所有的"动物实验"都有必要等问题。在结论段，作者指出，如果"动物实验"确实必须进行，那么"实验动物"也应该受到人道的对待。

Key Points

In this essay, the author discusses a controversial issue—Animal Testing. Concerning this issue, two controversial viewpoints are presented; one is about the necessity and morality of animal testing; the other one questions the necessity of animal testing and worries about the rights of tested animals. The author puts his thesis statement at the essay's end, which seems to be a compromise between the above mentioned viewpoints: Animal testing seems unavoidable, but we must treat the tested animals in a more humane way.

In order to develop his argument, the author uses the following methods: 1) He **compares the positive and negative aspects** of animal testing; 2) He **cites statistics** from some organizations to make the reader aware that animal testing is very prevalent; 3) He **gives examples** of the fields where animal testing has been carried out; 4) He also applies **the cause and effect method** of argumentation to explain why animal testing seems unavoidable.

By a combined use of these various methods, the author easily comes to his conclusion.

Having made an analysis of this sample essay, let's draw some conclusions about the various methods of argumentation.

I won't explain the first four methods listed here since I have just given a detailed explanation about their application in the sample essay.

Let's start with the 5th method: **Chronological**(按发生时间顺序排列的) **argumentation**, which is a journal-style format which progresses point by point, with details about each point given in the order in which it occurred.

The next method is **description argumentation**, which is similar to the chronological argument structure except that, instead of systematically moving from the argument as it was presented at one moment to how it was presented at the next moment, it is a point-by-point explanation of a place, person, or thing.

In our own writing practice, it is not necessary to put all these methods into use; instead, we can decide which way to argue according to different topics we are to discuss.

> 常见的论证方法有以下几种：比较/对比法、引用数据法、举例法、因果关系法、按时间顺序论证法、按事物联系论证法等。通常可以采用两种不同的论证模式：传统的论证模式和罗杰斯论证模式。传统的论证模式通常先提出有争议的主题，然后提出作者的观点。在辩论的过程中，首先以充分的论据来证明作者所持的观点，然后说服读者为什么相反的观点不成立，最后进行总结。罗杰斯论证模式主要通过以下步骤展开：首先提出有争议的主题，之后对与该主题相反的观点进行阐述，并指出作者对这些反对观点持理解和开放的态度，然后阐述作者观点并进行论证，在结论段试图通过论证来说服反对者。这两种论证模式的主要不同在于对相反观点的处理上，是先论证作者的观点还是先提出反对观点。

When planning an argumentative essay, we need to consider viewpoints different from our own. How we accommodate differing points is of vital importance to the success of our argumentation. Our willingness to consider opposing viewpoints will leave readers with the impression that we are fair-minded which may increase their openness to our position. More importantly, we can prove that our own position is more valid by pointing out the limitations or weakness of opposing viewpoints.

Now here are two common strategies to address opposing viewpoints.

Please read the following two essays and try to identify what strategy the author is using to address opposing viewpoints.

Essay 1

Who Should Implement and Dominate Scientific Research Projects

It is universally acknowledged that scientific research plays a vital role in a nation's long-term development and planning. So, when it comes to which side, whether the state or some private enterprises, should implement and dominate scientific research projects, opinions tend to be that governments should totally be responsible for them. But as far as I am concerned, I disagree with this statement, and I will explain why this is the case.

It must be admitted that business tycoons' funding and carrying out scientific research has its own strength. **To begin with**, delegating the management of these scientific research projects to private companies enable governments to concentrate more energy and capital on settling some urgent issues, such as popularising compulsory education, reducing unemployment rate and strengthening the construction of infrastructure. **Besides**, the private firms carrying out scientific research can promote the rapid transformation of science and technology to productivity. That is to say, when a scientific research is proven to be practical, the companies will patent their invention and then put it into practice, which will promote the rapid development of technology and improve people's living standards. In addition, investment in scientific research can raise the prestige of the businesses, which would make them gain more competitive advantages.

Certainly, there is no denying that private businesses controlling scientific research is never without the downsides. **For one thing**, unlike the projects implemented by the state, the privately funded research programmes may lack unified planning and arrangement. **For another**, some private company sponsors are mainly motivated by profit, who are much less likely than the government to pay for unprofitable research projects. The profit incentive causes some scientists to have to concentrate their energy only on projects which are more likely to generate profits.

Taking into account all these factors, we may reach the conclusion that the research funded by private companies and the research supported by governments both have their own merits and demerits. We should not depend too much on one while neglecting the other. So what we need to do is to make full use of their advantages and staying away from the disadvantages.

Essay 2

Charter Schools and Public Schools(School Choice)
Mark Liles

 Considering the many challenges facing public schools, it's understandable that many people would be eager to pursue new options. Supporters of school choice point out that under the current public school system, parents with economic means already exercise school choice by moving from areas with failing or dangerous schools to neighborhoods with better, safer schools. Their argument is that school choice would allow all parents the freedom, regardless of income level, to select the school that provides the best education. Schools would then have to compete for students by offering higher academic results and greater safety. Schools unable to measure up to the standards of successful schools would fail and possibly close. Activists within the school choice movement can be applauded for seeking to improve public education, but the changes they propose would in fact seriously damage public education as a whole.

 One of the biggest dangers of school choice is the power behind large corporations specializing in opening and operating charter schools. Two notable companies are Green Dot, which is the leading public school operator in Los Angeles, and KIPP, which operates 65 schools in 19 different states. These companies represent a growing trend of privatization of public schools by large corporations. It is feared that these corporations could grow to a point that public control of education would be lost. Education policy would be left in the hands of entrepreneurial think tanks, corporate boards of directors, and lobbyists who are more interested in profit than educating students. Education should be left in the hands of professional educators and not business people with MBAs. To do otherwise is not only dangerous, it defies common sense.

 In **Essay 1**, the author discusses the issue of public vs. private sponsorship of scientific research.

 In the introduction, **the author first points out the importance of scientific research and then offers two opposing opinions about the sponsorship of scientific research**. At the end of the introduction, the author presents his thesis statement: He disagrees with the notion of complete government sponsorship.

 Then, in the essay's main body (please look at the words in color), the author **first** discusses reasons why it is necessary for private businesses to carry out scientific research. **Then**, the author continues his discussion by pointing out the downsides of total control of scientific research by private businesses. **In the end**, the author arrives at a thoughtful compromising position, one which rejects a dominant role for the state's sponsorship of research.

 Having made an analysis of Essay 1, we can form a clearer outline of this commonly used strategy of addressing two opposing viewpoints. Please look at the structure and pay attention to **the sequence of argument and refutation**.

In **Essay 2**, the author **first introduces a supportive view of school choice and acknowledges its reasonableness** by summarizing reasons in favor of it.

Then the author points out the central flaw of school choice, which presents a major challenge to its proponents. He then puts forward his own viewpoint.

It is worth noting that the author does not appear to make superficial judgments when introducing the opposing viewpoints; instead his summary seems unbiased.

Different from the **classical model of argumentation** in Essay 1, we can clearly identify a different strategy of addressing the opposing viewpoints in Essay 2, which is known as **Rogerian strategy**(罗杰斯论证).

Let's look at the outline of a typical Rogerian model of argumentation:

First, we present the issue; **then** summarize the opposing arguments, **then** we state our own points and discuss the reasons why the reader should accept our points.

Summary

Before we finish Lecture 2, let's make a brief summary of today's key points.

In this lecture, we have detected various methods of presenting argument; meanwhile, we also discussed two models of addressing the opposing viewpoints.

讲座 3　议论文写作的准备阶段(Pre-writing an Argumentative Essay)

知识概要　本讲座主要阐述了议论文写作准备阶段需要注意的事项：确立合适的论点以及提出论点的方式，同时还介绍了如何创建议论文的基本结构。**主要内容**：1. 议论文写作首先要确立论点，好的论点首先必须具有争议性，其次必须是具体的。2. 论点的提出可以采取下列方式：解决问题式、反驳异议式以及思维路线式。3. 议论文通常由导论、论证和结论三个部分构成。

关 键 词　好论点的标准(criteria for a good thesis statement)；
论点提出的方式(ways to put forward a thesis statement)

Lead-in

In this lecture, we'll go over **the pre-writing stage** of an argumentative essay.

Objectives

I shall first give you some useful instructions on how to write the thesis statement of an argumentative essay. Then we will start to draft the outline of an argumentative essay.

高级综合英语写作教程（慕课版）

Tasks

Let's start with the first topic: how to write a thesis statement.

To write **an effective thesis statement**, we should keep the following criteria in mind. **First, we should avoid factual statements and make sure that our thesis statement is debatable.** Actually, we have already mentioned this point in the first lecture of Week 12 when we considered the features of good argumentation. No need for more discussion of this. **The second key point is that our thesis statement needs to be narrow and specific.**

> 议论文的论点应该符合以下标准：首先，议论文的论点必须是有争议的观点，不应仅仅是事实陈述；其次，论点必须是特定且具体的，要避免空泛的描述。

In order to have a detailed analysis of the second key point, let's read the following two thesis statements and try to find out which one is more suitable.

1. Drug use is detrimental to society.
2. Illegal drug use is detrimental because it encourages gang violence.

The first statement is too broad to argue. First, what is included in the category "drug"? Is the author talking about illegal drug use, recreational drug use (which might include alcohol and cigarettes), or all uses of medication in general? Second, in what ways are drugs detrimental? Is drug use causing deaths? Is drug use changing the moral climate or causing the economy to decline? Finally, what does the author mean by "society"? Is the author referring only to America or to the global population? Does the author make any distinction between the effects on children and adults? There are just too many questions that the claim leaves open. The author could not cover all of the topics listed above, yet the generality of the claim leaves all of these possibilities open to debate.

In the second thesis statement, the topic of drugs has been narrowed down to illegal drugs and the detriment has been narrowed down to gang violence. This is a much more manageable topic.

We can also use qualifiers such as "typically" "generally" "usually" or "on average", which can also help to limit the scope of our claim by allowing for the almost inevitable exception to the rule.

Now, let's consider how to write a thesis statement.

Three ways to write a thesis statement are recommended here.

1. The Question/Answer Format

For example, we can put forth our statement like this:

What can you do to make your marriage divorce-proof? The most important way to make your marriage divorce-proof is to make sure you have carefully prepared for that commitment.

In this way, our answer to the question is our thesis statement. By structuring our thesis statement in a question-answer format, we can successfully arouse the readers' attention.

2. Refute Objections

In this format, we first state one side of the argument and present a statement that refutes it.

While some people think there is no way to divorce-proof your marriage, studies have shown that there are fewer divorces when people carefully prepare for that commitment.

In this way, we can indicate that we have thoroughly considered the controversial opinions on a chosen issue.

3. Roadmap

A "roadmap" format tells in just a few words or in a single sentence each of the main points we will cover.

While some people think there is no way to divorce-proof your marriage, studies have shown that there are fewer divorces when 1) people carefully prepare for that commitment by taking the time to get to know the other person before becoming engaged; 2) by spending time with one another's family and friends; 3) by talking about hot-button issues like finances; and 4) by getting extensive premarital counseling.

This is an example of a really strong thesis statement in which we state a claim, our stance on that claim, and the main points that will back up our stance.

✎ 三种常见的提出论点的方法：解决问题式、反驳异议式以及思维路线式。

Key Points

With the analysis of the thesis statement, we now come to the key point of Week 12's lecture—**the standard outline of an argumentative essay**.

Generally speaking, **a typical five-paragraph topic analytical essay comprises one introductory paragraph, three evidentiary body paragraphs, and a concluding paragraph.**

In **the introductory paragraph**, we could begin our essay by presenting the full range of opinions concerning our topic. Then we need to explicitly state our thesis to make our position clear on the topic and support our argument. In doing so, our readers will immediately know where we stand and it will be easier for them to evaluate the evidence presented.

In **the evidentiary portion of the essay**, we should elaborate on our main argument and provide solid evidence to back up our own position.

In **the concluding paragraph**, we should wrap up the essay by restating why the topic is important and recapping our thesis statement.

Depending on our audience and our purpose for writing, the three body paragraphs could be structured differently. We could choose to provide **the three sub-claims of our main argument** in the body and provide solid evidence to support each of them. This is usually how we should organize our essay.

> **Introduction**
>   —Thesis statement
> **Body**
>   —Sub-claim 1
>   • Topic sentence
>   • Supporting evidence
>   —Sub-claim 2
>   • Topic sentence
>   • Supporting evidence
>   —Sub-claim 3
>   • Topic sentence
>   • Supporting evidence
> **Conclusion**

In this method of organization, it is suggested that we address only one sub-claim in each body paragraph and explicitly state our claim in the topic sentence. In addition, the three sub-claims should be presented in the same sequence as they appear in our thesis statement. This way of organization is straightforward and easy to follow, and thus it is the most frequently adopted structure by novice writers.

Alternatively, we could **choose to build up our evidentiary body by addressing the opposing viewpoints**. Two possible methods of organization are presented as follows:

> **Introduction**
> **Body**
>   —Addressing the opposing viewpoints
>   • Introducing the opposing views
>   • Acknowledging its plausibility
>   • Refuting the opposition
>   —Presenting your sub-claim 1
>   • Topic sentence
>   • Supporting evidence
>   —Presenting your sub-claim 2
>   • Topic sentence
>   • Supporting evidence
> **Conclusion**
>
> **Introduction**
> **Body**
>   —Presenting your sub-claim 1
>   • Topic sentence
>   • Supporting evidence
>   —Presenting your sub-claim 2
>   • Topic sentence
>   • Supporting evidence
>   —Addressing the opposing viewpoints
>   • Introducing the opposing views
>   • Acknowledging its plausibility
>   • Refuting the opposition
> **Conclusion**

The difference between the two possible structures depends on where we want to address the opposing viewpoints, which we discussed in the second lecture of this week's lecture series. No matter which structure we adopt, it is suggested that we clearly indicate how we focus on different sides of the issue.

> 议论文的结构通常由引论、正文和结论三部分组成。根据辩论主题和读者的不同，在正文部分，可以采取以下三种形式：1) 把论点分为若干分论点并逐一展开论证；2) 先驳斥相反观点再提出作者自身的论点并进行论证；3) 对论点展开讨论，然后驳斥相反观点。

Summary

At the end of Lecture 3, let's try to make a summary of today's main points.

In Lecture 3, we have provided some useful instructions for the pre-writing stage. We have talked about general criteria and different formats for composing a thesis statement and the suggested outline for argumentative essays.

讲座 4 议论文写作 (Writing an Argumentative Essay)

知识概要 本讲座主要阐述了议论文的常见类型以及议论文写作中常用的过渡词语和表达方法。**主要内容**：1. 常见的议论文主要有以下三种类型：阐述利弊/优缺点的议论文、问题分析型议论文、问题解决型议论文。2. 根据不同的读者和写作目的，在议论文主体的论证部分可以采用不同的结构。3. 议论文中常用的过渡词语和表达方法。这些表示比较、转折、顺序等的关联词汇使论证时的语句过渡更为自然、论证更为有力。

关 键 词 三种不同的议论文 (three types of argumentative essays)；议论文常用的过渡性表达短语 (transitional expressions for argumentative essays)

Lead-in

In this lecture, we are going to continue with the key points of Week 12, **the writing of an argumentative essay**.

Objectives

First, we shall summarize the different types of argumentative essays, **then** we'll consider how to write problem-solving essays, and finally, we'll learn useful transitional expressions to achieve coherence in argumentative essays.

Tasks

Generally speaking, commonly existing argumentative essays can be divided into three different types. The first is **the argumentative essay which tries to expose controversial attitudes or the pros and cons of a certain thing or issue**. Next is **the topic analytical essay**, in which the author tries to analyze a certain problem in its various aspects. The third type is **the problem-solving essay** which tries to find solutions to certain problems. As in Lecture 3 of this week's instruction, we discussed the suggested outline of the first two essay types; here we would like to focus on writing the problem-solving essay.

✎ 议论文比较常见的类型有以下三种：正反观点/利弊型议论文；分析型议论文；问题解决型议论文。

Key Points

Let's begin with the suggested outline of **a problem-solving essay**.

In **the introductory part**, the author tries to grab the readers' attention by introducing the context of the issue; he then presents his thesis statement with the proposed solution.

The paragraphs of **the main body** of the argument can be divided into **three segments**:

The first segment deals with the analysis of the problem, considering the causes and effects of the problem.

The second segment deals with the solution of the problem: 1) it tries to propose a solution that addresses the problem; 2) it discusses why this solution is an ideal (or at least plausible) solution; 3) the author then tries to figure out how that action or set of actions can be implemented.

A third segment of the body of the argument can be optional; it deals with counter arguments and concessions, trying to address concerns about or opposing claims for the solution and acknowledging the shortcomings of that solution.

In **the conclusion part**, the author restates the significance of the problem and reminds the reader of the benefits found in his solution. Finally, actions are called for regarding the implementation of the solutions.

> 问题解决型议论文的常见结构如下：起始段导入问题，提出作者的论点。主体部分则通过分析问题产生的原因和相关后果，提出解决问题的方法，以及如何实施这些方法；此外，主体部分还可以讨论一些与自己意见相左的观点。在结论部分重申问题的意义，提醒读者通过解决该问题可能获得何种好处，从而呼吁读者采取相应的措施。

Paragraph 1: Introduction
  A. Attention-grabbing hook
  B. Introduce the problem (context)
  C. Thesis statement (main-idea sentence) stating proposed solution

Body:
- **Paragraph 2: The problem**
  Consider causes and effects of the problem
- **Paragraph 3: The solution**
  A. Propose a solution that addresses the problem.
  B. Discuss why this solution is an ideal one.
  C. How can that action or set of actions be implemented?
- **Paragraph 4: Counter arguments and concessions (optional)**
  A. Address concerns about or opposing claims for the solution.
  B. Acknowledge the shortcomings.

Paragraph 5: Conclusion
  A. Restate the significance of the problem.
  B. Remind the reader of the benefits to this solution.
  C. Call to Action.

Now, let's look at the directions for a sample essay, which can illustrate the suggested outline for the problem-solving essay which we have just introduced.

The Internet has transformed the way information is shared and consumed, but it has also created problems that did not exist before. What are the most serious problems associated with the Internet and what solutions can you suggest?

According to the directions, the writer is supposed to compose an essay concerning the problems accompanied by the use of the Internet and then put forward solutions to these problems.

Here is a revised essay from an online article. **Please read it carefully and pay attention to the words in colors which indicate different parts of the essay.**

The Use of the Internet

The enormous growth in the use of the Internet over the last decade has led to radical changes to the way that people consume and share information. Although serious problems have arisen as a result of this, there are solutions.

One of the first problems of the Internet is the ease with which children can access potentially dangerous sites. For example, pornography sites are easily accessible to them because they can register with a site and claim to be an adult. There is no doubt that this affects their thoughts and development, which is a negative impact for the children and for society. Another major problem is the growth of online fraud and hacking. These days, there are constant news stories about government and company websites that have been hacked, resulting in sensitive information falling into the hands of criminals.

It is important that actions should be taken to combat these problems. Governments should ensure that adequate legislation and controls are in place which will prevent youngsters from accessing dangerous sites, such as requiring more than simply confirming that one is an adult to view a site. Companies must also improve their onsite IT security systems to make fraud or hacking much more difficult by undertaking thorough reviews of their current systems for weaknesses. Parents and children should also play their own role. On one hand, parents need to closely monitor the activities of their children and restrict their access to certain sites. On the other hand, children should increase their safety awareness and become more self-disciplined when they are hooked on the Internet.

To conclude, the Internet is an amazing technological innovation that has transformed people's lives, but not without negative impacts. However, with the joint action by governments, businesses and individuals, it can be made a safer place for everyone.

✎ 本文属于问题解决型议论文，主要探讨了互联网的使用给人们的生活带来的诸多变革和问题。面对这些问题，有何解决之道？作者在引论段引出该话题之后，便指出了本文的写作目的：如何解

决互联网带来的负面问题。主体部分分为两段，作者先陈述了与互联网相伴而生的两个问题：一是孩子们很容易接触有潜在风险的网站，二是网络诈骗和黑客现象。然后，作者从各个角度进行了分析，指出：政府应该加强立法，监管未成年人进入危险网站；公司应该加强技术安全防范；父母和孩子也应该注意网络安全。在结论段，作者指出互联网虽然伴随着负面影响，但是在多方共同努力下，一定会营造出一块净土。

Let's look at the outline of this essay in detail. **In the introductory part**, the author describes the context of the topic: the widespread use of the Internet has changed people's way of dealing with information. Then the author puts forth his thesis statement: Though this phenomenon has caused serious problems, solutions can also be found.

In the second and third paragraphs, the author tries to analyze the two existing serious problems and provides feasible solutions found in the efforts of three different parties.

Finally, **in the conclusion part**, the author restates his thesis statement by confirming the solution to the problems.

By structuring the problem-solving essay in this way, the author can cater to the readers' logical thinking process.

Language Focus

We now come to the last part of Week 12's instruction: learning some **effective transitional expressions** for argumentative essays.

There are several types of transitional devices, and each category leads the readers to make certain connections or assumptions about the areas being connected.

Here is a list of some common transitional devices that can be used to cue our readers in a certain way.

Here, we can get **some useful expressions to indicate how to continue, how to compare and how to prove**.

To add

and, again, and then, besides, equally important, finally, further, furthermore, nor, too, next, lastly, what's more, moreover, in addition, first (second, etc.)

To compare

whereas, but, yet, on the other hand, however, nevertheless, on the contrary, by comparison, while, compared with, but, although, conversely, meanwhile, after all, in contrast, although this may be true

To prove

because, for, since, for the same reason, obviously, evidently, furthermore, moreover, besides, indeed, in fact, in addition, in the case of, that is

For instance, if we want to continue our discussion, we may use transitional words such as "moreover" or "in addition" and so on.

If we want to compare two objects, we may use phrases such as "by comparison" or "conversely" and so on.

If evidence is needed, we can use signal words such as "for the same reason" or "in the case of" and so on.

There are **more expressions to show exception and time**.

> **To show exception**
> yet, still, however, nevertheless, in spite of, despite, of course, once in a while, sometimes

> **To show time or sequence**
> immediately, thereafter, soon, after a few hours, finally, then, later, previously, formerly, first (second, etc.), next, and then

> **To repeat**
> in brief, as I have said, as I have noted, as has been noted

> **To emphasize**
> definitely, extremely, obviously, in fact, indeed, in any case, absolutely, positively, naturally, surprisingly, always, forever, eternally, never, emphatically, unquestionably, without a doubt, certainly, undeniably, without reservation

For instance, we can use "despite" or "nevertheless" to indicate the existence of exceptions. If we want to indicate time, we can use phrases such as "previously" or "next".

Meanwhile, if we need to repeat or to emphasize prior concepts, we can use phrases such as "in brief" or "without doubt" and so on.

Also, we can get **some useful expressions to show sequence, to give examples and to summarize or conclude**.

> **To show sequence**
> first (second, etc.), A (B, etc.), and so forth, next, then, following this, at this time, now, at this point, after, afterward, subsequently, finally, consequently, previously, before this, simultaneously, concurrently, thus, therefore, hence, next, and then, soon

> **To give an example**
> for example, for instance, in this case, in another case, on this occasion, in this situation, take the case of, to demonstrate, to illustrate, as an illustration

> **To summarize or conclude**
> in brief, on the whole, sum up, to conclude, in conclusion, as I have shown, as I have said, hence, therefore, accordingly, thus, as a result, consequently, on the whole

Novice writers may find it very difficult to use these transitional phrases, but constant practice will lead them to proficiency.

✎ 议论文的习作中如果能够恰当地使用一些表示比较、转折、递进、顺序、举例等的关联词汇，能够使论证过程更为自然，论证更为有力。

Summary

Let's sum up what we've learned. First, we've gotten an overview of argumentation and we have learned the features of good argumentation. We then learned various methods to present argument; after that, we analyzed the organization of argumentative essays. We've finished Week 12's learning with an analysis of transitional expressions in argumentative essays.

All these items will be helpful as you write your own argumentative essays.

Ⅲ. 写作练习

1. Which of the following statements are proper to be used as a thesis statement in an argumentative essay?

1) Foreign languages should be taught in nurseries or kindergartens.

2) There are many languages in the world.

3) Olympic champions bring honors to their motherland.

4) Olympic champions make more contribution to the motherland than scientists.

2. Match the following statements with their respective logical fallacies.

1) Boxing is a dangerous sport because it is unsafe.

2) Clocks are structured in a certain way, and so is the universe. Since the clock is man-made, then the universe must also have a maker.

3) The barber is the "one who shaves all those, and those only, who do not shave themselves". The question is, does the barber shave himself?

4) He is a complete liar. How can you take his words?

    a. Weak Analogy

    b. Attacking the Person

    c. False Dilemma

    d. Circular Argument

3. Try to fill in the blanks with proper transitional words to complete the following essay.

Receiving a university education is important to many young people, 1) _____ they can find employment easily in the future. Those people who support government spending on education think that some students do not enroll because of learning costs. My personal view is that students should pay tuition, 2) _____ the disadvantaged can receive financial assistance from the government.

If higher education is not free of charge, students will study hard and take this educational opportunity seriously. They understand the financial cost of completing a degree, 3) _____ they make a conscious effort to finish all assignments and pass all exams in order to gain the qualification on time. 4) _____, in cases where young people have free access to education, they will possibly take it for granted and fail exams from time to time.

Another benefit of charging tuition fees is that it can lighten the burden on the government. More money can be used in primary and secondary education, 5) _____ can reduce illiteracy and prepare the next generation for university-level courses. Subsidies can be provided for those students who enroll in post-graduate courses to promote technological innovation.

6) _____, young people from less well-off backgrounds can be exempted from tuition. This can encourage these young people to attend college to acquire knowledge and skills, which can improve their career prospects. This can close the gap between haves and have-nots and help build a fair society. 7) _____, tuition fees may force them to drop out of college and make it difficult for them to reach their potential.

8) _____, the government should provide financial support according to students' needs to ensure that they have access to education. Students from deprived backgrounds should be exempt from tuition fees, while the abolition of tuition for all students is not realistic.

1) A) however   B) while   C) because   D) so
2) A) so   B) however   C) still   D) while
3) A) in contrast   B) so   C) because   D) since
4) A) In contrast   B) Finally   C) Because   D) Since
5) A) what   B) which   C) that   D) when
6) A) To begin with B) By far   C) All in all   D) On the other hand
7) A) Conversely   B) Initially   C) Primarily   D) Secondly
8) A) To begin with B) To summarize   C) By far   D) On the other hand

4. Please list the pros and cons for college students to take a part-time job, and then write an essay on the following topic: Should College Students Take Part-time Jobs?

第13周
学术论文写作 I（Academic Writing I）

▶▶ I. 概述

学术论文写作主要是为撰写英文论文做准备，这部分内容将介绍学术论文写作的要素、步骤和注意事项，包括整体介绍、准备题目、展开文献综述、做开题报告、撰写论文引言、描述材料和方法、报告和讨论结果、撰写研究结论、撰写摘要以及引用文献。这些内容将在第13周和第14周讲解。

本周课程内容包括：学术论文写作介绍、如何拟论文题目和主旨陈述、如何写文献综述、如何写开题报告、如何写引言。

▶▶ II. 慕课讲稿

讲座 1 学术论文写作介绍（Overview of Academic Writing）

知识概要 学术论文包括引言、材料与方法、事实与数据、研究结果或发现、讨论（研究结果）及结论。写作时一般包括以下五个步骤：选题、开题报告、事实/数据收集及评估、撰写初稿及各稿修改、终稿样张。学术文体使用半正式或正式措辞，并且在表述上力求达到精确、客观。**主要内容**：1. 识别不同类型的学术写作；2. 了解学术论文的结构；3. 了解论文写作的步骤；4. 了解不同的写作文体。

关 键 词 basic component part（基本组成部分）；step of writing（写作步骤）；academic style（学术文体）

Lead-in

This chapter includes the following six parts: **lead-in**, **objectives**, **tasks**, **key points**, **language focus**, and **summary**.

The students especially find the written demands of their courses extremely challenging. On top of the complexity of the vocabulary of academic English they have to learn a series of conventions in style, referencing and organisation. Academic Writing is a flexible seminar that allows students to practise the academic writing skills which are most important for their studies. The framework of the unit has been made as simple as possible to allow users to find what they want quickly. It will include 10 lectures:

1. Overview of Academic Writing;
2. How to Prepare the Title and Thesis Statement;
3. How to Present a Literature Review;
4. How to Make a Thesis Proposal;
5. How to Write the Introduction;
6. How to Describe the Materials and Methods Used in Research;
7. How to Report and Discuss the Results of Research;
8. How to Write the Conclusion;
9. How to Write the Abstract;
10. How to Cite the References.

Objectives

- Identify different types of academic writing assignments.
- Learn the organization of an academic paper.
- Know the steps of paper writing.
- Get to know some elements of the style of academic writing.

Tasks

Some of the terms used to describe different types of academic writing assignments can be confusing. Students need to be clear about the basic terms.

1. Basic terms

Students may have to produce various types of written work as part of their courses. Discuss the following writing assignments with your partner. Then complete the table to show their main purpose and usual approximate length.

Type	Purpose	Length
report		
project		
essay		
thesis/dissertation		
article/paper		

Answer:

A report is a description of something a student has conducted in an experiment or in a survey. It is as short as 1,000-2,000 words. **A project** refers to research conducted either individually or in a group on a subject chosen by the student(s). It is usually 1,000-3,000 words long. **An essay** is actually a short piece of writing used to assess coursework or on a particular subject chosen by the teacher. An essay needs to be 1,000 to 5,000 words long. **A thesis or a dissertation** is a long piece of writing on a certain subject chosen by the student for final assessment in pursuit of Master's/PhD degree. Generally, the student is supposed to complete one between 30,000 to 70,000 words. The last type is **an article or a paper**, which refers to a piece of writing published in an academic journal. The proper length of such a piece is between 5,000 to 10,000 words.

Type	Purpose	Length
report	to describe something a student has conducted, e.g. an experiment/a survey	1,000 – 2,000
project	research conducted either individually or in a group on a subject chosen by student(s)	1,000 – 3,000
essay	a piece of writing used to assess coursework/a particular subject chosen by the teacher	1,000 – 5,000
thesis/dissertation	a long piece of writing on a certain subject chosen by the student for final assessment in Master's/PhD course	30,000 – 70,000
article/paper	writing published in an academic journal	5,000 – 10,000

Now let's take a look at the terms concerning organization of those texts mentioned above.

2. Organization of texts

Pay attention to the following terms in italics:

Shorter texts, e.g. essays, are normally organized in the form:

Introduction > Main Body > Conclusion

[Depending on subject area], **longer texts**, e.g. dissertations and articles, may include:

Abstract > Contents > Introduction > Main Body > Case Study > Discussion > Findings > Conclusion > Acknowledgements > Bibliography/References > Appendices

Key Points

First of all, let's have a bird's view of the component parts of an academic writing.

Component parts of an academic paper

1) **Introduction**, which presents the background of the research and the issue to be dealt with;

2) **Materials** and **methods** used in the research;
3) **Facts** and **figures** used in the analysis, presentation of various perspectives on the central issue and forms of evaluative argument;
　* Learning how to present this data and make sound arguments in a coherent and convincing way is a very major part of learning to write well.
4) **Research results** or **findings**;
5) **Discussion of research results** and **conclusion**.

Each of these parts is important in itself, yet they do not call for equal attention or equal treatment in the paper. You may elaborate upon some of them more than the others.

✎ 学术论文每一部分本身都很重要，但你可能会更详细地阐述其中一些部分。

Steps of paper writing

A postgraduate student also needs to be familiar with steps of paper writing.

Paper writing generally follows five steps, which are:

1) Topic selection;
2) Thesis proposal;
3) Data collection and evaluation;
4) Creating first draft and subsequent revisions of the paper;
5) Finalizing of the paper.

The first three steps constitute the main preparatory stages. Careful preparation helps academic writing proceed smoothly and effectively.

Good writing is largely a matter of effective imitation and disciplined thinking about the nature of your argument and how to present it. Therefore, obtain copies of highly regarded scientific papers in your research area, including papers in the journal to which you plan to submit your current work. Notice how these papers are written.

For example: How are they structured, and how long do the various sections tend to be? What types of subheadings, if any, tend to be included? How many figures and tables, and what types are typical? Especially if you are a non-native speaker of English, what seem to be some standard phrases that you could use in presenting your own work? Using published papers as models can prepare you to craft a manuscript that will be suitable to submit.

Research and academic writing are often a recursive process, especially in the preparatory stages. It is only after constant efforts, repeated modification and alternations that you get everything finalized. Sometimes your thesis will be done in collaboration with a thesis advisor.

Language Focus

Academic writing attempts to be **precise**, **semi-formal**, **impersonal** and **objective**. However, this will vary among disciplines. Study the style of this paragraph and underline any examples of **poor style**.

A lot of people think that the weather is getting worse. They say that this has been going on for quite a long time. I think that they are quite right. Research has shown that we now get storms etc. all the time.

Using these guidelines, we can analyze the paragraph above.

"A lot of people think…" is an imprecise expression. Readers will ask: how many is a lot? The word "weather" needs to be replaced by "climate". The other imprecise expressions include "quite a long time" "Research" and "storms", etc. Additionally, the original paragraph uses informal verbal phrases such as "getting worse" and "going on"; and informal pronouns such as "They(say)" "I(think)" and "we(now get)".

A lot of people think…	Imprecise—how many is a lot?
…the weather…	Imprecise—weather is short-term
…getting worse…	Informal
They say…	Informal, use of pronoun
…going on…	Informal phrasal verb
…quite a long time.	Imprecise—how long is this?
I think…	Informal, personal phrase
Research…	Vague—whose research?
…we now get…	Informal
…storms etc…	Vague
…all the time.	Over-generalized

The paragraph can be rewritten:

It is widely believed that the climate is deteriorating. It is claimed that this process has been continuing for nearly 100 years. This belief appears to be supported by McKinley (1997), who shows a 55% increase in the frequency of severe winter gales since 1905.

It is difficult to give rules for academic style which apply to all subject areas. The following are **general guidelines for academic style**:

a) Use standard English instead of idiomatic or colloquial vocabulary.

b) Avoid contractions: *don't*, *can't*. Use the full form: *do not*, *cannot*.

c) Use the more appropriate formal negative forms, such as *no*, *little and few*.

Namely, use *no* instead of *not…any*.

Use *little* instead of *not…much*.

Namely, use *few* instead of *not…many*.

For example, instead of saying "The analysis didn't yield *any* new results.", we say

"The analysis yielded *no* new results."

This problem *doesn't* have *many* viable solutions. → <u>This problem *has few* viable solutions.</u>

d) Avoid the following (informal words such as *like*, *thing*, *lots of*, *little/big*, and *get* phrases).

For example, avoid using *like* for introducing examples. Use *such as* or *for instance*.

Avoid using *thing* and combinations: *nothing* or *something*. Use *factor*, *issue* or *topic*.

Avoid using *lots of*. Use *a significant/considerable number*.

Avoid using *little/big*. Use *small/large*.

Avoid using *get* phrases such as *get better/worse*. Use *improve* and *deteriorate*.

e) Limit the use of "run on" expressions, such as *and so forth* and *etc*.

These semiconductors can be used in robots, CD players, *etc*. →

<u>These semiconductors can be used in robots, CD *players, and other electronic devices*.</u>

f) Avoid adverbs that show your personal attitude: *luckily*, *remarkably*, *surprisingly*.

g) Avoid using two-word verbs such as *go on* or *bring up* if there is a suitable synonym. Use *continue* or *raise*.

h) Avoid addressing the reader as "you". Instead, use passive voice.

You can see the results in Table 1. →<u>The results can be seen in Table 1.</u>

i) Be as precise as possible when dealing with facts or figures. Avoid phrases such as *about a hundred* or *hundreds of years ago*. If it is necessary to estimate numbers, use *approximately* rather than *about*.

j) Do not use question forms such as "What were the reasons for the decline in wool exports?" Instead use statements: There were four main reasons for the decline…

 学术文体在表述上要精确、客观，避免使用模糊或口语化表达。例如，"A lot of people think…"和"quite a long time"是不精确的表达方式，因为读者会问：多少是很多？多久是很久？还要避免使用口语化的动词短语，如"get 短语"和表示"继续"的"go on"等。避免使用主观性代词"I"或don't/can't 这类缩略表达，或非正式的否定式，如"not…many"等。

Summary

Writing an academic text in English, you need to:

◇ Know the basic component parts
◇ Follow the steps of writing
◇ Write with structural complexity
◇ Avoid casual style
◇ Distinguish formal and informal words and phrases
…

The checklist for writing in academic English is not complete. Use the Internet, books, textbooks to find out what other conventions could be applied to using academic English.

讲座 2 如何拟论文题目和主旨陈述
(How to Prepare the Title and Thesis Statement)

知识概要　论文题目通常由名词短语、动名词短语和介词短语构成，应尽量简短。主旨陈述应提出有力的论点，而非浅触某一论题。主旨陈述应确切，避免模糊不清或过于宽泛，也应避免使用 everyone, everything 或绝对化词语。学术写作多使用正式动词。**主要内容**：1. 理解命题中的关键动词；2. 学会缩小论文题目；3. 学会初拟主旨句；4. 了解正式文体中的常用动词。

关 键 词　prepare a title（准备题目）；thesis statement（主旨陈述）；formal verb（正式动词）

Lead-in

1. Most academic written assignments begin with a title, and students must be quite clear about what question the title is asking before starting to plan the essay and do research concerning the topic. This understanding will then determine the organisation of the essay. For example: *Education is the most important factor in national development. Discuss the above statement.* Here the key word is *discuss*. Discussing involves examining the benefits and drawbacks of something.

2. In preparing a title for a thesis or a paper, you need to choose all words in the title with great care. A good title is defined as the fewest possible words that adequately describe the contents of the paper. Words that appear at the start of the title, such as "Studies on" "Investigations on" and "Observations on", are superfluous and therefore waste words. An opening "A" "An" or "The" is also an unneeded word. They are useless for indexing purposes. Sometimes you need a title for a presented paper to be "catchy", so people will want to come to your session and hear your paper.

 小心地选择题目中的所有单词，使用尽可能少的词来充分描述论文的内容。出现在标题开头的短语，如"Studies on""Investigations on"和"Observations on"是多余的，可以删除，也无须使用冠词"A""An"或"The"开头，因为它们对于索引毫无帮助。

Objectives

- Understand the key verbs in the title of written work.
- Learn to narrow down the title of a paper.
- Learn to draft the preliminary thesis.
- Know verbs used in formal writing.

Tasks

The commonly used verbs in essay titles include:

> define, describe, analyze, compare and contrast, examine, state, evaluate, suggest, summarize

Task 1

Underline the key words in the following titles of written assignments and consider what they are asking you to do.

a) Define Information Technology (IT) and outline its main applications in medicine.

b) Compare and contrast the appeal process in the legal systems of Britain and the USA.

c) Evaluate the effect of mergers in the motor industry in the last ten years.

d) Trace the development of primary education in China. Illustrate some of the issues currently facing this sector.

Answer:

a) define: give a definition; outline: describe the main features

b) compare: examine the similarities; contrast: look at the differences

c) evaluate: consider the value

d) trace: describe the main features; illustrate: give examples

Task 2

The following terms are also commonly used in essay titles. Match the terms to the definitions on the right.

analyze	give a clear and simple account
describe	make a proposal and support it
examine	deal with a complex subject by giving the main points
state	divide into sections and discuss each critically
suggest	give a detailed account
summarize	look at the various parts and their relationships

> **Answer:**
> analyze: look at the various parts and their relationships
> describe: give a detailed account
> examine: divide into sections and discuss each critically
> state: give a clear and simple account
> suggest: make a proposal and support it
> summarize: deal with a complex subject by giving the main points

Key Points

Next, you need to pay special attention to the key points. The first is still on how to prepare the title.

1 Prepare the title

1) The title of your paper may not be exactly the same as your research question or your thesis statement, but **the title should clearly convey the focus, purpose and meaning of your research**.

In terms of the structure of a title, it is mainly a noun phrase, gerund phrase, or a prepositional phrase. Sometimes, it can be a complete sentence. But for beginners, sentences are not recommended. The followings are some acceptable titles:

> Juvenile Delinquency as the Result of Television
> Death Penalty—Is It Beneficial or Unfavorable?
> Children's Punctuation: An Analysis of Errors in Period Placement
> Abnormal Muscular Tension Caused by Paspertin: Report of 12 Cases

2) **Narrow down the title if it is general, and make it specific.** "Sino-U.S. Relations" or "Hemingway's works" are general topics. It is important to realize that a huge topic usually requires you to do a book-length project. For a typical research paper, it's much better to do a thorough job on a smaller topic than treat a big topic in a superficial, touch-and-go fashion. A much more specific topic can save your hours of aimless reading in the library. The narrower titles could be:

> Henry Kissinger's Role in the Normalization of Sino-U.S. Relations
> Sportsmanship Reflected in Bullfight Scenes in *The Sun Also Rises*

论文题目应该清楚地传达研究的重点、目的和意义。如果题目过于宽泛，就需要缩小题目的范围，使之具体化。

2 Prepare the Thesis Statement

The second key point is on how to prepare the thesis statement. Your thesis statement may be the answer to your research question and/or a way to clearly state the purpose of your research. Thesis is the sentence or two that states what your essay is about. It includes **topic**, the **central point**, and sometimes **a preview** of the main ideas. A preview(预告) here means a description of the major ideas that you release in advance before more details are available in the paper.

Here is an example:

◇ Working mothers have changed the character of the American family by contributing a second paycheck, by popularizing day care, and by creating a new division of labor in the home.

In the example, what are the topic, central point and preview of the main ideas respectively? In this case, the topic is on working mothers. The **central point** is an argument, "Working mothers have changed the character of the American family". The **main ideas to be discussed** include three aspects: the contribution of a second paycheck; the popularization of day care; a new division of labor in the home.

The thesis statement is supposed to be specific. Here is an example of a too broad statement:

◇ The Catholic Church's influence on the formation of labor unions in the nineteenth century was extremely significant.

Revision:

◇ The Catholic Church, by means of the pulpit and the purse, greatly influenced the labor movement in the United States during the final decades of the nineteenth century.

Additionally, **the thesis statement is generally located near the end of the introduction**; sometimes, in a long paper, the thesis will be expressed in several sentences or in an entire paragraph.

✎ 主旨陈述通常是用来陈述论文内容的一两个句子。它包含论题、中心论点，有时还涵盖主要观点。主旨陈述要尽量具体，常放在引言部分的结尾处。

Language Focus

A feature of most academic writing is a tendency to use rather formal verbs to express the writer's meaning accurately.

◇ ...supply of energy required to <u>accelerate</u> the growth...

◇ ...the development that is <u>envisaged</u> here needs to be not only sustainable...

✎ In spoken English we would be more likely to use *speed up* and *imagined*.

Read the following sentences carefully and complete the exercises. Select the better alternative in each sentence.

a) The survey proved/yielded a surprising amount of information on student politics.
b) This question arose/manifested when older students were examined.
c) Darwin held/indicated very strong views on this issue.
d) One of the chimpanzees supplemented/exhibited signs of nervousness.

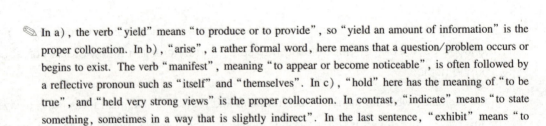

✎ In a), the verb "yield" means "to produce or to provide", so "yield an amount of information" is the proper collocation. In b), "arise", a rather formal word, here means that a question/problem occurs or begins to exist. The verb "manifest", meaning "to appear or become noticeable", is often followed by a reflective pronoun such as "itself" and "themselves". In c), "hold" here has the meaning of "to be true", and "held very strong views" is the proper collocation. In contrast, "indicate" means "to state something, sometimes in a way that is slightly indirect". In the last sentence, "exhibit" means "to show" while "supplement" means "to add something to it in order to improve it".

Answer: a) yielded   b) arose   c) held   d) exhibited

Summary

Here is a checklist for you to prepare the title and thesis statement.

> ◇ A good title is defined as the fewest possible words that adequately describe the contents of the paper and stimulate audience interest.
> ◇ A title is mainly a noun phrase, gerund phrase, or a prepositional phrase.
> ◇ The thesis statement should make a strong point about your topic; it should not simply name a topic.
> ◇ The thesis statement should express a proposition, an opinion, or a point of view. It should not simply repeat facts or summarize findings.
> ◇ The thesis statement should be specific. It should avoid vague or universal statements and avoid absolute or all-inclusive words such as "everyone" "everything" "good" or "successful".

讲座3 如何写文献综述（How to Present a Literature Review）

知识概要 文献综述要求学生对现有文献进行思辨式分析和评价，以引出研究的意义与价值。概要写作常用于概括文献资料，不仅要求替换原来的词语，也要求改变句子的结构和语言风格，且表达要清晰。按照 Swales 的观点，引用文献时常用三种时态：一般过去时、现在完成时和一般现在时。**主要内容**：1. 知道文献综述是什么及其重要性；2. 学会在文献中定位关键论点及议题；3. 学会概括及衔接论点不同的资料；4. 了解引用文献时常用的三种时态。

关 键 词 literature review（文献综述）; summarize source（概括资料）; tense in citation（引文中的时态）

Lead-in

The literature review is intended to critically present the available literature which is relevant to the research topic.

The student should review and analyze the existing literature to provide a better understanding of the subject. It shows the depth of knowledge the student has about the topic and exhibits his/her skills to critically evaluate and present the currently available literature.

It provides the reader with a better understanding of the available methods, the advantages and limitations of those methods and their utility in specific settings. It helps in rationalizing your choice of methods or procedures for the study. The use of literature reviews varies greatly among different disciplines, and that the student needs to consult his/her advisor to see what the conventions are in a particular discipline.

It thus locates gaps in knowledge and reveals areas where original research can be done. This is how one finds **a research question**.

> 文献综述旨在批判性地呈现与研究课题相关的现有文献。通过回顾和分析这些文献，学生可以更好地理解课题，并选择合理的研究方法或程序设计。文献综述也用于定位现有研究的空白，并揭示可以进行创新研究的领域，进而提出研究问题。

Objectives

- Know what a literature review is and its significance.
- Learn to locate the key points/issues in a text.
- Learn to summarize and combine sources and what to do when sources disagree.
- Know the three patterns of tense usage in citation.

Tasks

Task 1   Locate the key points/issues in a text.

When preparing to write an essay you may be concerned with only one aspect of a text, so your key points should relate only to the topic you are examining.

Suppose you are preparing an essay on <u>The application of DNA research to the development of vaccines</u>, what information do you think will be relevant to your research?

Read carefully the following text and underline the relevant parts.

New Light on the Plague

The plague, which first struck Europe in the sixth century, was one of the great disasters in history. In the fourteenth century it became the Black Death, when it may have killed one third of the entire population. The microbe that causes the disease lives on rats, and is passed on to humans by the bite of a flea. It still survives today, though outbreaks are less deadly: the World Health Organization receives reports of 3,000 cases annually. Scientists believe that the microbe was originally a stomach infection, but evolved into a more lethal disease about 1,500 years ago.

Now the genetic code of the plague bacterium has been "read" by scientists; a total of 465 million "letters" of DNA. They believe that this will help in the development of vaccines for the plague, one of which has begun clinical trials. In parts of Africa drug-resistant strains of the disease have evolved, which gives added importance to the work, as does the threat that the plague might be used as an agent of bacteriological warfare.

What is your answer to the question? **The suggested answer** is the second paragraph starting with "Now the genetic code of the plague bacterium has been 'read' successfully by scientists; a total of 465 million 'letters' of DNA." Do you agree? The first paragraph is mainly about the history of the plague and the disasters it has caused, so you may think the information is also critical since it highlights the social benefit of such research. However, if you examine the key words in the essay title again, such as "application" "DNA research" and "vaccines", you will agree that the initial paragraph seems to be less relevant to the student's present research.

Task 2 Make notes to identify the key points for your purpose.

Study the following example, and pay special attention to the key points in italic. Try to make notes from them.

Why Women Live Longer

Despite the overall increase in life expectancy *in Britain* over the past century, *women still live significantly longer than men.* In fact, in 1900 men could expect to live to 49 and women to 52, a difference of three years, while *now the figures are* 74 and 79, which shows that the gap has increased to five years. *Various reasons have been suggested for this situation*, such as the possibility that men may die earlier because they take more risks. But a team of British *scientists have recently found a likely answer in the immune system*, which protects the body from diseases. *The thymus is the organ which produces the T cells* which actually combat illnesses. Although both sexes suffer from deterioration of the thymus as they age, *women appear to have more T cells in their bodies than men of the same age.* It is this, the scientists believe, that *gives women better protection* from potentially fatal diseases such as influenza and pneumonia.

Sample note is as follows:

> ◇ British women live longer than men: 79/74
> ◇ Reasons? New research suggests immune system > thymus > T cells
> ◇ Women have more T cells than men = better protection

Let's take a look at the sample note, and compare it with the original sentences in italic. We can find that those key points presented by the paragraph have all been set down briefly as notes. The notes may help us easily memorize the key information that we have read in a rather long text. With the help of the notes, we can recall that now.

British women are expected to live longer than men. The average life span for the two groups are 79 and 74 respectively. What are the reasons? A new research suggests an answer lies in the immune system. The scientists have found that the thymus is the organ which produces the T cells which actually combat illnesses, and women appear to have more T cells in their bodies than men of the same age. That gives women better protection.

You can put all these types of notes together in one file. When you want to remember where you have found sources for a particular issue, you can search key words in the file. This is useful for dissertations, where you might have hundreds of sources.

Task 3   Use the skill of summarizing.

In reviewing literature students often have to summarize part of a book or journal article. The summary may be just one or two sentences, to explain the main idea of the article, and perhaps compare it with another summarized text, or it might be necessary to include much more detail. A good summary should not distort the original in main features, and the expression should be clear. Students need to follow a series of steps to summarize until the process becomes more automatic.

a) Read the text carefully and check key vocabulary.
b) Underline or highlight the key points/main ideas.
c) Make notes of these, taking care to use your own words/paraphrase.
d) Write the summary using the notes, re-organizing the order of the ideas where necessary.
e) Check the summary to make sure no important points/ideas have been omitted or distorted.

> 概要写作技能是写文献综述时必备的技能之一。开始练习时，学生可以刻意遵循一定步骤，直到形成良好的习惯。学生可遵循以下步骤：1) 仔细阅读原文，确认关键术语；2) 把核心观点及重要观点用下划线或彩笔标记出来；3) 做笔记，注意要改用自己的词语和句式；4) 基于笔记撰写概要，必要时调整观点之间的顺序；5) 检查，以确定没有遗漏或歪曲原文中的重要观点。

Key Points

Next, you need to pay special attention to the key points. The first is on how to combine different sources in a literature review.

1. Combining sources

Most essays require the writer to read more than one book or article. The differences between the ideas of different writers may be the focus of the essay. The writer needs to know the ways of presenting such contrasting views, especially when they seem to disagree.

Below are two sources used for an essay titled *Should Genetically Modified (GM) Foods Have a Role in Future Agriculture?* **Read the sources first, and then try to draft the essay extract.**

Source A   Genetic modification (GM) is the most recent application of biotechnology to food, which can also be called genetic engineering or genetic manipulation. The phrase "Genetically Modified Organisms" or GMOs is used frequently in the scientific literature to describe plants and animals which have had DNA introduced into them by means other than the "natural" process of an egg and a sperm. New species have always evolved through natural selection by means of random genetic variation. Early farmers used this natural variation to selectively breed wild animals, plants and even micro-organisms such as yogurt cultures and yeasts. They produced domesticated variants better suited to the needs of humans, long before the scientific basis for the process was understood. Despite this long history of careful improvement, such procedures are now labelled "interfering with nature".

Source B   Genetic modification (GM) is in fact far more than a mere development of selective breeding techniques. Combining genetic material from species that cannot breed naturally is an interference in areas which may be highly dangerous. The consequences of this kind of manipulation cannot be foreseen. It seems undeniable that these processes may lead to major benefits in food production and the environment. There is no doubt, for example, that some medical advances may have saved millions of lives. However, this level of technology can contain a strong element of risk. Our ignorance of the long-term effects of releasing GM plants or even animals into the environment means that this step should only be taken after very careful consideration.

Here is the model essay extract. Read carefully and answer the following questions.

Model writing—Integrating sources

It has been claimed that GM technology is not different from breeding techniques which have been practised by man for thousands of years. **Source A** *states* that this process is similar to natural selection and *remarks*: "such procedures are now labelled 'interfering with nature'". On the other hand, **Source B** *considers* that, although GM technology could bring considerable benefits in medicine and agriculture, it is quite different from traditional processes of selection. He *believes* that crossing the species barrier is a dangerous step and that there is insufficient knowledge of the long-term results of such developments.

In the essay extract, the writer uses **a mixture of direct quotes and summaries of arguments**.

   a) Find an example of each.
   b) What phrase does the writer use to mark the point where he moves from dealing with Source A to Source B?
   c) List all the phrases used to introduce summaries.

The starting sentence in italic is the summary of Source A and Source B. The sentence inside quotation marks is a direct quote: such procedures are now labelled "interfering with nature". For Question b), the linking phrase the writer uses is "on the other hand". The phrases, "It has been claimed that..." "Source A states that..." "Source B considers that..." "He believes that...", are used to introduce summaries.

> **Answer**:
> a)(The underlined sentences)
> b) On the other hand
> c) It has been claimed that...; Source A states that...; Source B considers that...; He believes that...

When crafting an extended passage which contains numerous elements of information and analysis, students should make sure these points follow each other in a logical order. Sometimes an outline is needed so that they can make sure they have created a logical and rhetorically effective structure for their presentation of information.

The second key point is on how to avoid plagiarism.

Avoiding plagiarism

You have committed plagiarism when you:

- copy a phrase, a sentence, or a longer passage from a source and do not give credit to the original author;
- summarize or paraphrase someone else's ideas without acknowledging the source;
- allow someone else to write significant portions of your document for you without admitting to the help; and
- forget to place quotation marks around another writer's words.

To avoid the problem of accidental plagiarism, get into the habit of clearly documenting the words and ideas you obtain from other sources during the research phase. Now there are sites, such as CNKI, where you can scan your text for plagiarism. You need to consult your advisor about the sites.

Language Focus

According to John M. Swales, there are three patterns of tense usage in citations. **Past tense** is usually used in reference to single studies; in the given example, the investigation is conducted by a single researcher, Jones in 1987. **Present perfect tense** can be mainly found in reference to research areas; the first sentence in Pattern II starts with "There have been several investigations into...", indicating "the causes of illiteracy" becomes a research area which has involved different researchers. In Pattern III, **present tense** tends to be used to show the current state of knowledge, neither a single scholar nor a group of scholars. Now read again to deepen our understanding of the general differences.

Three patterns of tense usage in citation(John M. Swales, 182–183):

I. Past—reference to single studies

> ◇ Jones(1987) *investigated* the causes of illiteracy.
> ◇ The causes of illiteracy *were investigated* by Jones(1987).

II. Present perfect—reference to areas of inquiry

> ◇ There *have been* several investigations into the causes of illiteracy(Jones 1987, Ferrara 1990, Hyon 1994).
> ◇ Several researchers *have studied* the causes of illiteracy.
> ◇ The causes of illiteracy *have been* widely *investigated*(Jones 1987, Ferrara 1990, Hyon 1994).

III. Present—reference to state of current knowledge

> ◇ The causes of illiteracy *are* complex(Jones 1987, Ferrara 1990, Hyon 1994).
> ◇ Illiteracy *appears* to have a complex set of causes.

✏ 写文献综述时需要使用文中注(in-text citation)，通常使用以下三种动词时态。

一般过去时	描述单项研究	Jones(2000) investigated the causes of…
现在完成时	描述某领域从过去某时间点开始的持续研究	The causes of… have been widely investigated(Jones 2000, Keeley 2008, Martin 2020).
一般现在时	描述某领域的知识现状	The causes of…are complex(Jones 2000, Keeley 2008, Martin 2020).

- Sometimes, the present tense is also used with famous or important sources.

  ◇ Plato argues that…
  ◇ Confucius says…
  ◇ *The Bible* says…
  ◇ The Constitution states…

- Comparable options exist in the subordinate clause.

Pay special attention to the linking verbs in the subordinate clauses in the following two sentences.

◇ Jones(1987) found that illiteracy was correlated most closely with poverty.
◇ Jones(1987) found that illiteracy is correlated most closely with poverty.

The first sentence shows that the writer believes that the finding should be understood within the context of the single study. In the second, the writer implies that a wider generalization is possible.

Summary

A literature review can:

1. Provide the reader with a clear picture of the research development so far.
2. Explain the relationship of previous works to the present study.
3. Prepare for and justify the research questions or hypotheses of the present study.
4. Point out the areas of original research so as to avoid the appearance of repetition.
5. Add authoritative support for the present study.

讲座 4 如何写开题报告(How to Make a Thesis Proposal)

知识概要　申请开题时需提交开题报告，报告应明确论文题目、给出文献综述、明确研究方法、列提纲、讨论预期结果及可能遇到的困难，最后列出参考书目。提纲一般包括题目、主旨陈述、引言、方法、分析和讨论、结论。表达评判的词语常引出文献中的研究空白。**主要内容**：1. 学会构思开题报告；2. 了解自己论文的结构；3. 学会使用常见的开头句句型；4. 学会使用表达批判的词语以引出研究空白。

关 键 词　thesis proposal(开题报告); outline(提纲); "critique" expression(表达批判的词语)

Lead-in

Your main purpose when writing a proposal is to **propose a solution to a problem**. There are various types of proposal writing in the workplace and in academic circles. The following table may help students know the status of varied proposals. For example, employees need to submit a proposal to their supervisors to request permission to begin projects or gain promotions. Professors often submit proposals to obtain grants. Students are required to hand in a proposal to their professors in order to obtain permission to pursue research for their papers, theses or dissertations.

高级综合英语写作教程（慕课版）

Proposer	Target audience	Requesting
Engineering firms	Large corporations	Contract to design, build, or reconfigure something
Scientists	Government or corporations	Funding for research laboratories and materials
Academic institutions	Charitable trusts, corporations, other large agencies	Funding for new programs, buildings, equipment
Employees	Supervisors	Permission to begin new projects or gain promotions
Students	Professors	Permission to pursue research for papers, theses, dissertations

✎ 写开题报告旨在提出解决问题的方案。它广泛应用于职场及学术活动中。例如：员工提交方案以申请项目或获得晋升；教授们提交申报书以获得科研资助；学生提交开题报告以获得许可继续进行论文或学位论文的研究。

A thesis proposal is an outline of the proposed research that is designed to answer the research question or test the hypothesis. It should define the goals and objectives that are to be fulfilled by the study proposed. It is important to make a note of the existing gaps in the field and how this study will fill the existing knowledge gaps and highlight the originality of the work being planned. Your proposal should:

- Identify your topic.
- Make a literature review.
- Identify the methods and materials.
- Draft the outline (structure) of the research paper.
- Discuss the anticipated results as well as limitations and difficulties.
- Offer the preliminary list of references.

✎ 开题报告是一份关于研究工作的规划。它应明确研究目标，并且重在指出该领域现有的知识空白，以及这项研究将如何填补空白，突出工作的原创性。开题报告一般应包括以下部分：确定主题、进行文献综述、确定方法和材料、起草论文提纲(结构)、讨论预期结果及困难、初拟参考文献。

Objectives

- Learn to plan a thesis proposal.
- Know the structure of your research paper's (RP's) outline.
- Learn some opening statements.
- Learn to use "critique" expressions to indicate a gap in knowledge.

Key Points

✔ Outlining your thesis or paper

Using an outline can help you organize your material and can also help you discover connections between pieces of information.

A working outline might be only an informal list of topics and subtopics which you are thinking of covering in your paper. Sometimes, however, an advisor or instructor might require that a working outline be submitted at the beginning of your project. The working outline can be revised as you discover new material and get new ideas that ought to go into your paper.

A final outline enhances the organization and coherence of your research paper. The outline organization should be well suited to your purposes. Are you attempting to show the time order of some historical development, cause-and-effect relationship, the effectiveness of a type of experiment, comparison and contrast between one phenomenon and another, the process in which something is accomplished, the logic of some position or crafting a proof for an issue in mathematics?

A final outline can be written as **a topic outline**, in which you use only short phrases to suggest ideas, or as **a sentence outline**, in which you use full sentences to show the development of ideas more fully. The following is a template outline of research, which may not reflect all of the research you will be including in your final paper, but it should show that you have done enough research that you know the main topics and subtopics that you will be using.

Here is a template for working outlines. It includes title, thesis statement, introduction, methodology, analysis and discussion, and conclusion. For more information, read each of the component parts carefully.

✔ A "skeletal" sample of a working outline

- Title
- Thesis statement

Introduction

> ◇ Describe the problem.
> ◇ Show the importance of the problem.
> ◇ Show the scope of the review.
> ◇ Point out gaps in previous studies.
> ◇ How the results of the review will be applied.
> ◇ Identify the research questions you hope to answer.

Methodology

◇ Identify the method used.
◇ Explain the rationale(i.e. principles or reasons).
◇ Explain the procedures.
◇ Put in discussion of the experimental/mathematical methods/models used and what materials are being studied if the paper is in a scientific or technical field.
◇ Identify the criteria for evaluating the information found.

Analysis and Discussion(General Points to Consider)

◇ Evidence and ideas are presented from sources.
◇ Concepts are organized by subtopics.
◇ Sources are grouped by concepts instead of individual entities.
◇ Grouping may be related to research questions.
◇ Validity of sources is stated to support your ultimate answers to your questions.
◇ Each of your statements is cited by placing the number(s) and identifying the reference(s) which support your statement.

Conclusions and Recommendations

◇ Identify and synthesize findings.
◇ Systematically answer your research questions.
◇ Provide recommendations for
  ◆ future research;
  ◆ classroom applications;
  ◆ business applications;
  ◆ social, legal and political applications;
  ◆ applications in Engineering or in other projects in Physical Sciences;
  ◆ educational policies and procedures;
  ◆ program revisions, or other applicable situations.

Tasks

Task 1 The beginning paragraph of a proposal

Read the following text(the beginning paragraph of a proposal) and mark the opening statement.

High Angle-of-Attack Calculations of the Sub-sonic Vortex Flow in Slender Bodies
By D. Almosnino

1)_____The increasing interest in high angle-of-attack aerodynamics has heightened the need for computational tools suitable to predict the flowfield and the aerodynamic coefficients in this regime. 2) _____ Of particular interest and complexity are the symmetric and asymmetric separated vortex flows which develop about slender bodies as the angle of attack is increased.

> **Answer**: The opening statements are "The increasing interest in…has heightened the need for…" and "Of particular interest and complexity are…" The second sentence uses the emphatic inversion.

Language Focus

The first language focus is on how to make opening statements.

1 Making opening statements

It is possible to start immediately with a topic or thesis statement.

> ◇ The purpose of this paper is to…
> ◇ This paper describes and analyzes…
> ◇ In this paper, we report on…

However, this kind of opening is rare and unusual. In fact, statements like those above typically come at or near the end of a research paper introduction. **Here are some alternatives as opening statements of a proposal**. Notice some of them use the present perfect.

> ◇ Recently, there has been growing interest in…
> ◇ Many investigators have recently turned to…
> ◇ The relationship between…has been investigated by many researchers.
> ◇ Many recent studies have focused on…
> ◇ The…has been extensively studied in recent years.
> ◇ The possibility of…has generated wide interest in…
> ◇ The development of…is a classic problem in…
> ◇ The development of…has led to the hope that…
> ◇ The…has become a favorite topic for analysis…
> ◇ Knowledge of…has a great importance for…
> ◇ The study of…has become an important aspect of…
> ◇ A central issue in…is…

 学会使用开题报告的开头语。注意它们常用现在完成时。

The second language focus is on **"critique" expressions**, which are often used to indicate a **research gap**. They include "quasi-negative" subjects and alternative expressions. Probably the most common way to indicate a gap is to use a "quasi-negative" subject. By indicating a gap, the writer shows that the research conducted so far is not yet complete or sufficient. For example, "However, little information" "However, few studies" "None of these studies", etc.

To show your thesis advisor that you have done the proper background work, it might be a good idea to be more specific about what research and whose research has been lacking.

❷ "Critique" expressions

✔ Using a "quasi-negative" subject to indicate a gap (something is missing)

> ◇ However, little information/attention/work/data/research…
> ◇ However, few studies/investigations/researchers/attempts…
> ◇ None of these studies/findings/calculations have…

 表达"批判"的短语用于指明迄今为止进行的研究还不够完整或充分,例如"However, few studies""None of these studies"等。而较柔和的表达方式是使用对比句式"Research has tended to focus on…rather than on…"或者提到某个方面尚不清楚,例如"However, it remains unclear whether…"等。

The alternative expressions include contrastive statements, such as "These studies have emphasized…as opposed to…"; raising questions such as "However, it remains unclear whether…"; continuing a line of research such as "The literature shows that A is a useful technique for…This paper uses A to…"

✔ Using alternatives

You may prefer to avoid negative or quasi-negative comment altogether. Here are some alternatives.

a) A contrastive statement. A useful alternative is to use a contrastive statement.

> ◇ These studies have emphasized…as opposed to…
> ◇ Research has tended to focus on…rather than on…
> ◇ Although considerable research has been devoted to…rather less attention has been paid to…

b) Raising a question (something is unclear), a hypothesis, or a need.

> ◇ However, it remains unclear whether…
> ◇ It would thus be of interest to learn how…
> ◇ If these results could be confirmed, they would provide strong evidence for…
> ◇ These findings suggest that this treatment might not be so effective when applied to…
> ◇ It would seem, therefore, that further investigations are needed in order to…

c) Continuing a line of research (largely restricted to research papers written by same or similar research groups).

> ◇ The literature shows that Rasch Analysis is a useful technique for validating multiple-choice tests. This paper uses Rasch Analysis to...

In this example, the literature both admits and highlights the validity of Rasch Analysis. The paper continues with this method so as to consolidate it rather than indicate a drawback in it. The paper's author is probably one of the members in the same or similar research group.

Summary

A proposal helps you to organize ideas that can guide the research process. Proposals allow you to start the thought process needed to focus your ideas. A good research proposal will identify the topic, present a working thesis, and offer a plan to prove it. Think of your proposal as an outline for how you will pursue your research and structure your paper. The thesis proposal is to be orally presented within a given period of time. Your advisor or review committee will ask you questions or discuss with you the problems and offer their advice and suggestions before finally giving their approval of your research plan.

讲座 5 如何写引言（How to Write the Introduction）

知识概要 引言是论文正文第一部分。引言的写作通常遵循"三步"结构：明确研究领域、提出研究空白、填补空白。为了实现句式的多样性，可使用介词短语、不定式短语、从句、副词等不同形式引出句子开头，也可使用多样的句子结构。**主要内容**：1. 了解引言写作遵循的"三步"结构；2. 学会如何提出研究空白、填补空白；3. 学会使用多样化的句子结构。

关 键 词 introduction（引言）; three moves（引言"三步"结构）;
variety in sentences（句式多样性）

Lead-in

A good Introduction is supposed to:

> ◇ present with clarity the nature and scope of the problem investigated;
> ◇ briefly review the relevant literature to orient the reader;
> ◇ state the method of the investigation;
> ◇ state the principle results and conclusions suggested by the results.

✎ 引言要明确研究范围及性质、简述文献等。它通常遵循"三步"结构：明确研究领域、提出研究空白、填补空白。

Objectives

- Know the three moves used in the introduction.
- Learn to occupy the niche (a need or gap in knowledge).
- Improve the variety of sentence structures.

Tasks

The sample reading is taken from the Introduction section of a journal paper. **Read the two paragraphs and then answer the questions** based on what you have learned in Lecture 4.

Soft Capacitors for Wave Energy Harvesting

By Ahnert, K., Abel, M., Kollosche, M., Jørgen Jørgensen, P., and Kofod, G.

The problem of adequately supplying the world with clean, renewable energy is among the most urgent today. It is crucial to evaluate alternatives to conventional techniques. One possibility is energy harvesting from ocean waves, which has been proposed as a means of offsetting a large portion of the world's electrical energy demands. However, the practical implementation of wave energy harvesting has met with obstacles, and the development of new methods is necessary. Oceanic waves have large amplitude fluctuations that cause devices to fail due to excessive wear or during storms. A strategy to overcome these catastrophic events could be to base the harvesting mechanisms on soft materials.

Soft, stretchable rubber capacitors are possible candidates for energy harvesting that have already been tested in a realistic ocean setting. They were originally introduced as actuators, capable of high actuation strains of more than 100% and stresses of more than 1 MPa. With a soft capacitor, mechanical energy can be used to pump charges from a low electrical potential U to a higher, so that the electrical energy difference can be harvested. This is made possible by the large changes of capacitance under mechanical deformation. Although the method is simple and proven, it is still not clear to what extent the approach is practically useful, which is the concern of this paper.

...

Questions:

1. How many "critique" expressions (refer to Lecture 4) can you find in the passage? Underline or highlight them.
2. Look back at Lecture 4. Are these phrases strongly negative or slightly negative?
3. What word signals the shift from reviewing the previous research to indicating the gap in it? What other words or expressions could also indicate this shift?
4. Can you anticipate what next paragraph will do?

Question 1 At the end of the second paragraph, the authors indicate the gap in the previous research by raising a question—"Although the method is simple and proven, it is still not clear to what extent the approach is practically useful…"

Question 2 These phrases are slightly negative because they show the previous research on the method or approach is not complete yet.

Question 3 The signal word is *although*. Words or expressions such as *still* and *not* could also indicate this shift.

Question 4 Next paragraph may propose a new approach or device used for wave energy harvesting.

Answers:
1. Although the method is…, it is still not clear to what extent the approach is practically useful…
2. The phrases are slightly negative.
3. The signal word is *although*. Words or expressions such as *still* and *not* could also indicate this shift.
4. Next paragraph may propose a new approach or device used for wave energy harvesting.

✎ 在第二段结尾，作者提出了一个问题，指出了以前研究中的不足之处——"Although the method is simple and proven, it is still not clear to what extent the approach is practically useful…"。句中的 still not 在语气上不是强烈否定(strongly negative)，只是轻微否定(slightly negative)，因为它们表明以前对方法或途径的研究还不完整。

在评价某领域的先前研究时，(have) failed to consider, disregard, misinterpret, be limited to, be restricted to 等表示"未能考虑到、错误地解读了、受局限于"，因此表达出强烈的否定语气；而含有"只聚焦于、忽视、忽略了考虑、低估了、高估了、缺乏"等意思的单词和短语 ignore, overlook, overestimate, underestimate, neglect to consider, suffer from, concentrate on 语气是柔和的，表达了轻微否定。

Key Points

John M. Swales in his "Create a Research Space (CARS)" Model of Research writing established the general pattern of three actions (he calls them "moves") in the Introduction section. **Move 1** is establishing a research territory; **Move 2** is establishing a niche; **Move 3** is occupying the niche. The term "niche" here means a gap, an evident opportunity or need which the researcher's work can fulfill. The items in each move are either optional or obligatory. Take Move 1 as an example. In Move 1, the author must establish the research territory by introducing and reviewing the previous research in the area, but the author can choose whether or not to show the significance of the general research area. In Move 3, the author must occupy the niche, namely, fill the gap, by outlining purposes or stating the nature of the present research while other items from b to e are all optional.

1. **Three moves in Introduction part** (John M. Swales, 331)

高级综合英语写作教程（慕课版）

Move 1	Establishing a research territory a. by showing that the general research area is important, central, interesting, problematic, or relevant in some way. (optional) b. by introducing and reviewing items of the previous research in the area. (obligatory)
Move 2	Establishing a niche a. by indicating a gap in the previous research, or extending previous knowledge in some way. (obligatory)
Move 3	Occupying the niche a. by outlining purposes or stating the nature of the present research. (obligatory) b. by listing research questions or hypotheses. (optional) c. by announcing principal findings. (optional) d. by stating the value of the present research. (optional) e. by indicating the structure of the RP. (optional)

Now let's make a further study of Move 3.

2. Move 3: Occupying the niche

The third and final step in the typical RP Introduction is to make a proposal to fill the gap (or answer the question) that has been created in Move 2. The first element in Move 3 is obligatory. It has two main variants.

> Purposive(P)　The author or authors indicate their main purpose or purposes.
> Descriptive(D)　The author or authors describe the main feature of their research.

Note that Move 3 is typically signaled by some words in reference to the present text, such as the uses of *this*, *the present*, *reported*. These signals come early in the sentence. If the conventions of the field or journal allow it, it is also common for the authors to switch from the impersonal to the personal by using *we*, or more rarely *I*. These signals come early in the sentence.

> (P) The purpose of this paper is to…or the purpose of the present paper is to…
> (D) In this paper we present the results of three experiments.

It is more usual than "We present the results of three experiments in this paper." Got it? That is why we say "These signal words come early in the sentence".

> 按照 John M. Swales 提出的"三步"结构，在引言的结尾处要规划本研究的目的或性质。我们可以通过两类标志词来识别：目的性标志词(P)表明其主要目的；描述性标志词(D)描述其研究的主要特点。注意：句子开头通常会出现一些指示当前文本的单词或短语，例如 this, the present。请看下面两个例子。

(P) The purpose of this paper is to... 或者 The purpose of the present paper is to...
(D) In this paper we present the results of three experiments.
注意第二个例句的语序，它比起"We present the results of three experiments in this paper."更为常见。另外，作者常会在期刊允许的情况下，使用代词 we，从而转换到使用第一人称。

Read the third paragraph in the introduction of *Soft Capacitors for Wave Energy Harvesting*, and see **how it occupies the niche**.

For the purpose of a broad and realistic investigation, a minimal yet realistic model is proposed that takes into account the mechanical and dielectric properties of the soft capacitor material, including losses and limiting criteria. The model also includes cyclic mechanical driving, and an electrical control mechanism consisting of a switchable electrical circuit. The quality of the energy harvesting is characterized by efficiency and gain measures, which were evaluated for simulations on a very large set of varied system and material parameters.

...

> **Answer:**
> The paragraph is an example of Move 3. It states both the feature (Move 3a) and value (Move 3d) of the "minimal yet realistic" model. It includes those sentences such as "a... model is proposed that..." "The model also includes..." and "The quality of...is characterized by..." The sentences are descriptive.

Language Focus

✔ Variety in sentences

Sentences can vary in **length**, **structure**, and **complexity**. As you revise, vary your sentences so that they do not become tiresomely alike. You can:

> ◇ Vary sentence opening by using prepositional phrases, infinitive phrases, dependent clauses, adverbs, and so on.
> ◇ Use a variety of sentence structure.
> ◇ Avoid repetition of words. For example, it would be a bad habit of using phrases "It has been noted" "Now note" "Scholar X has already noted" again and again.
> ◇ The varieties of sentences differ a great deal between disciplines. For example, papers in the Humanities may have more "conversational" types of sentences than Engineering. A good strategy is, as you read the secondary literature, to look at how established scholars write and thus provide examples of potential sentence structure. But above all, be logical and concise, making sure ideas follow each other in a rational order, and that there are not too many superfluous expressions.

Example 1

◇ The American punk-rock songs of the early 1980s were musicians' way of expressing their criticism of the political establishment.

You may start the sentence with an infinitive phrase.

→To express their criticism of the political establishment, punk-rock musicians of the early 1980s wrote protest songs.

Example 2

◇ This part of the exhibit also features variable center distance in order to view the changes in stress concentration as center distance changes.

The whole sentence can be started with an adverb "additionally", and a coordinating conjunction "so" is used to connect the two independent clauses.

→Additionally, the exhibit shows variable center distance, so we can see how the stress concentrations change as the center distance changes.

Summary

Your introduction needs to follow the three moves. Above all, it should emphasize what is new and different about your approach. It should also demonstrate the overall significance of your research or approach by explaining how it fills a need, solves a current problem, or offers a useful application. To avoid lapsing into redundant patterns of sentences all beginning with subject followed by verb, you need to improve sentence varieties.

Ⅲ. 写作练习

1. Which of the English sentences is more formal and thus more academic?

1) 很多人认为该市的公共交通系统越来越差。

   A. **Lots of people think** that the public transportation system in the city is **getting worse and worse**.

   B. **It is widely believed** that the public transportation system in the city is **deteriorating**.

2) 自杀率，诸如儿童自杀率，正在上升。

   A. The suicide rate, **such as** child suicide, is **increasing**.

   B. **Sadly**, the suicide rate **like** child suicide is **going up**.

3) 不能总是相信那份报告中的数字。

   A. **You can't always trust the numbers** in that report.

   B. The **figures** in that report **are not reliable**.

4) 第二个因素是，大多数在贫民窟长大的儿童有可能成为罪犯。

A. **The second factor** is that **the majority of children** growing up in the slum **may** become criminals.

B. **The second thing** is that **most kids** growing up in the slum **will** become criminals.

5）一种疫苗可能会在来年被研制出来。

A. **Sometime soon they will find** a vaccine.

B. A vaccine **may be discovered in the coming year**.

2.

1) Which of the following titles is correct?

（从写作的角度来看，以下关于餐厨垃圾厌氧消化的研究，哪个题目更符合学术规范？）

A. The Anaerobic Digestion of Food Waste—Challenges and Opportunities

B. Studies on Anaerobic Digestion of Food Waste—Challenges and Opportunities

C. Anaerobic Digestion of Food Waste—Challenges and Opportunities

2) Fill in the blank with a suitable verb from the box. Use the correct verb form.

recognize clarify demonstrate suggest

① The evidence _____ that smartphone users are genuinely lower in analytical cognitive ability and have a more intuitive cognitive style.

② The results clearly _____ that girls learn more quickly.

③ This paper attempts to _____ the conceptual confusion between the two semantic terms.

④ Social class must be _____ as a leading factor in educational success.

3. Read the example and answer the questions.

Typically, *two main forms of educational research methods have been* **identified as** postmodern: discourse analysis（Lee & Petersen，2011）, and critical discourse analysis（Wodak & Meyer，2009）. Although postmodernism is not only limited to these two educational research methods, **as exemplified by** Brown & Jones（2001）who write about postmodernist action research. **According to** Lee & Petersen（2011）, DA is postmodernist in that it involves two prominent features which they **describe as** a "radical questioning of the nature of knowledge"（p. 139）which requires a "social analysis of the increasing textualization of the modern world"（p. 140）. Wodak & Meyer（2009）*explain* that CDA is postmodernist in its questioning of the relationships between language and power（p. 2）. As Edwards & Usher（2002）*argue*, however, the idea of research of modernity being "emancipatory" is highly problematic because of its underlying oppressive traditions.

Campbell, Madelaine (2018). Postmodernism and Educational Research. *Open Journal of Social Sciences*, 6, 67-73. Some modifications have been made.

Questions:
a) How many writers are mentioned?

b) What is the function of the words in italics?

c) Which word/phrase is used to mark the point in the text where there is a shift from one point of view to another?

4. Some words are used to illustrate weaknesses in the previous research in the literature review part. Talk with your partner to decide how "negative" they are.

definitely or strongly negative(- -) or **slightly negative**(-)

However, _____.

1) Graves' alignment was restricted to predicting the location coefficient

2) the researchers also suffer from the inability to create a model to combat cyber-crimes

3) the concept of public policy needs to be re-thought in this new light

4) an obvious limitation of this model is its limited scope

5) there exist second order effects as well which have gone unnoticed

5. The following sentences are given at the end of an introduction section. Decide whether they are purposive(P) or descriptive(D).

1) The paper aims to give…

2) The most important distinguishing feature of this approach is that…

3) Therefore, the fundamental research question that this study addresses is…

4) This study is designed to propose an easy-to-use and general-purpose approach…

第14周
学术论文写作 II（Academic Writing II）

❯❯ I. 概述

本周课程继续讲解学术论文写作，内容包括：如何描述材料和方法、如何汇报与讨论结果、如何写结论、如何写摘要、如何引用文献。

❯❯ II. 慕课讲稿

讲座 1　如何描述材料和方法
（How to Describe the Materials and Methods Used in Research）

知识概要　材料和方法部分旨在描述或证实当前的实验设计，大多使用一般过去时和被动语态，要求语言精确、术语界定明确且具体。该部分一般遵循"七步"结构：概览、目的和问题、对象及/或材料、地点、程序、局限性及数据分析。连接短语有助于加强逻辑连接并增加表达多样性。**主要内容**：1. 了解材料和方法部分的"七步"结构；2. 理解简洁法和扩展法这两种类型；3. 学会使用连接短语。

关　键　词　research method（研究方法）；seven moves（"七步"结构）；linking phrase（连接短语）

Lead-in

As we will see, there are disciplinary differences in Methods sections; even the heading **Methods** is not always used, as when authors use **The Study** as their section heading or **Materials and Methods**. In some fields, it is common to have subsections in Methods that might deal with materials, the apparatus used, definitions employed, the subjects or participants in the study, or the statistical procedures or mathematical models used. The section may vary

from very condensed one to elaborately extended one.

> 这部分的标题除了"方法"以外,也可能使用"该研究"或者"材料和方法"。在某些学科中,这部分会分成几小节,比如材料、使用的仪器、定义、研究对象或参与者、使用的统计程序或数学模型。这部分在有些论文中很简洁,有些则经过了扩展。一般来说,扩展方法在心理学、社会学、教育学和应用语言学的研究领域中有着广泛的应用。化学、材料科学、分子生物学等采用简洁的方法。公共卫生、政治学、医学研究等领域则大多采用折中的方法。

Objectives

- Get to know seven "moves" in Methods sections.
- Understand both the condensed and extended types.
- Learn to use linking phrases.

Tasks

Let's start with a reading sample. Here is the Methods section from a paper investigating hypothetical consumer behavior in buying stolen, pirated, or counterfeit goods from the black market. The Methods section includes two parts: participants and procedure, and questionnaire. Read it and then answer the questions.

Take the first part as an example. The authors give the total number of participants, explaining that they come from either the University of Canterbury or from the general public recruited in four malls. The researchers simultaneously mark out the number of each group (in brackets) and how many socio-economic levels are involved in dividing the second group of participants. Then, more specific information, such as the overall age range and the mean age, the final sample and the rewards all participants were given for their help, are available in this part.

Consumer Decisions in the Black Market for Stolen or Counterfeit Goods

Casola, L., Kemp, S., and Mackenzie, A. (2009).
Journal of Economic Psychology, 30, 162-171.

Method

1. Participants and procedure

A total of 80 (36 male) participants were recruited at the University of Canterbury (51 participants) and from the general population (29 participants). Participants from the general public were recruited in four different malls of the local city, representing four different socio-economic levels as indicated by land values. The overall age range was between 15 and 68 years of age, with a mean of 27 ($SD = 13$). All participants completed the same questionnaire. The final sample contained 53 current students and 27 non-students. All participants were given two $1 "scratch-and-win" lottery tickets in recognition of their help.

2. Questionnaire

The bulk of the questionnaire consisted of nine black market scenarios. Participants were asked to rate each scenario in terms of how unacceptable they perceived it was for the agent in the scenario to make a purchase from the black market. Participants circled a value between 1 and 7 on a rating scale where a score of 1 corresponded to "completely acceptable", a score of 4 was "reasonably acceptable", and a score of 7 was "not at all acceptable". The nine scenarios varied(3 x 3) the need of the agent and the original source of the goods offered in the market. The need of the agent could be survival; a need to save money; or not otherwise being able to afford the goods. The original sources of the goods (victims) were an individual; an organization or society. Two examples of scenarios were:

…

Half the questionnaires included scenarios in which all the consumers were depicted as male while in the other half they were always female. The only difference between these two questionnaires was the implied gender of the names and the pronouns used. The order of presentation of the scenarios was varied across participants. Finally, a demographic section asked participants their age, gender, occupation and income.

Questions:

1. Do you think the level of detail is sufficient or insufficient? In other words, is there enough information to allow the study to be adapted or replicated by others? If not, what would you need to know?
2. What verb tense dominates? Does active or passive voice dominate? Why is this the case?

Answers:
1. It is an extended Methods section with sufficient details in procedure. Additionally, it still needs to state how the data was analyzed.
2. Past tense and passive voice(Past passive) dominate in the Methods section because it describes what was done by the researchers several months or even years ago.

Key Points

This complex section could be analyzed by the pattern of seven "moves" proposed by Peacock(2011). The pattern consists of overview, research aim/questions/hypotheses, subjects and/or materials, location, procedure, limitations, and data analysis. The specific contents may differ from field to field. Take the third move, subjects and/or materials, as an example. In Business, Language and Linguistics, Law, and Public and Social Administration, a description of the subjects refers to a description of the people(groups of people) in the study; and in the sciences, it means a description of the materials and equipment.

Overview	a short summary of the research method, at or near the beginning of the Methods section
Research aims, questions, or hypotheses	a description of the research goals, the questions to be answered, or the hypotheses
Subjects and/or materials	in Business, Language and Linguistics, Law, and Public and Social Administration, a description of the people (groups of people) in the study and the items studied (for example, a Chinese text, Japanese drama, Cambodian temple architecture, Buddhist chants from Thailand, etc.); and in the sciences, a description of the materials, equipment, and so on
Location	a description of where the research took place and possibly why
Procedure	a discussion of the process used to obtain the collected data
Limitations	a focus on a shortcoming of the method, possibly accompanied by an explanation
Data analysis	a description of how the data was analyzed

It is important to keep in mind that the moves do not necessarily appear in the order given. The science fields investigated tend to follow the moves seen above. In the remaining fields, the move structure may be much more complex and variable. According to Peacock's research (see the following table), all Methods sections contain some explanation concerning procedures. We can see methods in the sciences do not generally include overviews; it is 100% for all fields. Language and linguistics are most similar to Business in terms of percentage in each move. In the fields of Biology, Chemistry, Physics, and Public and Social Administration, less than 10% of the Methods sections include a consideration of the limitations of the methods.

Do you agree on the analysis? You may discuss with your partner to find out other information illustrated by the table.

The Frequency of the Moves in Different Fields (Peacock, 2011)

Moves	Biology	Chemistry	Physics	Environmental Science	Business	Language and Linguistics	Law	Public and Social Administration
Subjects or materials	97	100	75	31	92	94	86	86
Location	36	8	0	67	47	58	58	75

（续）

Moves	Biology	Chemistry	Physics	Environ-mental Science	Business	Language and Linguistics	Law	Public and Social Administration
Procedure	100	100	100	100	100	100	100	100
Data analysis	86	100	67	78	72	67	56	50
Limitations	6	0	0	69	44	19	28	6
Research aims or questions/ hypothesis	3	0	6	11	36	22	58	67
Overview	3	0	0	50	25	19	42	54

The following Methods section is taken from a research paper in a Biology field. Read and discuss the questions with a partner. **How does the author give an account of the procedures? Are there any explanations or justifications for the procedures?**

DNA was extracted from tissue and feather samples using the Qiagen DNeasy Extraction kit. An addition of dithiothreitol was used for samples from feathers. Polymerase chain reaction(PCR) was carried out using two primers pairs for cytochrome B(CytB; Sorenson et al., 1999). PCR and sequencing was done following protocols in Mindell et al. (1997).

Answers:

There is no chronology here, no use of personal pronouns, and no explanations for the procedure. Also, notice that the fourth sentence concludes with "**was done following protocols in Mindell et al**". Naming procedures by citation(rather than describing them) only seems possible in fields with well-established and standardized procedures, as in some of the hard sciences. We can consider **this type of description as abbreviated or condensed**.

Now let's identify two types of methods.

Condensed methods state what the researchers did with little elaboration or justification. **Extended methods** present readers with a rationale of **why and how** researchers did what they did.

We need to get an idea of how fields might differ in terms of the condensed-to-extended continuum. Do you agree? The following table will show **Disciplinary Variation in Methods Section**. The extended methods are more commonly used in the research fields of Psychology, Sociology, Education and Applied Linguistics. Chemistry, Material Science, Mycology, and

Molecular Biology adopt the condensed methods in Methods Section. The intermediate methods can be seen in research areas of Public Health, Political Science, Medical Research, etc.

Condensed	Intermediate	Extended
Chemistry	Public Health	Psychology
Material Science	Political Science	Sociology
Mycology	Systematic Botany	Education
Molecular Biology	Medical Research	Applied Linguistics

However, it should also be noted that the Methods section will probably need to be more extensive if any of these conditions apply:

- The paper is aimed at a multidisciplinary audience.
- The methods chosen are new or controversial.
- The paper is essentially a "methods paper".

Language Focus

Here is the section of language focus in this lecture: using linking phrases in the Methods section of a research paper to enhance coherence and stylistic variety.

✓ Linking phrases in the Methods section

Using a linking phrase to justify a procedure in the methodology section.

The word "justify" means "to show that something is right or reasonable". Here, it means to show that the procedure/step is right or reasonable by offering a rationale. For example:

> ◇ Based on previous reports of HR mutations in APL, we performed direct DNA sequencing analysis.
> ◇ Because of its hygroscopic properties, the dye was stored and handled in ethanol solution.

Here we provide a few more linking phrases that operate to tie sections together and to add some stylistic variety. They include:

A. Initial purposive clauses or phrases;
B. Phrases making time links;
C. Causal or connective phrases.

The linking phrases will be specified by the following examples.

For example, we can use phrases indicating purpose: "*In an effort to evaluate…*" "*To *further test this hypothesis…*"; the phrases making temporal links: "*During the data collection…*" "*On arrival on campus, the participants …*"; phrases revealing the causes and logical connection: "*Based on the feedback from the pilot study*" "*In spite of these issues, we…*"

A. Initial purposive clauses or phrases

1. *In an effort to evaluate…*
2. *To further test this hypothesis…*
3. *In order to establish…*
4. *To determine the cost…*
5. *In the interest of obtaining useful data…*

B. Phrases making time links

1. *During the data collection…*
2. *Prior to collecting this information…*
3. *On arrival on campus, the participants…*
4. *In the follow-up phase of the study, we…*
5. *After the interview, subjects were…*

C. Causal or connective phrases

1. *Based on the feedback from the pilot study…*
2. *On the basis of the literature review…*
3. *In spite of these issues, we…*
4. *In light of these unexpected findings…*

✎ "方法"部分常用的连接短语有三类：目的短语、时间短语、原因短语或其他表示逻辑衔接的短语。例如：目的短语可以是"In an effort to evaluate…" "To further test this hypothesis…"；时间短语可以是"During the data collection…" "On arrival on campus, the participants…"；原因短语或其他表示逻辑衔接的短语可以是"Based on the feedback from the pilot study…" "In spite of these issues, we…"。

Summary

Here are some tips:

◇ The main purpose of Methods section is to describe (and if necessary defend) the experimental design.
◇ Most of this section should be written in the past tense.
◇ Exact and specific items are being dealt with and precise use of English is a must.
◇ Passive voice can often properly be used.

讲座 2　如何汇报与讨论结果（How to Report and Discuss the Results of Research）

知识概要　研究结果不只是呈现数据，还需要概述或解释数据，而讨论部分将解释该结果为何在当下有意义。可视化设计主要指各种图表。写研究结果时经常会使用作比较的语言以及定位陈述语。**主要内容**：1. 识别数据与结果；2. 学会读取可视化信息；3. 学会在概括时使用作比较的语言；4. 学会定位陈述语；5. 注意谓语动词一致性的特殊情况。

关　键　词　result of research（研究结果）；visual device（可视化设计）；comparative language（作比较的语言）；location statement（定位陈述语）

Lead-in

Before revisiting some of these concepts, we first need to explore the difference between data and results.

1. Data versus Results

Data consists of **facts** and **numbers**, and these are generally presented in tables and figures. **Results**, on the other hand, **are "statements in the main text that summarize or explain what the data show"**. A result is supported by data.

2. Results versus Discussion

- Another important consideration is the difference between results and discussion of results. You will say that it is hard to avoid commenting on the results as you present them. However, Discussion sections differ from Results sections in that **the Discussion section explains why the results are meaningful** in relation to previous, related work and the research question that was explored, or sometimes suggestions for future research.

- Two important linguistic characteristics of the Results sections are the use of **location statements** (i.e. where you find the data) and **comparative language** (i.e. for evaluation).

Objectives

- Identify the distinction between data and results.
- Learn to read visual information.
- Learn phrases to make generalized comparisons.
- Learn location statements.
- Note special verb agreements.

Tasks

Visual devices such as graphs and tables are convenient ways of displaying large quantities of information in a form that is quick and simple to understand.

Below are visual illustrations of some of the main types. Identify the types of the visuals, and then match the uses(a – e) to the types(1 – 5).

Uses: a) comparison   b) proportion   c) function   d) changes in time
  e) statistical display

图形和表格等可视化设计是以一种快速、简单易懂的形式显示大量信息的方便方法。

All the visuals have been put into order. Notice there are numbers to indicate the order.

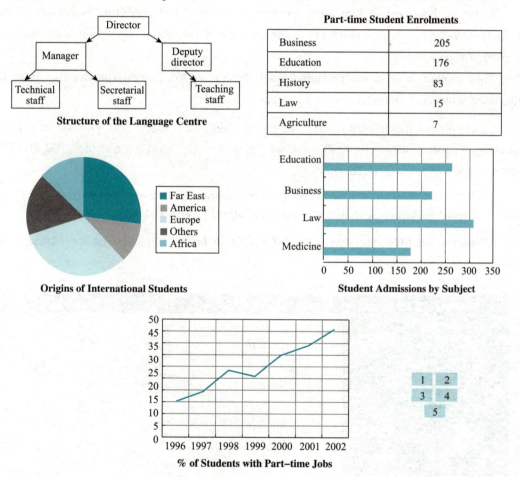

Take another look at the five types of visuals used in academic texts again. Have you got the answers? First let's identify the types.

Answers: No. 1 is a diagram; No. 2 is a table; No. 3 and No. 4 are both called charts(a pie chart and a bar chart); No. 5 is a line graph. A diagram is usually used to show how a machine, a system or an organization works. A line graph is a planned drawing, consisting of a line or lines, showing how two or more sets of numbers are related to each other. The diagram shows the function or roles of faculty members in the Language Center. No. 2, the table, gives statistical numbers. The pie chart is intended to make the proportion easier to understand while the bar chart visualizes the comparison. The line graph reveals changes in time.

Types	Uses
1. diagram	c) function
2. table	e) statistical display
3. pie chart	b) proportion
4. bar chart	a) comparison
5. line graph	d) changes in time

Learn the **language of indicating changes**. You can say *it grew/rose/increased/climbed (slightly/gradually/steadily/sharply)*, or *dropped/fell/decreased(a slight drop/a gradual fall/a sharp decrease)*.

Take another look at the previous visual illustration No. 5. You can describe it in the following sentences. Pay attention to the words in italics.

Sports center membership *grew slightly* in 1992, and then *rose steadily* until 1995, reaching a peak of 4900. In 1998 there was *a sharp rise*, then a peak of 6,700 in 1999, followed by *a slight drop* in 2000.

✎ 指示趋势变化的句式有 it grew/rose/increased/climbed(slightly/gradually/steadily/sharply),或者 dropped/fell/decreased(a slight drop/a gradual fall/a sharp decrease)。

Complete the following description of the table below, which is on the Marriage and Divorce Rates.

Country	Marriage rate	Divorce rate
Britain	10.7	3.4
United States	8.6	4.7
Turkey	8.0	0.5
Iran	7.8	0.5
Japan	6.2	1.8
Russia	5.2	3.2
Spain	5.2	0.8
South Africa	4.0	0.9

The a)_____ shows the wide variations in marriage and divorce rates in a b)_____ of countries. The c)_____ rate varies from 10.7 per thousand in d)_____ to 4.0 in South Africa, while the divorce e)_____ ranges from 4.7 in the United States to 0.5 in Turkey and f)_____. It appears that in the United States more than g)_____ of all marriages end in divorce, while in Turkey the h) _____ is less than 10%. This suggests that in countries such as the United States and Britain the high marriage rate may be a i) _____ of the high divorce rate.

> **Answers:**
> a) table b) range/variety c) marriage d) Britain e) rate
> f) Iran   g) half   h) proportion/figure i) result/consequence

The **table** shows the wide variations in marriage and divorce rates in a range/variety of countries. The **marriage** rate varies from 10.7 per thousand in Britain to 4.0 in South Africa, while the divorce **rate** ranges from 4.7 in the United States to 0.5 in Turkey and **Iran**.

The following description can be taken as a sample. Pay special attention to those underlined words. The last two sentences analyze the data of the United States, signal the difference between the U.S. and Turkey, and suggest the possible cause of the high marriage rate in both the U.S. and the U.K. "It appears that in the United States more than **half** of all marriages end in divorce, while in Turkey the **proportion/figure** is less than 10%. This suggests that in countries such as the United States and Britain the high marriage rate may be a **result/consequence** of the high divorce rate."

Key Points

Here is the section of key points.

✓ **Making comparisons**

When writing up the results, you may want to include **statements of comparison**. The useful sentence structure include:

A linking verb is followed by a comparative adjective form.

> ◇ _____ is (more than %) _____ -er (comparative adjective form) than that of _____.
> The median wage of a college graduate *is* now *more than* 70 *percent higher than that of* a high school graduate.

Use the comparative structure "as much…as" or "as many…as".

> ◇ as much _____ as/as many _____ as
> China produces *four times as many* engineers *as* the United States does.

Use "times" in the following structure.

> ◇ X times the _____ as _____
> Turfgrass is the main cultivated crop in Florida with nearly *four times the acreage as* the next largest crop, citrus.

The following sentence structures No. 1 to No. 4 may be more complex. Take No. 4 as an example. The density of water is *more than* 800 *times greater than that of* air. Here, *that of air* is the abbreviation of *the density of air*.

> 1. more/less than X times the _____ of _____ as _____
>   Greece consumes *more than double/more than two times the amount of* cheese *as* Denmark.
> 2. more/less than X times the _____ of _____
>   The guarana seed contains *more than two times the* caffeine *of* a coffee bean.
> 3. more than X times _____ -er than the _____ of _____
>   Each year, the average probability of dying from motor vehicle accidents in France was *more than* 12 *times higher than the* risk *of* drowning.
> 4. more than X times _____ -er than that of _____
>   The density of water is *more than* 800 *times greater than that of* air.

Here are **some other ways** that authors can **signal similarity/equivalence and difference/non-equivalence**. The first four cases (1-4) signal difference or non-equivalence: the conjunctive adverb "however" used to join independent clauses with a semicolon, the subordinating conjunction "while", the phrase linker "in contrast to" and the coordinating conjunction "but". Cases 5 to 9 indicate similarity/equivalence between things or groups of people.

Sentence connectors (conjunctive adverbs: however, nevertheless) which join two independent clauses with a semicolon	1. Like jargon, shortened forms are easily understood within a group of specialists; outside the group, *however*, shortened forms might be incomprehensible.
Subordinating conjunctions (while, although)	2. Analyses showed that 70.5% of students had access to both a desktop and a laptop computer, *while* only 0.6% of students (n = 11) had access to neither.
Phrase linkers	3. *In contrast to* the false positives, the false negative rate improves when the distance threshold increases.
Coordinating conjunctions (but, yet)	4. The results of some observers were poor, *but* those of others were satisfactory.

More likely than/less likely than	5. Women are *more likely than* men to have given the most "pro neighborhood" answer, and men more likely than women to have given the most "pro transportation" answer.
Like	6. The results shown in Figure 8 are very much *like* those of Experiment 5.
Alike	7. During the study period, real household income rose in both cities and suburbs *alike*, but more so among suburban households.
Similar to/the same as	8. The observation of smaller magnetization at low thickness is *similar to* results obtained for the Fe3O4 thin films.
Verbs such as compared with/compared to	9. Women had a mean score of 3.89, *compared with* a mean for men of 4.76.

Language Focus

Let's take a look at language focus of this lecture.

❶ Location statements

They are used while referencing to non-verbal material(tables, graphs, figures, photographs, etc.). The four patterns are listed below. Patterns a) and b) are more common than others.

a) Table 3 *shows/reveals/provides* the high rates.
b) The high rates *are shown in* Table 3.
c) The rates were high(*see* Table 3) or(*Table* 3) or(*shown in* Table 3).
d) The rates were high, *as shown in* Table 3. (*As shown in* Table 3, the rates were high.)

✎ 定位句式可用来引入图表、数字等非文字材料。在所列四种表达中，前两种更为常见。

❷ Special verb agreements

◇ A set of 200 questionnaires was distributed.

This sentence follows the standard rule that **the verb agrees with the subject noun**([in this case] **set**) and not the second noun([in this case] questionnaires).

A better way to understand this is that, in the phrase "a set of questionnaires" "of questionnaires" acts like descriptive adjective. For example in "A committee of women" "of women" describes the composition of the committee.

Note that this important rule does not apply in a few exceptional cases, such as when the first noun is a *fraction*, *a proportion*, or *a percentage*. In these special cases, **the verb agrees**

with the noun closest to the verb. Notice the agreement of the subject and verb in these sentences. For example:

A large proportion of students are distracted when they cross a street while talking on the phone".

> The linking verb here needs to be in the plural form "are", because it agrees with the plural noun closest to the verb, "students". This is probably because the phrase "large proportion" also functions as a modifying adjective. It is like "most" in the sentence "Most students are distracted when they cross a street".

More examples:

Only a minority of the cells were alive.

Only a small fraction of English speakers know more than 20% of all the grammar rules.

> 主谓一致的特殊情况。在句子 A set of 200 questionnaires was distributed. 中,谓语动词 was distributed 与单数主语名词 set 保持数的一致,而不是与第二个名词 questionnaires 保持一致。因为在该名词短语中,"of questionnaires"的功能类似描述性形容词。
>
> 但是需要注意,当第一个名词是 a fraction, a proportion 或 a percentage 时,谓语动词与离它最近的名词保持数的一致。例如:Only a small fraction of English speakers know more than 20% of all the grammar rules.

Summary

Here are some useful questions to ask yourself about writing the Results section of your paper:

1. Does the Results section deal with the topic that was proposed?
2. Is everything in the Results section relevant to the Methods section and the research questions?
3. Is the data logically and clearly organized?
4. Have you described the statistical and graphic information in an academic (and clear) manner?
5. Have you presented the major significant findings?
6. Have you stated the locations of the Results and Findings?
7. Have you compared or contrasted the data presented in the graphs you made?
8. Is there a clear distinction between your findings and those of other authors?
9. Have you documented all the information you have referred to?
10. Are the grammar, punctuation and spelling correct and acceptable?

讲座3　如何写结论(How to Write the Conclusion)

知识概要　结论是论文正文的最后一个部分,它应就研究的问题提供解答。讨论和结论有时合并成最后一个部分,形成"五步"结构,其中报告/总结主要结果并加以评论是两个不可或缺的步骤。结论中经常使用表达归纳的形式或单词和短语。**主要内容**：1. 回顾学术论文的整体结构（IMRD 模式）；2. 了解结论的一般结构；3. 学会使用表达归纳的形式或单词和短语。

关键词　conclusion（结论）；structure of five moves（"五步"结构）；generalizing phrase（概括性短语）

Lead-in

The last component in the body part of an academic paper is the Conclusion.

The Conclusion section gives meaning to and interprets the results in relation to the purpose of your study and the methods used to conduct it. The conclusion must grow out of the evidence for the findings in the body of the text.

The IMRD format（Introduction—Methods—Results—and—Discussion）shows the **overall structure of an academic paper**. Subsequently the four different sections have become identified with four different purposes（Swales，286）.

Introduction（I）	The main purpose of the Introduction is to provide the rationale for the paper, moving from a general discussion of the topic to the particular question, issue, or hypothesis being investigated. A secondary purpose is to attract interest in the topic—and hence readers.
Methods（M）	The Methods section describes, in various degrees of detail, methodology, materials（or subjects）, and procedures. This is the narrowest part of the RP.
Results（R）	In the Results section, the findings are described, accompanied by variable amounts of commentary.
Discussion（D）/ Conclusion	The Discussion/Conclusion sections give meaning to and interpret the results in a variety of ways. Authors make a series of "points", at least some of which refer to statements made in the Introduction.

✎ 我们重温一下论文的各个核心部分，包括引言（Introduction）、方法（Methods）、结果（Results）、讨论（Discussion），即 IMRD 模式。引言把对课题的一般性讨论转移到正在研究的特定问题上。方法部分描述了方法、材料和程序。结果既包括对结果的描述，也附有评论。讨论/结论说明了结果的含义和解释，提出一系列"观点"。

Objectives

- Review the overall structure of an academic text（IMRD format）.
- Know the structure of the Discussion/Conclusion sections.
- Learn generalizing phrases to present the conclusions.

Tasks

Read this text about dreams and write more than three **generalizations using the data**.

A recent survey on dreams, completed by over 10,000 people, found that 68% of all dreams came into the "anxiety" category. Being chased was the most common dream, recorded by 72%. Dreams about falling (which signify insecurity) are also very common, being recorded by 70%.

55% have dreamed about relatives and friends who have died. Many people believe that dreams can foretell the future, but only 42% have experienced this type. 28% of those surveyed have dreams about food, which seem to occur during periods of weight watching, but 23% have been pleased by dreams of finding money.

> Answers:
> a) Two common dreams are being chased and falling.
> b) A majority have dreamed about the dead.
> c) Dreaming about the future is quite common.
> d) Food dreams may be linked to dieting.
> e) A minority dream of finding money.

Key Points

This key point concerns **The Structure of Discussion/Conclusion Sections** (Swales, 368).

The pattern includes five moves: background information, summarizing and reporting key results, commenting on the key results, stating the limitations of the present study and, last, making recommendations for future research. The second and the third are obligatory moves according to Swales (2012). Meanwhile, Move 1 and Move 4 are optional although in some fields they are likely to be chosen. That is what the abbreviation PISF means.

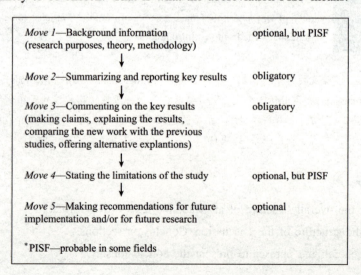

In most Discussion/Conclusion sections, the majority of the space is taken up by Moves 2 and 3, in which writers refer first to their study and then relate it to previous work in their field. These two moves are considered obligatory.

Move 2—Summarizing and reporting key results   obligatory

↓

Move 3—Commenting on the key results   obligatory
(making claims, explaining the results,
comparing the new work with the previous
studies, offering alternative explanations)

✎ 讨论/结论部分可能包括五个步骤：背景介绍、总结和报告主要结果、评论主要结果、说明本研究的局限性以及对未来研究的建议。其中第二和第三个步骤是必要的，并且占据主要篇幅。

Language Focus

❶ Two ways of making a generalization

a) Using the plural: *Computers are useful machines.*

b) Using definite article and a singular noun: *The computer is a useful machine.*

It is better to avoid absolute phrases such as "cats *are cleverer than* dogs". Instead use more cautious phrases such as "cats *tend to* be cleverer than dogs" or "*most* cats *are more intelligent than* dogs".

❷ Levels of generalization

In the Results section, **some statements may be quite specific** and closely tied to the data.

> ◇ As can be seen in Table 1, 84% of the students performed above the 12th grade level.
> ◇ Seven out of eight experimental samples resisted corrosion longer than the controls.

On the other hand, in the abstract or in a summary, **space restrictions may lead to a high level of generality**.

> ◇ The experimental samples resisted corrosion longer than the controls.
> ◇ The results indicate that the students performed above the 12th grade level.

In the Discussion section, we usually expect something in between these two levels. A common practice is to use one of the following "**phrases of generality**".

> ◇ Overall…
> ◇ In general…
> ◇ On the whole…
> ◇ In the main…
> ◇ With…exception(s)…
> ◇ The overall results indicate…
> ◇ The results indicate, overall, that…
> ◇ In general, the experimental samples resisted…
> ◇ With one exception, the experimental samples resisted…

结论中经常使用表达归纳的形式或单词和短语。表达归纳时,可使用名词复数形式,或者定冠词 the 加上一个单数名词。例如:**Computers** are useful machines. 或者 **The computer** is a useful machine. 通常也会使用表示归纳的单词或短语,例如:"Overall""In general""On the whole" "With one exception"等。

❸ Ways to express academic modesty

Learn the ways to express academic modesty by placing a limiting word or phrase in an initial sentence.

> ◇ Despite its limitations, this study does suggest…
> ◇ However exploratory, this study may offer some insight into…

在结论中,有时会在句首使用限定词或短语来表达谦逊的语气。例如:Despite its limitations, this study does suggest…等。

Summary

- There is usually a link between the starting point, i.e. the title, and the conclusion. If the title is asking a question, the conclusion should contain the answer. The reader may look at the conclusion first to get a quick idea of the main arguments or points.
- In some cases, the conclusion may be linked to the Discussion section.
- It is helpful for the reader to have a Discussion/Conclusion section that briefly looks back at what has been said (or key results that have been reported) and makes some comments about the main part (or key results).
- Avoid using absolute phrases and learn the ways to express academic modesty.

讲座 4 如何写摘要(How to Write the Abstract)

知识概要 摘要用于概括和突出论文的主要观点,其长度一般为 200~250 词,其中不可加引用的内容。摘要虽然被置于论文正文的前面，但通常是在完成论文的主要部分后才着手撰写。可以适当使用一些动词和短语使归纳内容的语气温和，以避免语气过于绝对。**主要内容**：1. 理解摘要的定义、作用和结构；2. 识别描述型和信息型摘要；3. 学会在归纳时使用语气温和的表达。

关 键 词　abstract（摘要）；descriptive abstract（描述型摘要）；informative abstract（信息型摘要）；soften generalizations（使归纳的语气温和）

Lead-in

Although the Abstract will appear at the beginning of the article, write the Abstract only after you have finished writing the paper's main sections.

An abstract summarizes and highlights the major points. Its primary purpose is to enable readers to decide whether to read the work in full, so prepare your abstract carefully. The abstract is simply a summary of what you will find in the article. It is not the article itself and, therefore, should never be quoted. For those who intend to turn a written paper into conference presentation, learning to write this sort of abstract is good preparation for writing an abstract for a conference.

An abstract is typically 200 to 250 words long. It is often published as an introduction to the complete paper and can also be published separately in periodical indexes and by abstracting services. For this reason, an abstract must be readable apart from the original document.

✎ 摘要用于总结并强调要点。因为摘要不是文章本身，因此其中不可加引用内容。摘要长度通常为200~250词。它可以与论文一起出版，也可以在期刊索引和文摘服务中单独出版。因此，摘要必须有较强的可读性。

Objectives

- Understand the definition, function and structure of the abstract.
- Identify descriptive or informative abstracts.
- Learn the ways to soften generalizations.

Tasks

Here is part of an abstract in a journal paper. The paper is entitled *Relation Between Interactive Learning and Prior Knowledge: Insights from a General Education Program of Science and Humanities*. The abstract is put at the very beginning of the academic text. There are six sentences altogether. **Discuss it with a partner and try to analyze the sentences and underline those stating the background, purpose, method, result(s) and conclusion.**

Relation Between Interactive Learning and Prior Knowledge: Insights from a General Education Program of Science and Humanities

Hin-Yan Chan, Chun-Yeung Lo, Andy Ka-Leung Ng,
Derek Hang-Cheong Cheung and Kai-Ming Kiang(2017)
The Journal of General Education, 66, 136-165.

ABSTRACT

①Possession of prior knowledge has been shown to critically influence students' learning in major courses. ②Yet the topic remains unexplored in the realm of general education in higher education. ③The study aims at investigating whether students lacking relevant high school knowledge background could benefit by taking two courses, one oriented toward science and one oriented toward the humanities, in a general education program at a university in Hong Kong. ④Interactive learning has been intensively practiced in the program to minimize the unfavorable impact brought up by a lack of prior knowledge among students.

⑤Data from an entry-exit survey show that a lack of prior knowledge does not limit students' learning in outcomes related to generic cognitive skills and subject matter content in both courses. ⑥An interactive learning approach is suggested to have mediated the problem of the lack of prior knowledge in students' subsequent learning in the two general education courses.

Have you completed the pair work? Now let's do the exercise together based on what we have learned in the previous lectures. The first two sentences introduce the significance of the topic and also indicate the research gap directly. Sentence③ provides the aim of the present study and some specific information on the courses investigated. The next sentence describes the method the authors have used. Sentence⑤ briefly reports the result and Sentence⑥ arrives at the conclusion.

> **Answers**: ①-② the background; ③ purpose; ④ method; ⑤ result; ⑥ conclusion

Key Points

Depending on the kind of information they contain, abstracts are often classified as descriptive or informative. **A descriptive abstract** summarizes the purpose, scope, and methods used to arrive at the reported findings. It is a slightly expanded table of contents and need not be longer than several sentences. **An informative abstract** is an expanded version of the descriptive abstract by summarizing any results, conclusions, and recommendations. The informative abstract retains the tone and essential scope of the original work, omitting its details. Structured (informative) abstracts have subheadings similar to those in a paper.

- Background
- Aim
- Method
- Results
- Conclusion

> 摘要通常分为描述型和信息型两种。描述型摘要用几个句子概述研究目的、范围、方法并报告结果/结论，它是在目录基础上稍作扩展。信息型摘要则会概述所有结果、结论和建议，并且有类似论文中的那些副标题，例如背景介绍、目的、方法、结果、结论。

Here is another reading sample of Abstract. Read it and answer the questions.

ABSTRACT

The Effects of Long-Distance Running on Male and Female Runners Aged 50 to 72 Years

Young Sandra

①The long-term effects of long-distance running on the bones, joints, and general health of runners aged 50 to 72 can help determine whether physicians should recommend long-distance running for their older patients. ②Recent studies conducted at Stanford University and the University of Florida tested and compared male and female long-distance runners aged 50 to 72 with a control group of runners and nonrunners. ③The groups were matched by sex, race, education, and occupation. ④The Florida study used only male runners who had run at least 20 miles a week for five years and compared them with a group of runners and nonrunners. ⑤Both studies based findings on medical histories and on physical and X-ray examinations. ⑥Both studies conclude that long-distance running is not associated with increased degenerative joint disease. ⑦Control groups *were more prone to* spur formation, sclerosis, and joint-space narrowing and showed more joint degeneration than runners. ⑧Female long-distance runners exhibited *somewhat more* sclerosis in knee joints and the lumbar spine area than matched control subjects. Both studies support the role of exercise in retarding bone loss with aging. ⑨The investigation concludes that the health risk factors *are fewer* for long-distance runners *than* for those less active aged 50 to 72. ⑩The investigation recommends that physicians recognize that an exercise program that includes long-distance running can be beneficial to their aging patients' health.

Key words: bone loss, exercise programs, geriatric patients, health risk, joint and lumbar degeneration, long-distance running, runners, sclerosis

Questions:
1. Analyze the structure of the abstract.
2. What tenses are used in the abstract? Is this usage common and conventional in your field?
3. How does the author of this abstract approximate the precise numbers in the paper? What do you think of this?

> **Answers:**
> 1. Sentences ①-④ construct **a descriptive section** by covering purpose, method and scope. Sentences ⑤-⑧ report **findings**. Sentences ⑨-⑩ are **conclusion and recommendations**.
> 2. Present tense is used both in the section of Purpose and in the section of Conclusion and Recommendations. However, past tense is mostly used in Method and Findings sections. The use of tenses here follows the general rule, and there would be exceptional cases in some fields. Give a tentative answer after having a discussion with your partner, or conduct a survey of several journal papers published recently in your field.
>   ◇ Purpose—present tense
>   ◇ Method and findings—(mostly) past tense
>   ◇ Conclusion and recommendations—present tense
>   ◇ Only suggestions are given in terms of the open question.
> 3. In the abstract, the author uses the phrases such as "were more prone to" "somewhat more" "are fewer...than..." to approximate the numbers in the paper.

Language Focus

✔ Language focus is on ways to soften generalizations

1. Three classic verbs for carefully stating a generalization are the verbs *appear(to)*, *seem(to)*, and *tend(to)*.

   > ◇ Children living in poverty *appear to* do poorly in school.

2. Another way to make a generalization more acceptable is to qualify (or limit) the subject.

   > ◇ *Many(A majority of/Some/In most parts of the world)* children living in poverty do poorly in school.

3. A third alternative is to add exceptions.

   > ◇ *With the exception of(Apart from/Except for)* those enrolled in specialized programs, children living in poverty do poorly in school.

4. Use weaker verbs.

> ◇ Many studies have concluded that excessive credit growth *contributed to* the global financial crisis. (The verb "contributed" is weaker than "caused".)
> ◇ The results *indicated* that there is a link between smoking and lung cancer. (The verb "indicated" is weaker than "established".)
> ◇ The survey results *suggest* that the reuse of sentences or sections from one's previously published papers is a questionable practice. (The verb "suggest" is weaker than "show".)

5. Use phrases to distance yourself from the data by attributing your point to someone else or to other studies.

> ◇ *Based on the limited data available…*
> ◇ *According to this preliminary study…*
> ◇ *In the view of many scholars…*

✎ 归纳时一般使用温和的语气，以避免表述绝对化。这里介绍5种表述方法。
方法1：使用3个表示归纳的经典动词(短语) appear(to), seem(to), and tend(to)。
方法2：限定主语。例如句子"*Many(A majority of/Some/In most parts of the world)* children living in poverty do poorly in school."，用于限定主语 children 的限定词是 *Many(A majority of/Some/In most parts of the world)*。
方法3：列举例外。例如句子"*With the exception of(Apart from/Except for)* those enrolled in specialized programs, children living in poverty do poorly in school."，用于表达例外情况的短语是 *With the exception of(Apart from/Except for)*。
方法4：使用弱动词(weaker verbs)。例如句子"Many studies have concluded that excessive credit growth contributed to the global financial crisis."，动词 contributed 在语气上比 caused 弱。
方法5：将个人观点归于其他人或其他研究，使个人与数据保持距离。例如：
　　Based on the limited data available…　　根据获取的有限数据……
　　According to this preliminary study…　　根据这项初步研究……
　　In the view of many scholars…　　在许多学者看来……

Summary

The abstract usually addresses five questions:
- What is the background of the study in the research field?
- What is the purpose of the study?
- How were the data collected and analyzed?
- What were the results or major findings?
- What are the conclusion or recommendations?

讲座 5　如何引用文献(How to Cite the References)

知识概要　引用文献一般包括文中注和参考文献两部分。本讲座详细讲解了 APA 和 Chicago Manual 两种格式。转述动词指在文中注中用于转述他人研究的动词。在不同的学科中，使用频率高的转述动词也是不同的。**主要内容**：1. 为避免抄袭，应学会使用恰当的直接引用、释义以及概述方法；2. 了解不同的参考文献格式(以 APA 和 Chicago Manual 为例)；3. 学会使用高频转述动词。

关　键　词　cite the reference(引用文献)；style of referencing(参考文献格式)；reporting verb(转述动词)

Lead-in

✓ **Main systems of referencing**

"**Style**" refers to the way you present information and write what you have to say. Style guides prescribe conventions for writing and documenting your sources. There are numerous styles but the four main styles are MLA, APA, Chicago Manual and IEEE.

> 1. MLA(Modern Language Association) style: used by the vast majority of high schools, colleges, and in literature, linguistics, and the humanities programs.
> 2. APA(American Psychological Association) style: widely used in the scientific community.
> 3. Chicago Manual of Style: typically used in books, magazines, corporate publications, and other popular outlets.
> 4. IEEE(Institute of Electrical and Electronics Engineers)

Styles aim to bring consistency to the way in which information is presented. They are designed to **promote intellectual integrity** and **protect writers against plagiarism** by specifying the ways in which information should be reported, quoted, paraphrased, and summarized.

✎ "格式"指论文采用的表达和撰写信息的方式。格式指南规定了撰写和引用资料的惯例。常见的四种格式是 MLA、APA、Chicago Manual 和 IEEE 格式。
　　MLA(现代语言协会)格式：被绝大多数高中、大学、文学、语言学和人文学科所采用。
　　APA(美国心理协会)格式：广泛应用于科学界。
　　Chicago Manual(芝加哥手册格式)：通常用于书籍、杂志、公司出版物和其他流行渠道，其"注释-书目"类格式常用于艺术、历史和人文学科。IEEE(电气与电子工程师协会)格式适用于电气与电子工程方面。

Objectives

- Learn to properly make direct quotations, paraphrases and summaries to avoid plagiarism.
- Know different systems of referencing (such as APA and MLA).
- Learn the most frequently used reporting verbs.

Tasks

Decide which of the following need references.

a) A mention of facts or figures from another writer

b) An idea of your own

c) Some data you have found from your own research

d) A theory suggested by another researcher

e) A quotation from a work by any author

f) Something that is agreed to be common knowledge

What are your answers? Among all cases, only a), d) and e) need reference. Are your answers all correct?

Key Points

In order to give references accurately, it is important to follow the following procedure:

a) When reading and note-making, keep a careful record of the details of your sources. For a long piece of writing such as a dissertation, a card index is useful.

b) Find out which system of referencing is used in your subject area. You can do this by studying current textbooks and journals and checking departmental guidelines.

c) Use summary, quotation or mixture of the two methods to give the reference.

Volumes have been published on the rules and recommendations of both styles. The MLA publishes the widely used *MLA Handbook for Writers of Research*, as well as the *MLA Style Manual and Guide to Scholarly Publishing* which offers more detailed guidance for graduate theses, dissertations, and papers to be published in journals. The APA offers a variety of style guides, including *Mastering APA Style and the Publication Manual of the American Psychological Association*, as well as extensive information online. **Numerous online writing labs** (OWLs) sponsored by university writing programs, also provide extensive resources to help you brainstorm, outline, and write papers, as well as avoid plagiarism, which include the online writing labs in Purdue University, University of Wisconsin and University of North Carolina.

There is a lot of bibliographic software, such as EndNote which may be quite useful.

📎 学生可以参考 MLA 手册及《MLA 格式手册和学术出版指南》，它们为研究生论文、学位论文以及论文在期刊上的发表提供了详细的指导。关于 APA 格式，可以参考《掌握 APA 格式》及美国心理协会的出版手册以及大量在线信息。需要使用 Chicago Manual 时，可以参考《芝加哥格式手册》。

一些大学的在线写作实验室（OWLs）也提供了广泛的资源，帮助你集思广益、列提纲、撰写论文，并讲解如何避免抄袭。其中包括普渡大学、威斯康星大学和北卡罗来纳大学等大学的在线写作实验室。

当撰写参考书目时，EndNote 是个很好用的软件助手。

The key point is **What to Cite**. You are supposed to cite whenever you borrow or include in your paper:

> ◇ Exact wording in phrases, full sentences, or passages found in magazine and newspaper articles, books, journals, reports, advertising, and other print sources.
> ◇ Exact wording in phrases, full sentences, or passages from TV and radio broadcasts, interviews, speeches, panel discussions, conversations, and other oral communications.
> ◇ Summaries of the original ideas, findings, or conclusions of others that you found in your research.
> ◇ Photographs, drawings and illustrations, charts and graphs, diagrams and schematics, and other pictorial Images.
> ◇ Websites or pages on the Internet.
> ◇ Citing styles. [This section will only cover APA style and MLA style.]

I. APA style

APA (the abbreviation for American Psychological Association) style is most commonly used to cite sources within the social sciences. The following resource, revised according to the 6th edition, second printing of the APA manual, offers examples for the general format of APA research papers, in-text citations, endnotes/footnotes, and the reference page.

Who should use APA?

It describes rules for the preparation of manuscripts for writers and students in:

> ◇ Social Sciences, such as Psychology, Linguistics, Sociology, Economics, and Criminology
> ◇ Business
> ◇ Nursing

Before you adopt this style for your paper, you should check to see what citation style your discipline uses in its journals and for student research.

❶ In-text citation: author and year

In-text citations include the author's surname or corporate name, the publication year, and the page number, separated by a comma.

✔ Short quotations

For example, in the short quotation:

> Discourse-based interviews and text-based interviews have been described as "talk around texts"(Lillis, 2001, p. 6).

The author's surname "Lillis", the publication year "2001" and the page number "6" are all given in the brackets at the end of the sentence.

However, if the author's surname, in this sentence, "Lillis" is provided in the text, there is no need to repeat it in the citation.

> Lillis(2001) describes discourse-based interviews and text-based interviews as "talk around texts"(p. 6).

✔ Multiple sources

If multiple sources are cited in the same in-text citation, they are arranged alphabetically and separated by a semicolon.

> At a local scale, the notion of place is not only a space that we occupy; it is also a part of who we are. This relationship between location and identity can easily be observed through behaviors displayed both during national holiday celebrations and during all-out war(Crang, 2014; Gruffudd, 2014).

In this example, Crang is put before Gruffudd according to the alphabetic order.

✔ Long quotations

If a quotation has more than 40 words, it forms a block of text indented half an inch(or 1.27 cm) from the left margin. Contrary to other quotations, it is not within quotation marks.

In the following example, the page number 35 in the parentheses comes after the full stop. Yagoda(2004) states that we read with our ears all the time:

> When we "get into" a book, the pleasant enveloping feeling brings us back to the childhood state of being read to by our parents. Bad writing keeps clearing its throat to wake up from our reverie. Psychologists report that all of us, whether or not we move our lips when we read, subvocalize, or silently recite the text to ourselves. (p. 35)

✓ Modified quotations

If alterations or clarifications are made to a quotation, they are added in brackets within the quotation.

"It [yoga] is neither a religion, nor a creed; it is a need of life [emphasis added], as the breath we breathe" (Krishnananda, 2000, p. 80).

If words or sentences are omitted from a quotation, they are replaced by an ellipsis.

"Yoga is a…need that will be felt by every individual…Yoga is the science of existence" (Krishnananda, 2000, 80).

✓ Paraphrase or summary

- The safety of energy drinks has not yet been established (Reissig et al., 2009).
- In their study of energy drinks, Reissig et al. (2009) suggested that energy drinks may not be entirely safe. They also indicated that more research is needed.

The abbreviation "et al." ([ˌet ˈæl]) is here used after a name or a list of names to indicate that the opinion was held by more than two people.

If source material is paraphrased rather than quoted, the page number is optional.

- According to some, the relationship between art and society is reciprocal (Mueller, 1935, p. 374).

Or you can omit the page number.

- According to some, the relationship between art and society is reciprocal (Mueller, 1935).

❷ References section

The entries include all the elements needed to locate a source, such as the source's author, year of publication, title, and publication information. They are arranged alphabetically according to **the authors' surnames** in a list called References.

…

Bell, J., & Waters, S. (2014). Doing your research project: A guide for first-time researchers (6th ed.). New York, NY: Open University Press.

Colton, M. (1989). Attitudes of special foster parents and residential staff towards children. Children & Society, 3(1), 3-18. doi: 10. 1111/j. 1099-0860. 1989. tb00565. x

Kernis, M. H., Cornell, D. P., Sun, C, R., Berry, A., & Harlow, T. (1993). There's more to self-esteem than whether it is high or low: The importance of stability of self-esteem. Journal of Personality and Social Psychology, 65(6), 1190-1204.

United Nations Development Programme. (n. d.). Human development index(HDI). Retrieved from http://hdr. undp. org/en/content/human-development-index-hdi

…

If there is no author, the bibliographic entry is arranged alphabetically according to the title.

The first entry is a book, including Author. (Year). Title of Book(Edition). Location: Publisher.

The second entry is about an article in a scientific journal, including Author. (Year). Title of Article. Title of Periodical, Volume(Issue), Pages. DOI.

The third is about an article in a journal of social science.

The fourth is from web content; it includes Author. (Year). Title of Web Page. Retrieved from http://URL.

And in the fourth entry, there is no author, so the citation indicates the title instead. And there is no year of publication, the citation indicates "n. d. " for "no date".

II. MLA style

MLA is the abbreviation for the Modern Language Association. This section contains resources on **in-text citations** and **Works Cited pages**.

Who should use MLA?

MLA Style is typically reserved for writers and students preparing manuscripts in various humanities disciplines such as:

- English Studies—Language and Literature
- Foreign Languages and Literatures
- Literary Criticism
- Comparative Literature
- Cultural Studies

Common abbreviations include: ch. (chapter), ed. (edition), et al. (and others), no. (number), p. (page), par. (paragraph), pp. (pages), qtd. in(quoted in), sec. (section), trans. (translation), UP(University Press), vol. (volume).

❶ In-text citation: author and page

✓ Short quotations

In-text citations include the author's surname or corporate name and the page number.

> ◇ Culture is "what some persons feel or do, unlike others who do not feel or do the same things"(Wallerstein 91).

If the author's surname is provided in the text, there is no need to repeat it in the citation.

> ◇ According to Wallerstein, culture is "what some persons feel or do, unlike others who do not feel or do the same things" (91).
> ◇ Is it possible that culture is merely "what some persons feel or do, unlike others who do not feel or do the same things" (Wallerstein 91)?

✓ **Multiple sources**

If multiple sources are cited in the same in-text citation, they are separated by a semicolon. This rule is the same as that in APA style, but the number given here is the page number rather than the year of publication.

At a local scale, the notion of place is not only a space that we occupy; it is also a part of who we are. This relationship between location and identity can easily be observed through behaviors displayed both during national holiday celebrations and during all-out war (Crang 8; Gruffudd 556-557).

✓ **Long quotations**

As Coiro puts it:

> Milton's success in constructing himself as English literature's great, solitary author whose career, even its necessary interruptions, forms and overarching plan of vatic power has also obscured the involved history of the masque. Yet Milton's theatrical involvements at Cambridge, the masque's theatrical identity, and the masque's material existence as a printed book all tell a counterintuitive story—collaborative, theatrical, and historically and culturally embedded. (609)

❷ **Works Cited section (page)**

The entries include all the elements needed to locate a source, such as the source's author, title, publication information, and year of publication. They **are arranged alphabetically** according to the authors' **surnames** in a list called **Works Cited**.

…

Browne, M. Neil, and Stuart M. Keeley. Asking the Right Questions: A Guide to Critical Thinking. 10th ed., Pearson Prentice Hall, 2011

Hamblin, James. "How to Talk to Strangers." The Atlantic, 25 Aug. 2016, www.theatlantic.com/health/archive/2016/08/civil-inattention/497183/.

Martin, George R. R. A Game of Thrones. Bantam Books, 1996.

Mueller, John H. "Is Art the Product of Its Age?" Social Forces, vol. 13, no. 3, 1935, pp. 367-375. JSTOR, www.jstor.org/stable/2570399.

Tan, Amy. "Rules of the Game." *The Vintage Book of Contemporary American Short Stories*, edited by Tobias Wolff, Random House, 1994, pp. 497-508.

…

In **Entry 1**, the source has two authors; the bibliographic entry includes both names in the same order as on the title page. The first name is inverted, and each name is separated by a comma. **Entry 2** is from the web content, and thus it includes the author, title of the article, title of the website, posting or publishing date, URL. **Entry 3** is about a book; it includes the author, title of the book, publisher, and year. **Entry 4** is about an article in a scientific journal, including the author, title of the article, title of the periodical, volume, number, year, pages, title of the database, and URL. **Entry 5** is from part of a book; there are both the author and the editor. It is composed of the author, title of the short story, title of the book, editor's full name, publisher, year, and pages.

Language Focus

1 Reporting verbs

There is a range of **reporting verbs** that you may use when referring to your source material. In fact, a study by Ken Hyland (1999) identified more than 400 different reporting verbs; however, a much smaller number of verbs tend to predominate.

The following table **shows the most frequently used reporting verbs from a variety of disciplines**, with the most frequent on the left and the sixth most frequent on the far right. Pay attention to disciplinary differences (Swales, 213).

High-frequency reporting verbs differ from field to field, as shown by the table.

All these disciplines are divided into two categories: harder sciences and softer sciences. For Biology, which ranks the first in the category of harder science, the first six high-frequency reporting verbs are *describe*, *find*, *report*, *show*, *suggest* and *observe*. Among all the seven harder sciences, "report" "show" and "find" are widely used. The word "develop" is only included by the fields of Physics, Electrical Engineering and Mechanical Engineering, which may indicate these fields have more demands for innovations. On the contrary, among the six softer sciences, the word "develop" never appears. Strikingly, the word "suggest" is used in all six fields investigated. The next verb widely used in this category is "argue", which never appears in those harder sciences. The list of high-frequency reporting verbs will probably save our time while choosing words.

Discipline	Verbs and Frequency Rank					
	1	2	3	4	5	6
Harder Sciences						
Biology	describe	find	report	show	suggest	observe
Physics	develop	report	study	find	expand	
Electrical Engineering	propose	use	describe	show	publish	develop
Mechanical Engineering	describe	show	report	discuss	give	develop
Epidemiology	find	describe	suggest	report	examine	show
Nursing	find	suggest	report	identify	indicate	show
Medicine	show	report	demonstrate	observe	find	suggest
Softer Sciences						
Marketing	suggest	argue	find	demonstrate	propose	show
Applied Linguistics	suggest	argue	show	explain	find	point out
Psychology	find	show	suggest	report	demonstrate	focus
Sociology	argue	suggest	describe	note	analyze	discuss
Education	find	suggest	note	report	demonstrate	provide
Philosophy	say	suggest	argue	claim	point out	think

（以上来自 K. Hyland 和 Carson Maynard 的统计结果）

> 引用材料时，可以使用报告动词（Reporting verbs）。Ken Hyland（1999）的研究分别统计了硬科学和软科学中的高频报告动词。在硬科学排名第一的生物学中，前六个高频报告动词是 describe, find, report, show, suggest 和 observe。在所列的硬科学学科中，"report" "show" 和 "find" 得到了广泛使用。而 "develop（研发）" 这个词只被用于物理学、电气工程和机械工程领域，这可能表明上述领域对创新的要求更高。相反，在软科学学科中，"develop" 一词从未出现，而 "suggest（建议）" 一词遍布软科学各学科。另一个在软科学中常见的动词是 "argue（争论）"，但是它从未出现在硬科学学科中。

❷ Summary reminder phrases

In a longer summary, you may want to remind your reader that you are summarizing:

> ◇ The author goes on to say that/Reissig et al. go on to describe…
> ◇ The article further states that…
>   ◇ [Authors' surnames here] also state/maintain/argue that…
>   ◇ [Authors' surnames here] also believe that…
>   ◇ [Authors' surnames here] conclude that…
> ◇ In the second half of the paper, [author's surname here] presents…

Some of the following sentence connectors may be useful in introducing additional information.

| additionally | in addition to | also | furthermore | further | moreover |

Summary

- Always check the style guides in your discipline to learn more about proper documentation.
- Bibliographies include all the related sources you consulted in your research whether or not you cite or mention them at all in your paper.
- Your works cited should include only the sources that you cite.
- If your Works Cited/References page includes a source that you did not cite in your paper, delete it.

Ⅲ. 写作练习

1. Read the sentences taken from Methods section. Then rewrite them with passive voice in order to emphasize the recipient(接受者) of the action of a verb rather than the doer.

1) We conducted the study at the beginning of the semester and gave the final one at the end of the semester.
2) We developed two questionnaires for the survey, based on two earlier survey instruments that Taylor & Hussein (1985) and Guo (1989) made.
3) We recruited (招募) a total of 80 (36 male) participants at the University of Canterbury (51 participants) and from the general population (29 participants).
4) We computed the final scores into mean averages (X) and standard deviations (SD).
5) We collected rice straw from Hubei Province (China) in 2014.

2. Which of the English sentences is correct?

1) 把英语作为二语的 Level 1 学生，其写作动机高于 Level 3 学生。

　　A. The L2 writing motivation of Level 1 students is higher than Level 3 students.

　　B. The L2 writing motivation of Level 1 students is higher than that of Level 3 students.

2) 图 8 所示的结果与实验 5 的结果非常相似。

　　A. The results shown in Figure 8 are very much *like* Experiment 5.

　　B. The results shown in Figure 8 very much *like* those of Experiment 5.

　　C. The results shown in Figure 8 are very much *like* those of Experiment 5.

3) 女性的平均分为 3.89，而男性的平均分为 4.76。

　　A. Women had a mean score of 3.89, compared with a mean for men of 4.76.

　　B. Women had a mean score of 3.89, comparing with a mean for men of 4.76.

4) 分析了所有水果残渣的元素组成，如表 1 所示。

　　A. The elemental compositions of all of the fruit residues were analyzed, as were

shown in Table 1.

 B. The elemental compositions of all of the fruit residues were analyzed, as shown in Table 1.

 C. Shown in Table 1, the elemental compositions of all of the fruit residues were analyzed.

5) 该系本科生中有很大一部分被招募来参加这项研究。

 A. A large proportion of undergraduates in the department were recruited for the study.

 B. A large proportion of undergraduates in English Department was recruited for the study.

3. Here is the Conclusion section of the paper written by M. A. A. Mamun, G. Lawrie and T. Wright. Answer the following questions.

Conclusion

① This study provides a positive exemplar of how to implement an inquiry-based learning in an online environment while considering no immediate teacher or peer support. ② The findings suggest that the overarching POEE framework and effective use of the pedagogical tools such as multiple external representations, inquiry questions, and instructional guidance can potentially mitigate (减少) the need of immediate teacher and peer support in an online environment. ③ However, recent research also warrants more attention as challenges increase when scaffolding is employed in the self-regulated learning environments without direct teacher support (Palincsar et al., 2018). Some researchers argue the effectiveness of combining multiple scaffolding tools since these tools had varying effects on students' understanding of a problem (Zydney, 2010). Therefore, Ustunel and Tokel (2018) suggest that technology-based scaffolds and their integration within a learning setting must be considered carefully by designers taking into consideration both goals and contexts. ④ In line with this argument, this study recommends that there is need for studies in a larger scale and in other domains about the use of multimodal scaffolding, particularly the proposed POEE strategy in the self-directed online context without the personal, direct, synchronous guidance by a teacher or peer.

Four items are usually included in the **Conclusion** section:

 A. background information

 B. summarizing and reporting key results

 C. commenting on the key results, stating the limitations of the study

 D. making recommendations for future research

Please answer the following questions:

1. Which item is Sentence③ about?

2. Which item is Sentence④ about?

3. The authors use varied ways to express **academic modesty** in Sentence②. Find out such words, and write down at least **one word**.

4. Compare Sentence ② and the following sentences. Then decide from which section the following sentences are more likely to be taken from, **Introduction**, **Methods**, **Results**, or **Conclusion**?

  This data revealed that, in the self-directed online learning, synchronous feedback assisted students to evaluate, clarify, and confirm their learning. It also supported them through a structured learning progression so that they could proceed without direct supervision.

4. Compare the following pairs of sentences. Then decide which is softer in tone and thus academically respectable?

1) A. The present study *has offered an insight into* the uses of multimodal markers in tourism discourses.

 B. The present study *has solved* the uses of multimodal markers in tourism discourses.

2) A. Neural machine translation is a newly emerging approach to machine translation.

 B. *According to Kalchbrenner et al.*, Neural machine translation is a newly emerging approach to machine translation.

3) A. Smokers *develop more* blood clots.

 B. Smokers *are more prone to/are at higher risk of* blood clots.

4) A. We therefore *suggest* that min-invasive therapy *would be* effective in treating LIDP.

 B. We therefore *declare* that min-invasive therapy *is* effective in treating LIDP.

5. Now, do it yourself. Find a paper in your research field. Pay attention to the in-text citation as well as References/Works Cited/Bibliography sections, especially the details about how to order the entries and how to use italics and capital letters in titles. Find an example of each type: 1) a book by one author; 2) an edited book; 3) a source on the Internet; 4) an article in a journal.

第 15 周
国际会议（International Conferences）

❱❱ I．概述

本周课程将围绕学术会议演讲展开，内容包括：1. 概述；2. 投怎样的征文，投到何处：征文通知；3. 撰写会议论文摘要；4. 精心准备学术会议演讲；5. 参加学术会议、宣读会议论文和接受提问。

首先，学术演讲的种类繁多，口头演讲与书面论文差别巨大，作者根据自己多年参加学术会议的经验认为，演讲者应遵循相应的模式和规范，充分利用国际会议提供的各种机会，扩大与其他参会者的交流。

其次，演讲者应仔细阅读国际会议通知，可以在上面找到会议主题和论文要求等内容，然后按照相关要求撰写并提交论文。

再次，学术会议摘要应明确定义文章要研究的主题、某一问题研究的重要意义、研究问题时使用的方法以及研究中得到的主要收获和结论。完成演讲稿并准备好演示稿（PowerPoint，PPT）和讲义。将书面论文转换为口头演示文稿，在演讲中使用合适的直观教具来加强演讲效果。

最后，成功的会议演讲还需要注意事先反复排练，提前熟悉演讲会议厅以及会议厅内设备的操作和使用。此外，演讲过程中还需要注意使用适当的目光交流、语调调节、形体传意，并能够优雅从容地回答听众提出的问题。

❱❱ II．慕课讲稿

讲座 1　课程和授课教师简介（Introduction to Course and Instructor's Name）

知识概要　作者首先介绍了他在三十余年教学生涯中本人宣读会议论文及帮助学生宣读论文的经历，然后提供了本周课程概览：为什么要提交论文，如何选择提交的论文，如何找到信息来源和怎样发掘摘要的有用信息，怎样写出适合宣读且能被接受的论文，如何有效使用PPT及其他信息演示系统，如何使用手稿或其他媒介，如何排练论文报告以及在完成论文报告后应该做些什么。其次，作者介绍了口头报告与书面论文的巨大差异。由于学术报告的种类繁多，演讲者应遵循相应的模式和规范，充分利用国际会议提供的各种机会，扩大与其他参会者的交流。

关 键 词 口头演讲(an oral presentation)；专业化(professionalism)

Lead-in

I have been giving papers and helping our students present papers for over thirty years. My own style has changed a great deal over that time in response to the issues I discuss below. I have been able to help my students craft and improve their own presentations and I hope I can assist you too.

I want this mini-course to be practical as well as theoretical. But this course must also serve the needs of you, the student. Thus please, if questions arise as you view my presentation, PLEASE POST THEM. Such questions will help you, your fellow students, and all the instructors of this course.

Objectives

In this short course I want to provide a useful overview of why students should present a paper, how to choose what paper to send, useful information about how to figure out where to send an abstract, how to write that abstract, how to compose your accepted paper for oral delivery, how to best use PowerPoint or other information display systems, how to use handouts or other media, how to practice for and give your paper, and what to do after you have presented your paper.

Tasks

In the previous instruction module, you learned how to write a paper for advanced coursework or for possible publication. In this module we want you to understand how **different** an oral presentation should be from a written paper meant to be read. So take a moment and think of four ways an oral presentation is different than a written article.

What four differences can you think of?

Key Points

Why oral papers are different? We have seen graduate students and junior scholars essentially read a slightly edited version of a seminar paper, and usually such a presentation is a disaster.

You can read a scholarly article at your own pace, go back and reread a paragraph if you do not understand something, look up a term in the dictionary, stop and take a break if needed and so forth. But the audience for a conference paper cannot go back and re-hear a prior paragraph.

An oral presentation happens in real time! If the presenter's language is confusing, some audience members may get lost and never be able to pick up the thread of the argument. Likewise if they cannot properly hear the speakers, or are distracted by his body language and gestures, understanding is lost.

And if the handouts and PowerPoint presentations are poorly designed and badly used, confusion and distraction may result, leading to communication failure. Everybody does not process information at the same speed or have the same familiarity with the topic.

By simplifying and focusing your presentation, you will improve learning outcomes. There is no point in presenting information which cannot be retained.

Remember the best presentations provide valid and pertinent(有关的) information, with research or data to support that information, and are done in an engaging and audience-friendly manner.

When composing, find your balance between having fun and being informative, between sounding smart and being understood.

Professionalism. We found a large number of sites about presentations connected to business and government. This makes sense. In business promoting and selling projects, ideas directly relate to an individual's success. If you are using a PPT to make a presentation to a board of busy, senior directors, you need to meet **their** needs, not yours. So if you are going to make a presentation, you need to do it right the FIRST time.

Conferences are the life-blood of academia. At conferences scholars from around the country(and sometimes around the planet) converge to exchange ideas, comment on each other's research, and find out what others in the field are studying, find employment opportunities, join new collaborations, and much else. Through giving papers you can participate in the community of scholars. And sometimes representatives from the world of publishing, government, industry and much more are also attending, depending on the field. You can never know who might show up!

The diversity of presentations. Because of the vast variety of academic disciplines, there are many different types of presentations possible. What we present here is only a general overview—it is a very good idea for students thinking about presenting papers to talk with professors or other experts in their field to get more specific details.

Some types of papers:

(A) The individually presented paper, in which one person presents a paper he/she has composed. Sometimes papers are presented with two authors or even more.

(B) Panel discussions, where sometimes all papers are on one topic or area, and there is often one speaker who comments on all the papers.

(C) Workshops, in which the speaker may actually teach or show the audience how to perform certain tasks or use certain techniques.

(D) Poster sessions, particularly prevalent(流行的) outside the Humanities. Attendees read the poster and talk with their authors about the topic presented.

(E) And, as conferencing software has improved, there is a new kind of conference, sometimes called the "webinar". All members of the "audience" log on to a virtual presentation space, and listen to the speaker's presentation, and often have the ability via voice or texting to post their own questions and have discussions.

There can be huge differences in styles among these types. Papers on literary topics can be extremely wide ranging, speculative, or diffuse(啰唆的). In the physical sciences the whole paper can consist of explaining why a particular experiment was performed, how it was performed(with much detail), the results and the significance of those results. There can be considerable differences between the cultures of presenters and their fields of study in formality of language, style of dress, body language and so forth. Again, it is so important to seek the advice of those in the field to see what the norms are in your field.

Summary

1. There is a huge difference between a successful written article and a successful face to face presentation.

2. One can learn a lot from the "real world" about how to make truly successful oral communications. Follow the most professionally successful models.

3. It is good to seek advice from more senior professionals about particular standards and convention in your field regarding presentations.

4. There is a variety of types of conference presentations.

5. Conferences allow you to participate in a community of scholars.

讲座2 开始准备：投怎样的会议论文，投向何处？征文通知
(Getting Started: What Paper Should You Send and Where? The Call for Papers)

知识概要 大多数国际会议通知会详细介绍会议主题和论文要求等内容，演讲者应仔细阅读这些内容，并按照相关要求提交论文。

关 键 词 征文通知(call for papers)；听众(audience)

Lead-in

For this module, you need to read the material below.

Call for Papers

Conference on The Philosophy of Logic, Mathematics, and Physics (LMP)

Submission deadline: March 15, 2019. Acceptance notices should be received by 15 April 2019.

Conference date(s): June 10, 2019—June 11, 2019

Conference Venue: Department of Philosophy, University of Western Ontario, London, Canada

Details: The 19th annual Philosophy of Logic, Mathematics, and Physics Conference will take place on Monday-Tuesday, June 10-11, 2019, at the University of Western Ontario in London, Ontario, Canada. We are pleased to announce that Dr. Isaac J. Brane, (Miskatonic University, Arkham Massachusetts) will be giving the keynote address "M-Theory Symmetry and the Metaphysics of Physics" for this year's LMP. Click here for details on attending the conference banquet and lodging options in the University dormitory or at Best Western Inn London.

Call for Papers: Scholars (including graduate students) are invited to submit papers on any topic in philosophy of logic, philosophy of mathematics, and philosophy of physics. Each of these subjects will have their own conference track. Papers in philosophy of physics will be considered for the 16th Annual Clifton Memorial book prize. The contest will be adjudicated by philosophy of physics faculty members at University of Western Ontario. Select papers will be accepted for the online publication of the conference proceedings.

Submission Guidelines: The maximum paper length is 5,000 words, including footnotes and appendices (but not references). If the paper includes tables, figures, or equations, an appropriate number of words should be subtracted from the limit. Papers are to be prepared for anonymous review, and should be accompanied by an abstract (no longer than 300 words).

Deadline: Papers should be submitted in. pdf format via EasyChair by March 15th, 2019 at *https://easychair.org/conferences/?conf=2019lmp*.

Authors of accepted papers will be limited to 30-35 minutes for presentation, followed by a 20-minute period of discussion. Presenters are expected to bring their own laptops.

Please send any questions to the LMP Conference Committee: *uxwolmp2@gmail.com*.

Please post questions.

Objectives

In this module, we shall consider: 1) where to start in choosing what topic to write your oral paper on; 2) how to read the call for papers and proposals; 3) how to think about your audience as you compose your presentation.

Tasks

Young scholars should start out writing on a subject they know well and have written about before. So, imagine Jackie Ma wanted to pay you one million RMB to produce a 20-minute conference talk in one week. Give two subjects/papers/projects you could immediately start working on.

What were your examples?

Getting started. Most graduate students start by giving papers rooted in a course they had taken or in a project they were involved in. Often graduate students will turn a section or chapter of a dissertation into a paper for presentation. My first paper in Classics grew out of a course on Vergil's Aeneid and my first paper in Archaeology grew out of an excavation I participated which was located in Southern Italy. The first workshop I gave grew out of my work in creating online courses, and it involved teaching teachers how to create videos using inexpensive Macintosh software.

Key Points

Pick your conference carefully. Here the advice of colleagues and mentors, networking and a little research can help. The Internet is always useful, as is Facebook or its equivalents. I have always advised my graduate students (and some undergraduates) to join professional societies in their field, whose newsletters and Internet resources can be very helpful. But be careful. Make sure that you pick a conference that actually accepts papers like yours. Often the abstracts of accepted papers are published for you to read and study. But sometimes acceptance is just a matter of chance.

Call for proposals/papers. Conference program committees will typically send out a call for proposals a few months ahead of the conference. Now pause and read carefully this short (and edited by me) handout titled *Call for Papers*.

Have you read *Call for Papers* carefully?

As seen in the example, above, calls for papers have some common features. They will tell the purpose of the conference, who organized it, and where it will be held. They often request an abstract or proposal, typically 200-500 words in length, sometimes quite a bit longer as seen above. They will tell about the length and formatting of the abstract. They will provide the dates for submission and acceptance of abstracts.

Make sure you read ALL the directions in *Call for Papers* carefully. The word limit may or may not include bibliography (as here). There may be a specific way bibliography is to be cited within the abstract. There may be other formatting rules which the profession uses, such as the SME (Society for Mechanical Engineers) guidelines. The margins may have to be a certain size. Often you must make sure your name is NOT in the body of the abstract, since the judges (in theory) should not know whose work they are judging.

Some conferences will collect abstracts and post them so that those attending the conference can better select which papers they wish to attend. You may be asked to define your paper's subject area, so your paper can be part of the right "track", that is, a series of paper sessions on similar themes. You may be asked if you will use multimedia during your presentation.

As noted before, you may have the option of submitting four or more abstracts to create a whole "panel" on one topic, for example, five papers on *The Dream of the Red Chamber*. For a panel proposal you will need to submit all the abstracts for the papers of the panel at once. Often the date for the acceptance of panels is a month earlier than the due date of submission of abstracts for individual papers. The logic is that, if your panel is turned down, you can still submit your own individual paper.

The title of the paper should be informative, but, often in the Humanities, speakers like to add some humor. I once almost titled a paper on the angry dead in the *Aeneid* "Arms and the Man and Zombies" but I relented. Increasingly abstracts are submitted electronically, often in docx or pdf format. Some more elite, specialized conferences will publish their own conference proceedings (会议论文集), and submitted papers are often considered for publication. Again, please respect the submission deadlines posted.

After the submission deadline has passed, the conference committee will then select the best proposals (usually, but not always, using blind review) and put the conference program together. Be aware when you submit to a conference that there are different acceptance rates. For example, the Society for Classical Studies meetings, at which publishers and future employers meet, probably rejects 60 percent or more of abstracts submitted. When your paper is accepted, start thinking about the logistics of attending the conference, such as getting an airplane ticket or booking a hotel room.

Know your potential audience. This can be a tricky matter if your paper is highly specialized. For example, I am a Senior Classics scholar, but when I go to our Society for Classical Studies meetings, most of the papers presented I can only vaguely follow, because I am not an expert in that particular author, text, historical period and so forth. In my opinion, it is good, when composing your abstract and final presentation, to make some attempt to provide matter of interest to the non-specialists and to connect to the interests of your audience.

Summary

1. Choose a topic that you have already worked on in a class, seminar, or project.
2. Most conferences put out a "Call for Papers" which gives detailed information about the conference, what sort of papers it is looking for, and the requirements for submission and presentation.
3. Pay close attention to the details of the Call for Papers and respect deadlines.
4. The audience for your paper can vary wildly, depending on the subject and the nature of the conference. It is generally a good idea to have information in the paper that would be of potential interest to individuals who do not work in your area of study.

讲座3 撰写会议论文摘要(Writing the Abstract)

知识概要 学术会议摘要字数应该在200到800之间,摘要应明确文章要研究的主题。摘要一般包括某一问题研究的重要意义、研究问题时使用的方法以及研究中得到的主要收获和结论。

关 键 词 简单清晰(simplicity and clarity);收获(contribution);方法(means)

Lead-in

For this lecture, you need to read the two abstracts.

Example Abstract One

A Comparison of Anomic and Quartz Clock Hardware Used in Space Applications

Accurate and stable frequency reference sources, whose oscillations allow for extremely precise time regulation, are critical for a variety of commercial ground-based, and aerospace applications, especially involving navigation (Von Braun 2003). For any piece of flight hardware, there are many requirements that are generic (size, weight, durability, power consumed etc.) with other properties being unique to that particular application (output power, axial ratio, gain, throughput, etc.), but the key requirement for frequency reference sources concerns phase noise and signal stability (Armstrong 2010). Those required to design measurement protocols for such systems must weigh various requirements and options. This paper, focusing on issues of low-noise signal stability, provides an analytical overview of the similarities and differences of single distributed oscillators used in many communication satellites, master oscillators used in most military applications, and atomic clocks used in military and navigation systems, with a look forward to research in atomic-clock-on-a-chip project (Goddard 2018).

Example Abstract Two

Using Zoom™ and Globesmart™ to Enhance International Business Online Teaching

Due to a pressing need to expand markets and lower costs, universities are experimenting with online instruction (Postman 2001). A key challenge is how to bridge the physical distance between the instructor and class members and how to reduce the feelings of isolation and even alienation experienced by students, which has been well documented (Ignoramus 2008). Drawing on my fifteen years of experience as an instructor and advisor for the online MBA at Friedmann University, I will discuss and then demonstrate two technologies I use to make my online courses highly relevant and engaging. Zoom™ is a powerful web conferencing tool which allows the real-time delivery of course materials (PPTs, Excel files, screen sharing, videos, etc.) while allowing students to connect via video and voice. Globesmart™ is an online resource that allows students to research business-related cultural information on almost 100 countries. This workshop will demonstrate my approach to delivering online instruction and show how to incorporate Zoom™ and Globesmart™ to deliver content, enhance student interactions, and structure relevant assignments. During the workshop I will use content provided by the participants to demonstrate these technologies. I will also provide a "getting started" worksheet.

In order to present a conference paper, you need first to write an abstract, often between 200-800 words. Realize that writing the abstract is in many ways harder than writing the paper, because your abstract is in competition with dozens or hundreds of other abstracts, and you have limited space to promote your ideas.

Objectives

To produce a good abstract you need to be precise, clear, and able to show evidence that you have the necessary knowledge, have done the preliminary background research, have adopted proper research methods, have thought through what you want to discuss, and can cover the material properly in the given amount of time. Below I provide a very general guide on writing the abstract.

As noted before, every field has its own standards, culture, language and academic customs. Consult instructors and experienced professionals, and look online for copies of abstracts similar to yours.

Tasks

Now pause and carefully read the first example abstract.

Have you read the abstract carefully? Now answer the following questions about the abstract.

1. How does it show the issue under consideration is important?
2. How does it show what the central issue is?
3. How does it show for whom the paper is written?
4. How does it show knowledge of the pertinent scholarship?
5. How does it also offer something extra?

Answers

This abstract starts off by 1) explaining the vital function of frequency reference sources, and then 2) focuses on the issue of phase noise and signal stability. 3) The paper is aimed clearly at those required to design measurement protocols for such systems. 4) Internal footnotes show the scholarly sources 5) and it offers something extra in exploring the development of an atomic-clock-on-a-chip.

When you write your abstract, your goals should be simplicity and clarity. This does not mean using simple words or "dumbing down" your message. What it means is to strip down your presentation to the core idea and make those ideas show clearly.

Before you get started, get a clear idea of what is your main point and what are the means by which you prove that point. For some scholars, outlines or even flowcharts of ideas can help clarify their thoughts. Also, talking about your ideas with friends, colleagues or mentors can be very productive.

Key Points

To compose an abstract you will need to create:

1. **A title.** As noted, the title should be informative, but not too technical or dull. As long as the meaning of the title is clear, even a little wit is allowed. For example, which title would work better—"Resource Management Techniques of Spenisiforms" or "The Food Hunting Strategies of King Penguins"? "Who Moved My Cheese?" instead of "Food Location Behaviors Used by Household Mice".

2. **A statement of why your topic is important.** It is good to situate your paper in the context of your field and its issues, so that others will understand why they will want to hear your paper.

3. **A statement about what contribution to the field will be made by your paper.** Remember, the nature of this contribution will vary greatly due to the conference. The short abstract seen above did not claim to do original research, but rather to gather and summarize important information useful for a certain type of engineer. Other conferences will demand much more original work.

4. **A sample of your methodology and a demonstration** of how you prove your points, according to the best practices in the field.

5. **Sufficient proof** of your knowledge of scholarship and **secondary literature** concerning the issue you have chosen.

When you have finished the abstract, it is a good idea to have a friend or colleague look it over to see if it really makes sense. Make sure that its language is clear and that you show how all its components fit together and follow each other in a logical fashion.

Another popular type of presentation is the **workshop**, where the speaker engages the audience more directly, like in a classroom, and perhaps teaches a skill, as in this example. Now pause and carefully read the second example abstract.

Have you finished reading the example carefully? How is this workshop abstract similar to the one you studied before? How is it different?

1) The title provides a clear idea of the workshop's content.
2) It demonstrates why the issue is important (the needs of universities motivate experiments in online teaching).
3) It describes a major issue (student engagement vs. student alienation).
4) It gives evidence that the software under consideration will help solve such problems.
5) While it does not show methodology as such, it does indicate this software has been tested in the context of a long-term online MBA program.
6) Articles of two scholars are referred to.
7) What it offers that the previous paper did not is an opportunity for the workshop participants to experiment with this technology using content that the attendees provide.

To repeat what I have mentioned before, customs and conventions about an abstract's structure and language can vary a great deal between fields. Looking over example abstracts and consulting with those having more experience is always a good strategy.

Summary

1. Before you begin composing your abstract, make sure you have a very clear idea of what your core idea is and how you want support that idea, and what you want your audience to take away from your presentation.
2. In composing your abstract, make sure every part of your abstract (and subsequent paper) supports these purposes, including structure, language and rhetoric.
3. In composing your abstract, be able to state clearly why the issue you deal with is important, what is your original contribution, and the means by which you will prove your point.
4. Be aware of the conventions in your field to demonstrate the proper use of language, sources and methodology.

Now, in the next lecture, we shall consider writing the paper which you will orally deliver, which should differ in important ways from an article meant to be read.

讲座 4　精心准备学术会议演讲(Crafting the Oral Presentation)

知识概要　因为学术会议演讲的听众是从演讲者处获取信息，而许多演讲者在演讲过程中会使用直观教具(例如 PPT)，因此本讲座主要介绍如何将书面论文转换为口头演示文稿、如何在演讲中使用合适的直观教具来增强演讲效果。

关 键 词　转换(convert); 视觉的(visual); 听众(audience)

Lead-in

You have written a paper which was well received, and sent off an abstract which was accepted. But now you need to write the script for the oral presentation.

This can be challenging because you must condense a much longer paper into fifteen minutes. As noted, listening to a paper is very different from reading a paper. However, learning to present your work is an important academic exercise which invites critical engagement with your work, which in turn enables you to improve your writing and thinking skills.

Objectives

Because many presentations include visual elements(e.g. PowerPoint), this lecture offers guidelines for converting a written paper into an oral presentation and creating visual material that is appropriate for that presentation.

Tasks

There are more extensive guides for this process which can be found on the Internet and elsewhere. Use them. And there are different conventions for oral papers in different fields, so you should consult those with knowledge and experience to assist you when you compose your first oral presentation.

Close your eyes and imagine you were listening to this passage during a conference. As you listen, what do you think what is wrong with it?

Ready Player One thus dialectically forecloses on what Dinshaw describes as the queer potentialities of amateur reading by reducing reading to a purely ludic game of memorization and textual association, as if seduced by consumerist version of Barth's plaisir du texte. Thus it rejects the inherently deconstructive and, at times, transgressive ways that amateurs play with ideologically authorized texts and traditions and thereby produce alternative readings that trouble the careful binaries through which the oppressive illusion of heteronormativity is maintained. The novel phantaphasmagorically reproduces as Real(in the Lacanian sense) and heteronormative the ideologies that Kücklich, following Jameson's late Marxist praxis, accuses of interpellating their fans into exploitative late capitalist means of production.

Take a moment and write down some problems with this passage.
Believe me, I have heard worse.
- This passage would be hard to understand even when read, much less spoken.
- Note the complex sentences, the dense references to theory and theorists, the lit-crit jargon, the name dropping.
- And think of other common faults we see in oral presentations PPT slide text is too small, or on a background of the wrong color. Sometimes image quality is poor.
- Presenters use cool, but very distracting, special effects for text and images. Some presenters do not speak clearly, or rush through their talk. Some have a PowerPoint presentation that seems unconnected to their talk and is full of spelling errors.

When you are preparing your draft, keep in mind that your audience will rely on listening comprehension, not reading comprehension. That means that your ideas and language need to be clear and to the point, organized in a way that makes it possible for your audience to follow you. Keep focused on what is absolutely essential for your audience to understand. All the rest is, so to speak, icing on the cake(装饰性的).

Key Points

Length. Over the years, I have found that I need to write about 2,100 words for a fifteen-minute presentation. I think this is pretty good general figure. But your own practice should be the guide.

As with the written paper, remember to do the following early on:
1) Introduce yourself.
2) State your thesis clearly.
3) Explain why this issue is important.
4) Explain what your contribution is.
5) Give an outline of your subsequent methodology and conclusions.

Clarity and effectiveness. The lessons you learned in previous modules about writing clearly and effectively also apply to oral presentations. Here are some points to remember:
A. Each paragraph should have a clear point.
B. Paragraphs should logically follow one another.
C. Pay attention to transitions as you move from one topic to another. You may see the

connection, but do not assume your audience will. Context is important.

D. Avoid wordy expressions, such as "undertake to examine" instead of simply "examine".

E. Avoid clichés like the plague.

F. If you are unsure about some aspects of English pronunciation, grammar and usage, consult a dictionary or other sources.

Quotes. While your written article may have many quotes, there is no time for that in an oral paper. When a quotation is necessary, use a signal phrase to introduce the source to your audience. For example, you can say: "As theorist Sandra Somebody states…" or "Theorist Sandra Somebody has argued that…" Also, your handout can provide the text of longer quotes if needed. When needed, you can put charts, tables, graphs, even images in the handout.

The conclusion is important. Your audience has just listened to many of your arguments, but they may have already forgotten some of them. Make sure to remind them how you came to your conclusion and why your scholarly project and analysis matter. For example, you can start your conclusion by stating: "As my presentation has shown, SSSS's relationship to HHH is contingent on factors(a, b, c). In conclusion, I would like to argue that…"

Here you summarize your main points and give your conclusion.

And be sure to thank the audience for listening to you.

Incorporate slides and visual materials Depending on your field of study or the nature of the conference, you may need to show some visual materials. You may even need to show movie clips and sound clips. Whether it's a pie chart to show percentages, or a powerful photograph to convey a point, visuals can be much more effective than words. Most presenters write the oral text, and then create the slide show. A better method is to create both at the same time, always asking yourself which is the more effective way of transmitting a given point—through words or images? A proper graphic can both save time and help the audience to better understand the topic.

Remember to keep your visuals clean and simple. A successful visual presentation should be in sync with(与……同步) the spoken part of your presentation. You can coordinate your talking/reading points with your visual presentation by marking your paper whenever you move to a new slide.

Make sure that you address the visual material that the audience is viewing on the screen. Do not assume that the audience will "get it". Many people may still be thinking about your previous point and need your direction to understanding the relevance of the visuals you are showing them. Pointing out what your listeners are looking at allows them to follow your argument, and perhaps, even better understand it! But be selective when you choose your images/visuals/graphics. Ask yourself: **Does this visual demonstrate my**

argument? How does it relate to my point? Avoid mere eye-candy（华而不实之物）, that is, fancy pictures that have no informational value. Likewise, do not use complex and unneeded transitions between slides.

Because your audience is listening to you, and also reading, try to keep the written part of a slide short. Reading all your points from the slides can be tedious for your audience, so short summaries (approximately 2-5 words) may work best on a slide. Too much text overwhelms your listeners. If your slides include text, make sure the font size is large enough and that the color of the font works well with the slide's background. Legibility is key. Make sure you can be seen from the back of the room.

As you move through your lecture, give your audience enough time to look at each slide. Do not seem rushed. You may have looked at your slides many times, but your audience needs time to absorb them and understand why each slide is relevant.

Standardize the appearance of your slides—same font, colors, placement of graphics and text, etc.

SPELL CHECK! It is very easy to overlook typos when you integrate visuals, but the audience members can see them. Be sure to proofread.

Use high quality images. Sometimes it is easier to find images online to use for presentations. However, the quality of online images varies dramatically, and sometimes you may need to scan images in order to retain a professional look for your slides. It is therefore important to begin preparing your presentation well in advance and avoid last minute additions of low-resolution images.

If you are using movie clips, realize you must subtract their running time from your speaking time, or you will exceed your allotted time.

Practice makes perfect. Practice your talk even before your final draft. The exercise of reading the paper out loud will help you find mistakes in your draft, such as misspellings and unfinished sentences and missing words, and it will help you judge the general flow and coherence of your paper. And, if possible, have another person listen too.

Summary

1. Compose the oral paper as something to be heard and understood immediately, not as something that can be read and reread.
2. Language and syntax should be simpler, and the flow of argument should be clear.
3. Visuals can sometimes transmit information better than language, but make sure the visuals are effectively produced and work well in conjunction with the spoken text.
4. Practice!

Now on to my last lecture, which has advice about the mechanics of attending a conference, giving the paper, and then taking questions. Onward!

讲座 5 参加学术会议、宣读会议论文和接受提问（Tips on Attending a Conference, Presenting the Conference Paper, and Taking Questions）

知识概要　当演讲者已经完成演讲稿并准备好直观教具和讲义之后，还需要注意以下事项：首先，事先反复排练演讲；其次，提前熟悉演讲会议厅以及会议厅内设备的操作和使用；再次，在演讲过程中使用适当的眼神交流、语调调节以及形体传意；最后，优雅从容地回答听众提出的问题。

关 键 词　排练演讲（practice one's presentation）；目光交流（eye contact）

Lead-in

You have composed the oral part of your presentation, and have your PowerPoint presentation and handouts ready. But you still have to show up at the conference, present the paper and take questions. These are not trivial matters. My objectives for this, my final lecture, is to give you some advice about these matters.

Objectives

As noted before, I am focusing on only one kind of presentation, and some varieties of presentation in the fields of business, science or health care can be very different. There are many resources online with information on these matters. Consult them. Also, you may have associates or professors who have attended the conference like the one you are scheduled to speak at, so please, make use of their expertise.

Tasks

Review Task 1　To prepare for this lesson, it is good to review major points made in the previous lecture. So what do you think was my major point regarding the basic principle of writing the oral paper that you will present?

Review Task 1 Answer. My central point was that the paper must be composed to optimize listening comprehension, not reading comprehension. Thus the structure of argument must be clear, the sentences shorter, the syntax simpler.

Review Task 2　In the previous lecture, what do you think were my two major points regarding the basic principle of composing your PPT?

Review Task 2 Answer. My central points were that 1) your slides should be readable and not distracting (right font size and color, short sentences, no distracting special effects), and that 2) the presenter must properly coordinate his/her presentation between what is spoken and what is shown. (Make sure transitions are smooth, and always make sure the audience understands the relationship between what is being said and what is being shown.)

Now we can move forward to our lecture.

Practice, practice, practice! Ideally, at least a week before you present the paper, start seriously practicing presenting it. You should start practicing even while you are writing initial drafts, for what might seem workable in print may fail when read. Then, when you have a good working draft ready, read it aloud, ideally with a trusted friend (or friends) who can give you feedback.

Are your ideas presented clearly? Do you speak clearly? Do your spoken text and visuals work well together? Did you maintain proper eye contact, with right posture and body gestures? Did you stick to the time limit?

You can annotate (给……加注解) your script, such as giving guides to the proper pronunciation of hard words, notes about when to change slides, notes to remind yourself to look up and maintain eye contact. Make yourself notes such as "breathe" or "slow down" if you have a tendency to get nervous and speak too quickly.

I tend to print out my paper in 20 point font or bigger, making it easier to read. Some presenters read from their laptops. I find this distracting, and others do too. I always make sure there are page numbers on the printed sheets I read from.

Keep up to date with how your conference is being managed. Don't book your hotel room at the last minute, for hotels fill up. Sometimes conference rooms and time will be changed at the last minute. If at all possible, check out the location and layout of the room before you actually present; also look at its multimedia set-up. Often presenters may have to switch computers or plug in hookups (连接) to allow sound. Make sure you figure out these matters before you present.

Often the session chair will ask you in advance for your CV so he/she can say something about you and your work. Always have a copy of your CV you can access. If you have a handout, make sure you arrange for how it will be distributed before you begin speaking. Check in advance how many copies you will need.

Different conferences have different rules, but often the speakers in a session sit in the front row, or at a separate table. Also, some sessions, for reasons of time, hold all questions until the end, while others allow some questions at the end of each talk.

It is often a good idea to make sure you have water at the lectern. Keep to the assigned time limit. Sometimes a session chair will have cards or other signaling devices to tell you your time is nearly up. Make sure you thank the audience when you are finished.

On the day you are to give your paper, try to show up early at your room to introduce yourself to the session chair and the other members of your session. The session chair may have important information about how the session will be conducted. Make sure you stay for the whole session.

Don't be nervous about being nervous. When you begin your presentation, smile. Be calm, and breathe deep. Be mindful of your posture: stand straight and hold your head up. Talk clearly, loudly, and energetically. But don't talk too fast: remember that there could be people in the audience whose native language is not English.

Don't speak in monotone for your whole presentation. Modulate your voice. Take advantage of pauses to look up at your audience, and give your audience time to react to what you say. Be careful that you continue to face the audience when you refer them to your visuals. Do not read off your visuals. If you stare at the same spot the entire time, your presentation will be ineffective(and awkward).

Pay attention to your bodily motion and how you present your paper. Even though you are nervous, try to avoid showing any indication of discomfort through fidgeting(坐立不安；烦躁) or excessive use of your hands as you speak. Try to keep your hands on the lectern. Your hands can also be used discreetly(谨慎地) to help you more effectively transition from page to page as you read.

Handling Comments and the Question and Answer portion. Some presentations are part of a panel format, where, after all the papers are presented, a commentator briefly speaks about all the papers, trying to tie what has been said together. Do not worry; the commenter is there to help you look better. You may think you can remember all he/she has to say about your work, but this cannot be assured, especially if you are nervous while listening. Make sure that you write down his/her comments, critiques, suggestions, and questions. The commenter's advice will help you strengthen your work as a researcher and conference presenter. Be grateful for any questions and comments.

The Question and Answer portion of a session can be scary. Remember to breathe and take the questions in stride(泰然自若地). It might help to write down the question being asked before you attempt to answer it. This will help you digest the question in full and allow you to answer it thoroughly. Smile. If needed, ask for a question to be repeated.

Always be thankful for comments. If possible, after the session make yourself available to members of the audience who may have more questions for you or want to give you encouragement or clues. Such interactions are an important part of academic life, and can have unexpected positive outcomes.

Finally, prepare for the unexpected. Sometimes rooms are changed at the last moment, presenters do not show up, there is distracting noise in the next room, hardly anybody appears to hear your paper, people keep entering and leaving and banging doors, or some mentally challenged person constantly asks rambling, confused questions. Stay cheerful; as Vergil put it, "Someday you will remember even this with pleasure".

Summary

Here are five key points:
1. Make sure you practice your presentation beforehand.
2. Try in advance to inspect where you will present and its technology.
3. Include in your script notes to help you present properly, such as references to slides, not reading too quickly, and maintaining eye contact.
4. When speaking, be careful about proper eye contact, voice modulation, and body movement.
5. Take questions gracefully.

Ⅲ. 写作练习

1. Please decide whether the following statements are true(T) or false(F).

1) The title of your presentation is as important as an advertisement to a product.
2) The title of your thesis paper is a perfect choice for your title slide.
3) A piece of writing often consists of two factors: the sequence in which different parts of an argument are provided to the audience, and the relationship the speaker has used to link these parts together.
4) Numbering seems overtly blunt in writing, so in oral presentations it is not helpful for signposting major points or pieces of evidence.
5) When you want to stress a word in a sentence, you can say the word more slowly.
6) The speaker lives in his own little world of research, so it is correct that he believes that all the background information needed to appreciate the meaning of his work is common knowledge.
7) Transitions show the relationships between the ideas and are the glues that hold your presentation together.
8) It makes your slide look more technical if you add some brackets into it.
9) You can use parallel structure to mark transitions between main sections. Use completely different phrases to mark each transition, and then emphasize it with a brief pause to let your audience catch on.
10) It is a good idea to type every word of your script on your slide.

2. Could you revise the following titles of presentations to be more concise?

1) The Lingo-cellulose Biomass Fuel Chain: a Review
2) Development of a Portable Device for Work Analysis to Reduce Human Errors in Industrial Plans
3) Effect of Crop Rotation Diversity and Nitrogen Fertilization on Weeds Management in a Maize-based Cropping System

3. Translate the following sentences into English.

1) 项目委员会很遗憾告知您递交的论文将不予发表。
2) 本次论文选拔程序极具竞争性，只有 200 篇提交稿件通过了。
3) 你可以在这个网站获取审稿建议。
4) 希望这些建议对您有用。
5) 我们期待在今年 8 月的会议上相见。
6) 今天的发言者将会和我们分享一些关于新能源的想法。
7) 接下来，我们将进入提问环节。
8) 您的发言仅剩 2 分钟了。
9) 您对这个问题怎么看？
10) 我觉得我们已经讨论了所有的要点。

4. Imagine you are going to give an oral presentation at an international conference in your research field. Write a "Literature Review" script to the presentation and rehearse it. And then present it to your group or class.

写作练习参考答案

✓ Week 1

1. 1)-5）BABAB　　6-10）BABAA
2. 1）terrorist；2）skinny；3）wordy；4）mean；
   5）cunning；6）extravagant
3. 1）yielded；2）arose；3）demonstrate；4）held
   5）emphasized；6）exhibited；7）concerned
   8）carried out
4. 1）C；2）PW；3）S；4）S；5）C；6）S
   7）PW；8）S
5. 1) This **signing**（改为：signature）of the document is ineligible.
   2) I **received**（改为：won）third place in the contest.
   3) She understands **deeply**（改为：fully）that I would do everything for her.
   4) We can keep in contact **by means of**（改为：by/through）WeChat.
   5) As the price for an apartment in Beijing is **very expensive**（改为：unreasonable/too high）this year, I cannot afford it.
   6) The government has made **good**（改为：considerable）progress in solving environmental problems.
   7) Our university **provides convenience for study**.（改为：Our university makes it convenient to study/makes study convenient.）
   8) I support him **in my mind**.（改为：heartily/sincerely）
   9) He is a person **of much ambition** and full of great expectation**of future**.
      （改为：He is an ambitious young man, full of great expectations.）
   10) Self-conception **is the basis of**（改为：underlines；注：be 动词使用过多，会使句子表达不够有吸引力，应尽可能避免）one's attitude towards success and failure.

✓ Week 2

1. 1) one of the youngest Supreme Court justices
   2) served as editor of the *Yale Law Journal*
   3) skills, knowledge, confidence
   4) judicial philosophy
   5) has many fans there, often speaks there
2. 1)-5）CCFCF　　6)-10）CCFCF
   11)-15）CCFCC　　16)-20）FCFCC
3. 1) grabbed　　　　2) cleaning up
   3) offers　　　　　4) ridiculous dialogue
   5) install a traffic signal　6) high humidity
   7) to cure　　　　8) in the south
   9) peeling shutters　10) assign term papers

✓ Week 3

1. Paragraph 1:
   Topic Sentence: 1)
   Supporting Sentences: 2); 3); 4); 5)
   Paragraph 2:
   Topic Sentence: 6)
   Supporting Sentences: 7); 8); 9); 10); 11)
   Concluding Sentence: 12)
2. 3)
3. 1) you→he or she
   2) you→I; your→my
   3) one→I
   4) you→we
   5) they are→he or she were

✓ Week 4

1. 1) First you will need a sheet of paper that is 30cm by 30cm. Fold it in half lengthwise. 2) Next, open the paper and fold one corner toward the center crease. 3) After you have made the final fold, fold the other corner down, in the same way, along the dotted line. 4) Then fold each side along the diagonal dotted line toward the center. 5) Now, turn the paper over. With the paper turned over, fold one side over along the dotted line. 6) Next, fold the other side along the other dotted line. 7) The last step is to tape the

body of the plane together. You now have a paper airplane that is ready for a test flight!

2. 1) The first step in creating a flower arrangement is to choose an attractive container, but the container should not be the focal point of the arrangement.

   2) Following signs is one way to navigate a busy airport; looking for a map is another.

   3) The firefighters told the third-grade class the procedures to follow if a fire occurred in their school.

   4) They emphasized that children should leave the building quickly. Also, they should move at least 100 feet away from the building.

   5) To lower fat consumption in your diet, first learn to read food product labels. Next eliminate those products that contain trans-fats or unsaturated fats.

   6) After you place the pill on the cat's tongue, hold its mouth closed, rubbing its chin until it swallows the pill.

✔ **Week 5**

1. 1) A; 2) B; 3) B; 4) B; 5) A
2. 1) A; 2) B; 3) A; 4) A; 5) B
3. 1) writing; apply; University; companies; from
   2)

> From: John Doe
> To: staff@buct.co.cn
> Subject: re post of research assistant
> Attachment: John's CV
>
> Dear Sir or Madam,
>
> I am writing to apply for the position of research assistant advertised on your university website. My major is Computer Science and I will graduate from Beijing University next year. I had experience in computer programming and worked for big companies. I participated in my supervisor's research project last semester and had been trained to be a research assistant.
>
> I am looking for a position of research assistant which will allow me to improve my skills and develop as a researcher. I am available for interview any time. Enclosed is my CV. I should be very much obliged if you let me know your decision at your earliest convenience.
>
> Best regards,
> John

4.
> From: John Doe
> To: Jane Doe
> Subject: Fix the date for the interview
> Attachment: none
>
> Dear Ms. Doe,
>
> I appreciate your acknowledgement of my application for the position of research assistant. Thank you for the opportunity and I will be ready for the interview next Monday morning as what has been scheduled.
>
> Looking forward to seeing you soon!
> Best regards,
> John

✔ **Week 6**

1. 1) c; 2) d; 3) b; 4) a
2. 3)
3. 1) India; 2) India; 3) Brazil; 4) South Africa; 5) Russian; 6) Russian
4. The charts show the breakdown of China's population in three separate years of 1990, 2000, and 2018.

   It is clear that the greatest proportion of population is the age group of 15-64. It rose from 66.7% in 1990 to 70.1% in 2000. In 2018, it remained the largest proportion, reaching 71.2% of China's population.

   The percentage of people who are over 65 had increased from 5.6% to 7% by 2000 before soaring to 11.9% by the end of 2018.

   However, the percentage of the age group of

0-14 had dropped from 27.7% in 1990 to 22.9% in 2000. In 2018, the percentage decreased to only 16.9%.

　　Overall, it can be seen that middle-aged people and adolescents constituted the largest proportion of China's population while the country may become an aging society in the future.

✓ Week 7

1. 3)—4)—6)—1)—5)—2)
2. 1) b, c; 2) a; 3) d; 4) e; 5) f
3. *The Human Body* is a unified and coherent paragraph.

　　The first sentence states the main idea of the paragraph and claims the superiority of the human body over the rest of the creation. It enables the reader to expect the following ideas in the paragraph that explain and illustrate the qualities and attributes of the human body.

　　The second, third, fourth, fifth, sixth, and seventh sentences compare, contrast, elucidate and justify the main idea or topic sentence. They establish the main theme with logical explanations and transitions. They create a graphic picture in the minds of the reader with suitable and appropriate language expressions. In brief, they develop the main idea of the paragraph.

　　The eighth and the ninth sentences interpret and analyze the limitations of the human body and prove the strength of the topic sentence. They, further, lead the main idea into a concluding thought.

　　Finally, the tenth sentence concludes with the idea that the human body should be well preserved for a proper functioning of the system and that a healthy mind can work only in a healthy body.

4. The second paragraph does not support the thesis since it talks about "eating healthier is beneficial to the environment".
5. 3)—1)—2)
6. **Introduction**

   6) The use of prepositions in English has always been problematic for language learners.

   5) These small connecting words do not necessarily exist in other languages, or may not have exactly the same meanings.

   8) This makes teaching of this area very difficult, and research indicates that no single method has yet proved successful.

   2) The essay which follows gives a brief history of prepositional theory and discusses two major teaching strategies from a cognitive linguistic perspective.

   Conclusion

   7) In conclusion, it is apparent that the most effective element in teaching of English articles is the reinforcement of the notion of countability.

   4) The evidence presented here suggests that learners do not use articles randomly, but that they choose articles according to whether or not the noun is countable.

   3) The concept of definiteness in relation to articles remains, however, more problematic, and needs further investigation.

   1) Despite these problems, it is possible for teachers to make a positive contribution to learners' knowledge in this important area.

7. 1) specific detail opening
   2) open with a quotation
   3) question opening
   4) thesis statement opening

8. 1) looking to the future
   2) posing questions
   3) close with a recommendation
   4) summary closing

✓ Week 8

1. 4)
2. I had to find help because I could not be late! I tried to ask a passing businessman for help, but my words all came out wrong.
3. 1) Clearly the writer is not too fond of the subway.
   2) *Sight:* a broken clock showing 4:30; dried chocolate syrup; the child's messy face; some paper trash rolls by like a soccer ball; a poster; deep, blue skies; a lone palm tree; sapphire waters
   Smell: smelly staircase

Hearing: a crying child; two old men are arguing; a little noise

4. 1) Your last day in high school

   2) A scary airplane ride to another city

   3) Buying your first car

   4) Your brother's embarrassing wedding ceremony

   5) What I did last New Year's Eve

5. noisy, well-lit, old, wooden, anxious, prim

6. 1) This paragraph describes how Mom took good care of her rose garden.

   2) No sentence can be deleted because each sentence has its own function that contributes to the main idea of the paragraph.

   3) a. While she was walking, she would rip out any weeds that threatened her delicate beauties.

      b. She also trimmed the old flowers to make room for their bright replacements.

7. a. 4 b. 6 c. 2 d. 1 e. 3 f. 7 g. 5

8. Titles will vary.

Background: My trip to Mexico City in September 1985 was not my first visit there, but this unforgettable trip helped me realize something about life.

Beginning: I flew to Mexico City on September 17. The first two days were uneventful. I visited a few friends and did a little sightseeing. On the evening of the eighteenth, I had a late dinner with some friends that I had not seen in several years. After a very peaceful evening, I returned to my hotel and quickly fell asleep.

Middle: At 7:18 the next morning, a severe earthquake measuring 8.1 on the Richter scale hit Mexico City. I was asleep, but the violent side-to-side movement of my bed woke me up. Then I could hear the rumble of the building as it was shaking. When I looked at my room, I could see that the floor was moving up and down like water in the ocean. Because the doorway is often the strongest part of the building, I tried to stand up in the doorway of the bathroom. As I was trying to stand up, I could hear the stucco walls of the building cracking. I was on the third floor of a six-story building, and I thought the building was going to collapse. I really believed that I was going to die.

End: In the end, approximately 5,000 people died in this terrible tragedy, but I was lucky enough not to be among them. This unexpected disaster taught me that life can be over at any minute, so it is important for us to live every day as if it is our last.

✓ **Week 9**

1. 1) as a result of; 2) resulted from;

   3) because of; 4) due to; 5) reasons

2. 1) therefore; 2) as a consequence;

   3) resulted in; 4) effect; 5) accordingly

3. 1) caused; 2) owing to; 3) consequently;

   4) because; 5) factor; 6) resulting in;

   7) is attributed to; 8) impact

4. 1) There are 3 parts in the introduction, namely Sentences 1-4, Sentence 5, and Sentence 6.

   2) Sentences 1-4 introduce the topic: Brexit, which is also an effect. Sentence 5 explains the importance of discussing the causes for Brexit. Sentence 6 is the thesis statement, pointing out 3 causes for Brexit.

5. 1) A major reason for Brexit is the rise of nationalism across the world.

   2) Brexit would bring about negative impacts on trade.

✓ **Week 10**

1. 1) unlike; 2) likewise; 3) similarly; 4) whereas;

   5) conversely; 6) on the other hand; 7) by contrast; 8) on the contrary; 9) as...as; 10) too

2. 1) In contrast to Covid-19, SARS caused fewer symptoms.

   2) Both COVID-19 and flu are similar in terms of how the disease spreads.

3. 1) The last sentence is the thesis statement.

   2) It is not a so-what thesis statement because it not only tells what the differences are, but also the purpose of explaining the differences—"to clear up the confusion".

4. 1) There are three parts in the concluding paragraph, namely, Sentence 1, Sentence 2 and Sentences 3 & 4.

   2) Sentence 1 is a restatement, telling the thesis

313

statement again. Sentence 2 is a summary, reinforcing the main idea, the major difference. Sentences 3 & 4 are the final remarks, giving comments on the current situation and predicting the future.

5. 1) ① The way the convention was held
   A. Democrats
   B. Republicans
   ② The way the pandemic was treated at the convention
   A. Democrats
   B. Republicans
   ③ Outreach
   A. Democrats
   B. Republicans
   2) The point-by-point pattern is used in the body.

✓ Week 11

1. A, D
2. 2), 4), 6)
3. 1) It is defined broadly. It is the topic sentence.
   2) After a broad definition the writer adds a series of short examples to support the definition.
   3) An emphatic order, saving the most important detail for the last.
4. For my grandmother who was born before the turn of the century, it was rude to start eating before everyone else was served. It was also very rude for children or younger people to interrupt older people when they were speaking. For my dad, who grew up during the Second World War, it was rude not to say hello to a clerk in the store, and he thought my brothers and I were rude when we made unfavorable remarks about him.

✓ Week 12

1. 1), 4)
2. 1) d; 2) a; 3) c; 4) b
3. CDBABDAB
4. **Pros**
   1) It helps to develop the consciousness of being independent.
   2) It helps accumulate skills to communicate with other people in the society.
   3) It can enrich experiences for possible future careers.
   4) It can put the book knowledge into practice.
   5) It helps students release the financial burden to some extent.
   6) It can make the students more skillful to balance their time.

   Cons
   1) It can affect their time for study and may cause poor academic performance.
   2) It may reduce their time to stay with friends and families.
   3) Students will be forced to step into the society at an early stage.

   Should College Students Take Part-time Jobs?

   In many countries it is common for students to take part-time jobs while they are still in college, while in other societies this is virtually unheard of. In the latter situation, students are expected to spend all of their time on their studies and consider schoolwork their "jobs". In my opinion, students benefit more from a more balanced lifestyle, which may include working at a part-time job. Therefore, I believe that it is a good idea for students to work while studying.

   While it is true that a student's most important goal must be to learn and to do well at his studies, it does not need to be the only goal. In fact, a life which consists of only study is not balanced and may cause the student to miss out on other valuable learning experiences. In addition to bringing more balance to a student's life, part-time work can broaden his range of experience. He will have the opportunity to meet people from all walks of life and will be faced with a wider variety of problems to solve. Furthermore, work helps a student to develop greater independence, and earning his own pocket money can teach him how to handle his finances. Finally, a part-time job can help a student to develop a greater sense of responsibility, both for his own work and for that of the team he works with.

   For all of these reasons, I firmly believe that most students would benefit from taking a part-time job while they are in college. Of course, they must be careful not to let it take up too much of their time because study is still their primary responsibility. In sum, living a balanced life is the best way to be successful.

✓ **Week 13**

1. 1) B; 2) A; 3) B; 4) A; 5) B
2. 1) C
   2) suggests; demonstrate; clarify; recognized
3. a) 8 writers.
   b) To introduce summaries.
   c) However.
4. 1) --; 2) -; 3) -; 4) --; 5) -
5. 1) P; 2) D; 3) D; 4) P

✓ **Week 14**

1. 1) The study was conducted at the beginning of the semester and the final one was given at the end of the semester.
   2) Two questionnaires were developed for the survey, based on two earlier survey instruments made by Taylor & Hussein (1985) and Guo (1989).
   3) A total of 80 (36 male) participants were recruited at the University of Canterbury (51 participants) and from the general population (29 participants).
   4) The final scores were computed into mean averages (X) and standard deviations (SD).
   5) Rice straw was collected from Hubei Province (China) in 2014.
2. 1) B; 2) C; 3) A; 4) B; 5) A
3. 1) C; 2) D; 3) suggest/potentially; 4) Results
4. 1) A; 2) B; 3) B; 4) A

5. (It is an open question, and the answers vary.)

✓ **Week 15**

1. 1) T; 2) F; 3) T; 4) F; 5) T; 6) F; 7) T; 8) F; 9) F; 10) F
2. 1) The Lingo-cellulose Biomass Fuel Chain [: a review]
   2) [Development of] a Portable Device for Work Analysis to Reduce Human Errors in Industrial Plans
   3) **How does** [Effect of] Crop Rotation Diversity and Nitrogen Fertilization **Affect the Way** on Weeds **are Managed** [management] in a Maize-based Cropping System?
3. 1) We are sorry to inform you that your submission was not selected for publication by the program committee.
   2) The selection process was highly competitive, with only 200 submissions selected.
   3) Reviewers' comments are available at the website.
   4) We hope the reviews will be useful to you.
   5) We hope to see you at the conference in August this year.
   6) Today's speakers will share their thought on new energy.
   7) Then, we'll have a Q & A session.
   8) You've just 2 minutes left to finish your presentation.
   9) What's your view on/reaction to this issue?
   10) I think we have covered all the main points.
4. (omitted)